Carol Anderson

New Faiths, Old Fears

American Lectures on the History of Religions
Sponsored by the American Academy of Religion, New Series
Number 17

This volume is the seventeenth to be published in the series of American Lectures on the History of Religions for which the American Council of Learned Societies, through its Committee on the History of Religions, assumed responsibility in 1936, and for which the American Academy of Religion assumed responsibility in 1995.

Under the program the Committee from time to time enlists the services of scholars to lecture in colleges, universities, and seminaries on topics in need of expert elucidation. Subsequently, when possible and appropriate, the Committee arranges for the publication of the lectures. Other volumes in the series are Martin P. Nilsson, *Greek Popular Religion* (1940); Henri Frankfort, *Ancient Egyptian Religion* (1948); Wing-tsit Chan, *Religious Trends in Modern China* (1953); Joachim Wach, *The Comparative Study of Religions, Christianity* (1959); Robert Lawson Slater, *World Religions and World Community* (1963); Joseph M. Kitagawa, *Religion in Japanese History* (1966); Joseph L. Blau, *Modern Varieties of Judaism* (1966); Morton Smith, *Palestinian Parties and Politics That Shaped the Old Testament* (1971); Philip H. Ashby, *Modern Trends in Hinduism* (1974); Victor Turner and Edith Turner, *Image and Pilgrimage in Christian Culture* (1978); Annemarie Schimmel, *As Through a Veil: Mystical Poetry in Islam* (1982); Peter Brown, *The Body and Society: Men, Women, and Sexual Renunciation in Early Christianity* (1988); W. H. McLeod, *The Sikhs: History, Religion, and Society* (1989); and Caroline Walker Bynum, *The Resurrection of the Body in Western Christianity, 200–1336* (1995); Wendy Doniger, *The Implied Spider* (1998).

New Faiths, Old Fears

MUSLIMS AND OTHER ASIAN

IMMIGRANTS IN AMERICAN

RELIGIOUS LIFE

Bruce B. Lawrence

COLUMBIA UNIVERSITY PRESS   NEW YORK

Columbia University Press
Publishers Since 1893
New York   Chichester, West Sussex
© 2002 Columbia University Press
All rights reserved

Library of Congress Cataloging-in-Publication Data
Lawrence, Bruce B.
New faiths, old fears : Muslims and other Asian immigrants
in American religious life /
Bruce B. Lawrence.
p. cm. — (American lectures on the history of religions ; no. 17)
Includes bibliographical references and index.
ISBN 0–231–11520–2
1. United States—Religion—1945–
2. Asians—United States—Religion.
3. Immigrants—Religious life—United States—History—20th century.
I. Title.
II. American lectures on the history of religions
(American Academy of Religion) ; new ser., no. 17.

BL2525 .L39   2002
200'.89'95073—dc21   2002073450

∞

Columbia University Press books are printed on
permanent and durable acid-free paper.

Printed in the United States of America
Designed by Audrey Smith

c 10 9 8 7 6 5 4 3 2 1

To Joseph Stagg Lawrence, my father,
a Hungarian immigrant, the marvel and
mainstay of my own immigrant imagination.

CONTENTS

Preface

New Faiths/Old Fears emerges from a series of five lectures sponsored by the American Academy of Religion. They were given in spring 1999 at nine different North American universities. Since then, the substance of the lectures has changed, but I want to acknowledge with gratitude both my hosts and several college groups who not only heard the original lectures but also offered critical insight into the issues raised, often from their own experience. They include students and colleagues at the University of Chicago Divinity School, where I was a visiting professor in the fall of 1998, and also my contact colleagues at Emory, Harvard, the Massachusetts Institute of Technology, Stanford, the University of Colorado, the University of Michigan, the University of Toronto, and the University of Washington. I also want to thank undergraduate students at Duke, especially those who contributed to my rethinking of this topic through their excellent term paper projects in that same spring of 1999. Above all, I want to thank Sandra Hernandez, who served as my research assistant during the final phases of transforming the lectures into a book; she made stylistic as well as bibliographic suggestions that proved invaluable. Nor would the lectures have evolved into the present book form without a yearlong seminar that I co-convened at the John Hope Franklin Institute during 2000–2001. Titled "Race, Religion, and Globalization," the seminar provided me with opportunities for collegial exchange and critical feedback that most scholars relish but that only a few are privileged to enjoy. I am in the debt of all the seminar participants and especially my fellow co-convenors, Gregson Davis and Walter Mignolo. Thank you, Gregson. Thank you, Walter.

Two other colleagues deserve special mention. Both are Americanists, and both have been generous to me, as well as patient with my efforts to poach on their field. Thomas A. Tweed of the University of North Carolina at Chapel Hill has talked through several aspects of *New Faiths/Old Fears* and made invaluable suggestions. Grant Wacker of the Duke Divinity School has also read and commented on the entire manuscript.

My major debt is to my father, Joseph Stagg Lawrence. A turn-of-the-century Hungarian immigrant to the U.S.A., he died prematurely in 1950. Yet his experience and his memory have continued to inspire me. He has been a lifelong mainstay for me and my three brothers, two of whom are graduates of Columbia University, the publisher of this book. As a collective and fitting tribute, I dedicate this book to him.

Finally, I acknowledge with unreserved gratitude the continuous support and frequent insight of my wife, miriam cooke. Neither she nor others are responsible for the final shape of this book, but I am in their debt for making it happen.

What are the New Faiths? The New Faiths are identified with Asia. Dominant among them, in numbers and influence, are Islam, Hinduism, and Buddhism, with Sikhism a distant fourth.[3] Although all population estimates are provisional, Muslims worldwide are perhaps 1.2 billion; Hindus, 790 million; Buddhists, 365 million; and Sikhs, 25 million. The numbers in the United States are fractional, and far less than those of the second American religion, Judaism, except in the case of Islam. Also, like the worldwide estimates, the number of American adherents to Asian religions is subject to conjecture: the total of American Muslims may number 5 million, but only 1.5 million count as recent immigrants, while American Hindus may reach 1 million; Buddhists, 700,000; and Sikhs, perhaps 100,000. Despite their relatively small collective total (less than 3 million in a population of 260 million), almost all summary accounts of American religion in transition begin by noting that these new immigrant communities are growing faster than all Christian groups combined.[4]

And all Americans, whatever their religious preference, became more acutely aware of Asian immigrants and their religious beliefs after September 11, 2001. In the early morning on that fateful day four commercial airliners were hijacked by Muslim militants allied to Osama bin Laden, a Saudi refugee living in Afghanistan. All four planes were then turned into weapons of mass destruction as they were guided to three destinations, two to the World Trade Center, the heart of New York City's commercial district, and a third to the Pentagon, the heart of the United States' operational planning as a military power. Only a cell phone call alerting those aboard a fourth plane about what had happened to the previous three gave some stunned passengers the courage to storm the cockpit and guide their own plane, passengers and hijackers together, to death in rural Pennsylvania, rather than to some other symbol of American power or prestige, with yet more lives lost, more buildings destroyed, and more innocents left to grieve.

Even now, Americans remain uncertain of the exact death toll from the carnage of that day. For grieving relatives and friends it makes a difference whether 6,000, as first reported, or closer to 3,000, in more recent figures, was the actual loss of life from September 11. Yet for most Americans what matters most is the consequence of that unprecedented event for foreign and domestic policy. Overseas, the U.S. military is engaged in a war on unfriendly terrain, in the mountain reaches of Afghanistan, seeking the terrorist leader, hoping to destroy his network, trying to decapitate the brutal government that supported him. In place of the Taliban, with or without the death of Osama bin Laden, with or without the elimination of al-Qaeda, the United States and its allies hope to forge a government friendly to American policy interests, even if not reflective of our own deepest social ideals. It is not a war the U.S. can win in the long term, since no foreign power has ever subdued and governed Afghanistan, and even "victory" there will not end the need for a continued military presence, as well as massive economic assistance to rebuild one of the poorest countries in Asia.

Simultaneously, another war is being waged within America. The war begun after September 11, 2001, on the domestic front will not be ended easily or quickly. That war is directed against domestic enemies who, it is presumed, have links to the Arab Muslim terrorists who carried out the brutal September attacks. Yet the links are not clear, the evidence merely circumstantial or inferential, and so a broad counterterrorist initiative has been launched by the attorney general. It will be implemented by the Federal Bureau of Investigation, in concert with the newly created Office of Homeland Security. Federal agents will detain and question thousands of young Arab Muslim Americans, some of them illegal immigrants but many legal citizens. As recently as mid-December 2001, it was reported that Justice Department officials were still trying to interrogate about five thousand Arab Muslim men in the Detroit area. What did they have in common? They were Arab and Muslim and between the ages of eighteen and thirty-three. They also had temporary visas that allowed them to come to the United States during the past two years, and they all came here from countries suspected of links to terrorism. Combined with talk of military tribunals to try terrorist suspects, the dragnet operation in Michigan has had a chilling effect on all American Muslims.

Nor will the spotlight of racial profiling be limited to Arabs or to Muslims. It will extend to other Asians, and North Africans, who look like Arabs, others who may be identified as both "alien" and Muslim, even though they may be neither. The new faiths of Asian Americans will be refracted through one faith, Islam. Muslims will come to epitomize what Anglo-Americans most fear about an expanding immigrant community: they will have different values, alternative allegiances; they will not conform; they will obstruct social harmony and diminish the collective good. Despite the repeated efforts of public officials, from the president to the first lady to members of Congress, to declare that Islam is not the enemy, the very accent on Islam will only confirm what many flag-flying Americans have already decided: they must be wary of all foreigners but especially those who look like Arabs, those who can be identified as Muslims.

Even before September 11, 2001, the new faiths had been stoking old fears of outside others and their impact on the dominant culture. But since September 11, and because all nineteen of the suicide hijackers have been identified as Arab Muslims, these fears cluster with increasing urgency around loss and disorder: loss of democracy, linguistic fragmentation, and cultural antagonism. It matters not that most Asian newcomers are neither Arab nor Muslim. They may be Indians with Hindu or Sikh or even secular loyalties, yet all have been lumped together, all have become fearsome, sometimes frightening because these same Arab/Asian others believe what is alien even as they look alien. Often they do have alien political views, and they certainly speak at least one language other than English. Defined and perceived as alien, they threaten American space. They threaten, or seem to threaten, to make American space itself alien to "true" Americans.

Do these reflexes sound like caricatures? They are. For me, at least, they do not convey the reality of who Muslims are, nor do they project what Asian as well as Arab Muslim immigrants represent for the future social good of the United States. Yet it is just these caricatures that inform much of what is debated as serious "academic" scholarship about Islam and other Asian traditions. Stereotypes and prejudices are no less real for having been crafted by academicians; if anything, they are more dangerous because they convey an aura of prestige and objectivity that justifies not just prejudice but also those who act out of prejudice.

During the years that have elapsed since I first gave these lectures, I have realized that the frame of reference is much larger, and infinitely more important, than was initially suggested by them. Back then, I had highlighted the notion of diaspora and, above all, the role of Asian Americans in weaving the religious as well as the social tapestry of late twentieth-, and now early twenty-first-century America. I had tried to bridge several gaps—the gap between religion and culture, the gap between religion and politics (reconnecting church and state), the gap between religious loyalty and ethnic identity, the gap between religious practice and civil law, and, finally, the gap between the norms of religious texts and the images of religious experience.

What I myself have experienced since then is an even larger gap, amounting to a double chasm, on both sides of my chosen topic. The first comes from the side of theory. There is a crucial need to expand the conceptual center of Asian American studies. My initial remedy has been to make all Asians equally important. The field is now weighted heavily toward East Asia. Pacific Rim immigrants or East Asian Americans are located in major urban centers, as well as within renowned universities. They have given a prominence to Asian American and especially East Asian American studies. An anonymous reviewer of this manuscript underscored the ubiquitous character of East Asia in Asian American studies. So ingrained is East Asia in the academic study of Asian Americans, it was noted, that neither Koreans nor Japanese nor Chinese are marked as *East* Asian. They are simply Asian, while others, whether they be South or Southeast Asians, are marked as South Asian or Southeast Asian; they stand out from the dominant Asian minority, which is East Asian.

But what are we to make of those non–East Asian Americans, whether they be South Asians or West Asians (aka Middle Easterners), who belong to the new Asian American profile of the twenty-first century? In what follows I try to remedy the dominant emphasis on East Asian Americans by providing South Asian accents, and also West Asian or Middle Eastern accents, in the cases I adduce and the arguments I advance.[5] Of special interest to me is the bridge role that Iranians play. According to current interest in colonial and neocolonial categories, Iranians are thought to be Middle Eastern, as though Middle East stands apart from both Europe and Asia. In fact, the Middle East, like the Far East, is a British colonial invention. It is more accurately labeled as West Asia, a geographically neutral referent. Iran, in particular, has played an enormous role in the history of both West and South Asia. Iranians are as much Asian as are Chinese or Japanese, and so I urge that Iranians be included in contemporary Asian American studies. Along with my major emphasis on South Asians, both Muslims and Hindus, I devote much of one chapter (chapter 4) to examining the Iranian difference within the spectrum of Asian American religious practices.

Yet the theory gap requires more than merely expanding the arc of Asian American referentiality. Beyond renewed attention to South Asian immigrants and their West Asian counterparts, one must also direct attention to other American minorities, minorities who are non-Asian yet share with Asian Americans some of the same experiences of dislocation and marginality from the dominant culture. Frequently, these same non-Asian Americans resist their redefinition as hyphenated or hybrid Americans. They see themselves as fully American. In the pursuit of life and liberty, along with happiness, they seek not just economic and political rights but also cultural citizenship, and they seek it within a polyvalent American ethos. Their fear, a long-standing one, is that they have been perpetually defined as alien, that they cannot relate either to one another or to previous indices of value apart from the dominant, which is the Anglo, culture.

Who are these non-Asian and non-Anglo Americans? They are first of all Native Americans. Though numerically few, Native Americans provide a crucial index as to how Anglo-American culture projects a frontier where Indians are still the Other. Indians are locked in an uneven relationship with the dominant culture: even as they run casinos patronized by Anglos, they seek restoration of property, especially burial grounds, long denied them in U.S. courts.[6]

The two epigraphs to the preface suggest how opposite is the experience of Native American citizens.[7] The first, from an Amerindian poet, underscores America as, above all, White America. It is not just white men who write white papers and create white monuments, it is also a white Jesus and a white God to whom white people pray. And that cycle of cultural production has been continuing for a very long time: names and faces might change, but in fact "ain't nothin' changed / ain't nothin' changed at all," laments the poet.[8] In contrast to this dire view is the hopeful one-sentence claim of a Tibetan spiritual leader: "We like America in its buffaloness." *Buffaloness* conjures the image of the frontier, of an open space mediated by tribes and tribal laws before the coming of the white man. But at the same time it is a space open to conquest: while buffaloness is a tribute to the untrammeled dignity of a large, free animal, it also critiques the folk who hunted and prized the buffalo as game.

Alongside Native American voices are those of African Americans. Victims of court injustice and denial of rights even with the official end of slavery more than a century ago, they embody the racism that has marked U.S. history since long before the first waves of Asian immigrants arrived at the turn of the twentieth century, and more recently, since 1965. All Americans, not just African Americans, "are imprisoned by the history of racial subordination in America," writes legal scholar Derrick Bell. While the way out of prison is to delegitimate racism, "we can only delegitimate it," argues Bell, "if we can accurately pinpoint it. And racism lies at the center, not the periphery; in the permanent, not in the fleeting; in the real lives of black and white [and red and brown and yellow and mixed] people, not in the caverns of the mind."[9]

The most evident face of racism is a system of hierarchical values imposed in the name of civil uniformity or cultural/religious assimilation; it denies dignity and overrides difference in the pursuit of "a higher good." Joining African Americans and Native Americans in the protest against hierarchical, conformist values are Latino Americans.[10] Their situation has its own internal complexity, not the least of which is the historical claim that they were part of the original America, that far from crossing the border to go north, it was United States expansionism that pushed the U.S. border south and so enveloped them. This issue of defining space as one's own is crucial. A young Chicano poet put it bluntly when she said: "No cruce la frontera, la frontera me cruzo a mi" (I did not cross the border, the border crossed me), referring to the U.S. appropriation of Mexican territory after the War of 1848. Not just because of their large and expanding numbers, but also because of their complex implication in the rewriting of American history, Latino Americans also merit comparison to Asian Americans.[11]

In what follows I will try to cross and recross several borders, theoretical borders challenging the assumed center of Asianness in America, geographical borders reinscribing the epicenter of American identity as piebald and plural. Over all discussion and analysis of Asian America hovers the specter of racism. Racism is a hierarchy of values that prizes one standard of ethnic, linguistic, and religious purity. In the United States racial prejudice becomes Anglo-English-Protestant prejudice against those deemed alien because they are neither Anglo in race nor English in speech nor Protestant in outlook. It also includes a class component because nearly all of those disadvantaged have a lower economic and class status than those judging them. It is my central thesis that without sustained attention to racialized class prejudice one can comprehend neither culture nor religion, neither the views of the dominant class toward immigrants and other marginal groups nor the hopes and the fears that Asian immigrants share with other disadvantaged folk in twenty-first-century America.[12]

New Faiths, Old Fears

Introduction

Your country? How came it yours? Before the Pilgrims landed, we were here. . . . Our song, our toil, our cheer, and warning have been given to this nation in blood-brotherhood. Are not these gifts worth the giving? Is not this work and striving? Would America have been America without her Negro people?
— W. E. B. Du Bois, *The Souls of Black Folk*[1]

I'm just a white person who stayed in the sun too long.
— Asian American motel owner, *Mississippi Masala*[2]

General Approach

The principal subjects of this book are recent Asian immigrants to the United States, especially those who have come here since 1965. The passage of a major bill in that year dramatically increased the number of Asian immigrants. Yet their adjustment within American sociocultural as well as political economic space was complicated, in part because Asian immigrants were neither the intended nor the sole beneficiaries of the U.S. Immigration and Naturalization Act, also known as the Hart-Celler Act.[3]

Latin American immigrants, for instance, almost doubled their percentage of the total pool of legal immigrants, while dominating the ranks of the illegal immigrants, between the 1950s and the 1990s. Four-fifths of all immigrants to the United States since 1970 have been either Latino or Asian, at the same time that arguments about immigration, and also about the cultural/religious loyalties of immigrants, have been channeled along disciplinary lines, reflecting the perspective of one academic field while too often ignoring quite different perspectives from other fields.

Introduction

The major challenge of talking about any form of American religion post-1965 is to account for difference between disciplinary assumptions and methods as much as it is about the differences among the immigrants themselves. And by focusing on race as a variable crucial to religion, one that ranks along with it but in a certain sense prior to it, I am following a line of reasoning that comes from sociology, specifically the research and writing of Howard Winant. "Once created and institutionalized, once having evolved over centuries, racial difference," observes Winant, "is a permanent, though flexible, attribute of human society."[4] One cannot avoid race, yet one is not limited to one notion of race or one approach to the complexity of racial difference. Especially crucial is the relationship between subjective approaches, which focus on racial identities, popular culture as well as "apparent" common sense, and structural approaches, approaches that derive from political movements and parties, state institutions and policies as well as market processes.[5]

In its broadest formulation the challenge for Asian Americans is to understand where they are, or can be, or should be, in the racialized pattern of American society. At the subjective level there is no longer the bipolar model of white/black or black/white. Always complicated by the presence of Native Americans, it is now multiplied by the recent immigration of Asians and Hispanics. Yet the multipolar, racially piebald profile of American society has not permeated the state or political society or the market to the extent that either common sense or foundational ideals would mandate.[6] At many levels, twenty-first-century America remains what Winant called a racially dual society: black and white are still the dominant categories. Polyvalent racial differences claim the lives and the imaginations of but a few, with the result that most Asian Americans, like their non-Asian counterparts, must choose among four levels of discourse concerning race and religion in the United States:

1. *Public policy.* Whether pursued at the national, state, or local level, public policy presumes a notion of the common good that is seldom articulated, except in statistical or economistic terms. Issues of race and religion alike are glossed as issues of professionalization and income distribution. While questions of religious affiliation are absent from the U.S. Census, religious diversity is thought to be a good thing, which supports mainstream or middle-class America, while racial difference is a bad thing, presumed to have a divisive affect on collective solidarity and national consensus.

2. *Law.* The court system frames issues in terms of citizenship, with individual rights and state responsibilities as well as resources directed only to legal immigrants. The plight of illegal immigrants in California has received extraordinary attention, but it is only symptomatic of a more diffuse national pattern that has made certain U.S. cities urban magnets for the majority of post-1965 immigrants, both illegal and legal.[7]

3. *Cultural studies.* The site of an internal debate between cosmopolitanism and pluralism,[8] it restages the age-old debate between universalism and particularism. Most recently, it has been recast as a debate within the circle of those who advocate cosmopolitanism, between critical cosmopolitans and liberal or universalizing cosmopolitans.[9] More interesting for the current focus on immigration and its cultural/religious consequence is the location of numerous theorists within the Asian American community. Seldom noted is the fact that some of the most acclaimed and oft-cited theorists within cultural studies are themselves immigrants or are identified with a particular subset of the immigrant community. Two examples, whose views recur in the following pages, are Arjun Appadurai, originally from India but long resident in the United States and now at the University of Chicago, and David Palumbo-Liu, originally from Taiwan but educated in the United States and now teaching at Stanford.

4. *Participants themselves.* One might say that they provide a ground-up rather than a top-down view of the immigrant experience and its religious dimension. Yet at least some of them are also part of the scaffolding project known as critical theory that provides the parameters and the arguments for cultural studies. It is a task almost unnoticed, but one that will become increasingly necessary: to locate the theorists themselves within the discourse about which they are theorizing. Appadurai, for instance, has been roundly criticized by David Hollinger for his views of transnationality.[10] Hollinger's critique is blunted, however, once one realizes that Appadurai is not speaking about all U.S. immigrants as participants in networks of long distance nationalism but only about the South Asian subset of which he himself is a representative as well as a spokesperson. Appadurai's discursive strategy may be universalist, but it masks a narrative perspective that is specific to South Asia, one that has to be understood from his speaking position, however occluded.

In most cases, the ground-up view presupposes that the stories make their own point, but they, too, are riddled with presuppositions and prejudgments. One of the least noted prejudgments is about race. A collage of narratives from Muslim women immigrants to Canada, for instance, identifies them by class and by sectarian loyalty without ever noting racial markers, either within these women's daily lives or in their perception of Canadian society at large.[11] Another approach is to embrace particular strategies for resistance. It has the benefit of foregrounding racial prejudice, but only as an external gaze: its individual essayists are resilient in crafting collective strategies and individual choices for resistance to stereotypes of the Asian immigrant, but they do not examine how those same normative degradations apply to their own reckoning of status and choice for location, education, and marriage.[12]

A graphic instance of how race suffuses all readings of immigrant religious outlook and practice occurred just as I was doing the final revision of this book. In June 2001 a Duke undergraduate working as a White House intern was ejected from a meeting on the faith-based and community initiatives chaired by President George W. Bush. Was he Christian or Jewish, was he Hindu or Buddhist? No, Abdullah al-Arian was Muslim, and since the meeting took place with other Muslims, many of them leaders of American Muslim groups, why would he be ejected? The official reason was this: a technical error in security clearance. The president, through his press secretary, apologized the next day, and even offered the ejected young Muslim student a tour of the West Wing of the White House and the Secret Service office! Yet the "technical error," even if it was a mere error, masks an evident fear: the ejected Muslim was not a South Asian Muslim nor an African American Muslim but an Arab Muslim. Not just an Arab Muslim but a Palestinian Muslim, and one whose father and uncle were both alleged to be pro-Palestinian activists—not only alleged to be activists but punished by the U.S. government for their presumed anti-American activity. The "error" visited on the son/nephew seems to have stemmed from secret profiling, and it reveals not just the difficulty of all groups' participating equally in the faith-based and community initiatives dear to President George W. Bush but also the impossibility of freeing Palestinians, whether Muslim or Christian, from the "terrorist" image that has been cast on all Arab Americans in recent years. Months later, in the aftermath of the September 11 bombings, with the psychic as well as physical harm they inflicted on American well-being, Arab Muslim Americans remain even more suspect—of disloyalty toward their adopted country at best, of terrorist intent toward public targets at worst.

Asian Americans may seem to have an easier time of it than Arab Amer-

icans, but they, along with Hispanics and other immigrants, also are framed
by the four levels of discourse just outlined. At two extremes stand the economistic and the culturalist views of twenty-first-century American society.
Both are projected as arguments. While the economistic argument characterizes those who tend to view immigrant issues through the eyes of law and
public policy, for cultural theorists and religious studies scholars, as also for
participants themselves, it is the culturalist argument that holds sway.

In both cases 1965 looms as a critical milestone.

The statement about 1965 as a watershed year for economic/public policy approaches to immigration is boldly etched by the Cuban American
economist George Borjas. Even though immigration from Asia was effectively banned after 1924, due to the enactment of the national origins
quota, Borjas, a Harvard professor, defends the need for a return to some
form of national origins quota in the aftermath of 1965. His argument is ele-
gantly economistic and statistical:

> The rekindling of the immigrant debate at the end of the twentieth
> century had its roots in the 1965 Amendments to Immigration and
> Nationality Act. The 1965 Amendments and subsequent minor legis-
> lation repealed the national origins quota system, set a worldwide
> numerical limit . . . , and enshrined a new objective for awarding
> entry visas among the many applicants: the reunification of families.
>
> The policy shifts in the 1965 Amendments had a profound impact
> on the number of legal immigrants. . . . Almost one million were
> entering (annually) by the 1990s [comparable to the First Great
> Migration to the United States, when 9 million immigrants entered
> between 1901 and 1910]. Moreover, many persons have come into the
> country illegally [about 7 million, according to Immigration and
> Naturalization Service (INS) estimates, by 2001]. . . . As a result of
> these trends, the proportion of foreign-born persons in the popula-
> tion began to rise rapidly, from 4.7 percent in 1970 to 7.9 percent in
> 1990 and 10 percent in 1998.
>
> The 1965 Amendments also changed the national origin mix of
> the immigrant population. . . . Over two-thirds of the legal immi-
> grants admitted during the 1950s originated in Europe or Canada, 25
> percent in Latin America, and 6 percent in Asia. By the 1990s, only
> 16 percent originated in Europe or Canada, 49 percent in Latin
> America, and 32 percent in Asia.[13]

What do these policy shifts and attendant population shifts portend? For Borjas, there is no doubt that the beginning and the end of the twentieth century present mirror-image challenges:

> There is an uncanny similarity in the key issues that fueled the immigration debates at the beginning and end of the twentieth century: a rapid increase in the number of immigrants, a huge change in their ethnic mix, and the perception that the new immigrants do not do as well as the earlier ones. American history has already revealed how immigrant policy responds when these "fundamentals" play themselves out in the political arena. The national origins quota system [enacted in 1924] was not born out of thin air; it was the political consensus that was reached after thirty years of debate to address the real or perceived problems. The current immigration debate revolves around the same issues. Will history repeat itself? Should it?[14]

The outcome for Borjas is clear: annual limits need to be set on total immigration (preferably scaling back to 500,000, as in the 1970s), and policies favoring more skilled workers need to be implemented. The outcome is less important for our purposes than the argument that precedes it. It is framed entirely above the fray of social concerns, yet it presupposes their heady, emotive tone. The historian Arthur Schlesinger, another Harvard professor, is deemed to be an authority predicting the fissiparous dangers of large-scale immigration. Schlesinger sees American identity threatened by the latest wave of immigrants. His fear is the old fear, that the newcomers will not only challenge that identity but replace it with anarchistic asymmetry. "The historic idea of a unifying American identity," warns Schlesinger, "is now in peril in many arenas. If separatist tendencies go unchecked, the result can only be the fragmentation, resegregation, and tribalization of American life."[15] Not only will there be loss of democracy and linguistic disunity but even possibly territorial disaggregation.

What all these economistic/policy/historicist arguments omit is the cultural component of the new immigrants, charted dramatically by the accent on Asians and the added texture that they provide to an already piebald American social fabric. Here is how two humanists, who are also religious studies scholars, chart that difference in their coauthored introduction to a textbook on Asian American religions:

Between 1960 and 1989 Asians accounted for 37 percent of the total immigration [to the USA]. As a result, the Asian-origin population doubled during the 1980s, rising to more than 7.2 million. By 1990 Asians constituted 3 percent of the US population, and, with Asians continuing to arrive in large numbers each year, demographers predicted the number would rise to 10 percent by 2050.

Over half these post-1965 Asian immigrants are Christian: most Filipinos are Catholic, and the majority of Korean immigrants are Protestant, but they also include almost a million Hindus, perhaps 700,000 Buddhists and the same number of Muslims, as well as 100,000 Sikhs.[16]

These transnational migrations—together with the effects of American conversions and the diffusion of Asian influences—have made the cultures of the United States more diverse than ever. . . . By the end of the nineteenth century, more forms of Christianity and Judaism flourished in America than anywhere else in the world. By the end of the twentieth century, however, a new global diversity had taken hold. America had mapped Asia and met its peoples and religions earlier . . . but after the 1960s diversity had become not just one feature of the American religious landscape; it was the major one.[17]

Tweed & Prothero

In short, though they agree on the centrality of 1965, culturalists and their economistic counterparts disagree on its significance: endless diversity is inherently lauded by Tweed and Prothero, while threat to the social fabric and its harmony is seen as more fundamental by Borjas. The radiant hope of multiculturalism is pitted against the looming disaster of socioeconomic unrest and perhaps political instability. Neither side accounts for the other; the two views seem both diametrical and incommensurate. To explore a middle ground one must account for much more evidence on both sides, and to do so one must begin by looking beyond the Asian beneficiaries of the immigration act to its other, non-Asian beneficiaries.

As crucial as is the Asian accent charted by Tweed, Prothero, and others, it is difficult to interpret its significance for the post-1965 period without also taking account of the major group that benefited from the Hart-Celler Act of 1965: the Latinos. While 49 percent of the legal immigrants during the final decades of the twentieth century were Latino, most of the illegal immigrants were also Latino. The Latino component alone may exceed 10 million, but in any case it numerically dominates the entire Asian component by a factor of two to one. Yet no major study to date has attempted to splice together the experience of Asian and Hispanic immigrants, or to understand both groups vis-à-vis other nonimmigrant minority groups, especially Native and African Americans, as well as the dominant Anglo group.[18]

My project, while concerned with immigrants, whether Asian or Latino, also extends to religion. It examines religious markings, both institutional and experiential, both familiar and unfamiliar. It emerges out of religious studies at the same time that it implicates other disciplines. It must necessarily confront a major aporia in all reflection to date on Asian immigrants. Just as there has never been an attempt to see Asian immigrants within a larger pattern of immigration to the United States since 1965, so there has been a near total omission of religion as a significant dimension of either immigrant identity or immigrant struggle within North American space. Instead, the indices of difference that are mapped across disciplines move from literary criticism to cultural anthropology to political economy. Religion, if considered, becomes a subset of cultural anthropology rather than religious studies proper.

This kind of synthesizing, polythetic study is all the more needed now because immigrant studies itself is undergoing a sea change. Studies of immigrants are entering what might be termed a third phase. If the first one was marked by temporal interest in the pre-1965 period, and the second by the racial shift to non-Anglo immigrants since 1965, the third phase is marked by a generational shift within the immigrant populace itself. Some of the second-generation immigrants from the post-1965 period are now working in the American academy. They are credentialed as professors even as they write about their own experience in becoming Americans who are still Asian (or Latino) in their self-understanding. In other words, if the first phase was to understand European immigrant patterns at the turn of the century, and if successive studies since 1965 have looked at discrete groups emerging since the passage of the 1965 law, current studies are now marked by an accent on local and individual experiences not available, or even attempted, in previous academic writing about immigrants and American culture.[19]

Specific Key Terms

Raymond Williams, the British cultural critic, has underscored the distinctive value of key terms. It is not merely what they say; the range of con-

Introduction

notation that they evoke also sets the stage for reflection and for debate, for an analytical yield that is at once distinct and productive of other insights. It is for that reason that the key terms of this book are also neologisms. I am introducing two key terms that do not have lexical referents; they cannot be found in the dictionary. Yet they do evoke a sense of immigrant experience and its religious dimension that, at least in my view, justifies the labor of reading them, reflecting on them, and applying them to the circumstances of Asian American immigrants since 1965.

The first term is *polyvalence*. It presupposes diversity, but unlike diversity, it accents not just perpetual variety and change but also stability and persistence. If diversity is a myriad of changing forms, polyvalence is the plumbing of depths within each form. Like its etymological analogues, *polytheism* and *polycentrism*, it connotes the many as equivalent to the one. The many are created and debated and re-created and adumbrated, yet they retain a referential link to the memory and the hope of each immigrant group. Polyvalence is neither essentialism nor fixity redeployed; it is negotiated equivalence without guaranteed permanence, it is pragmatic hope rather than utopian idealism. It is a value-added rather than a value-neutral projection of culture-specific norms.

The second term is also a neologism: *kaleidoculture*. It is the alternative to multiculturalism. Even when critical pedagogy is advocated, even when mestizo or Latino-style hybridity is counterposed to Anglo-Protestant cultural hegemony,[20] it is numerical increase that suffuses multiculturalism; many cultures rather than one is presupposed as an unquestioned good, yet the quality of the many is never hinted at, much less accented. Kaleidoculture, by contrast, makes a strong value judgment, one that is also informed by aesthetics. Like its etymological precursor, *kaleidoscope*, *kaleidoculture* evokes a changing spectrum of cultural values and experiences, each set of which is bright and scintillating, worthy of attention, examination, and appreciation as well as debate, critique, and transformation.[21]

Polyvalence and kaleidoculture extend the semantic range of the key terms that they both echo and supplant. Polyvalence echoes the technical language of chemistry: to be polyvalent is to have more than one power or capacity or value. Polyvalent culture also has an uncharted potential; polyvalence marks that potential without limiting it. Similarly, kaleidoculture adds value to the analysis of culture: while multiculturalism projects culture as irreducibly plural, kaleidoculture affirms culture as intrinsically var-

9

Culture & religion.

ied and alluring: the many faces of kaleidoculture, while changing, never cease to dazzle and to engage.[22]

Despite the value of economistic research and writing, I am troubled by its assumptions as well as its conclusions. They remain on the surface; they are two-dimensional. What they miss are the depth, the ambiguity, the three-dimensionality of cultural experience and its religious subset. While culture is not primarily religious, it cannot be understood without explicit and sustained attention to religious evidence. *The* key question is how to approach religious idioms/experiences while keeping race, gender, class, generation, and locational differences in tension. I want to argue that the polyvalence that characterizes twenty-first-century North America entails an increase in speaking positions and strategic advocacies available to immigrants.

The decisive analytic rubric is best defined as *racialized class prejudice*. Whiteness studies have demonstrated the pervasive influence of whiteness as an unmarked category projecting Anglo privilege. Class prejudice underscores how the economic and social and cultural resources of whiteness are denied to all nonwhites, but especially to one race that is underlined as occupying the other end of an unspoken U.S. hierarchical social order, namely, African Americans. Far from being freed of racial taintedness because they are neither white nor black, neither Anglo nor African American, other minority groups—Asians, Hispanics, and also Amerindians—are implicated in that persistent biracial patterning of norms and values. Racialized class prejudice applies to immigrants as much as it does to African or Anglo Americans; it also suffuses religion and politics.

Polyvalence holds out a twin hope: first, that citizenship can be cultural as well as political, with cultural citizenship demanding internal integrity, not external conformity, and second, that equivalent cultural citizenship can be extended to an expanded cluster of non-Anglos. Internally unlike each other, these groups need to be named and affirmed at the outset. Even though race has been defined overwhelmingly with reference to African Americans, cultural citizenship must extend to South Asians and Latinos as well as to African Americans. Racial difference, as Winant observed, did not begin in this century or even the last century. It has evolved over many centuries; the problem of race comes with the first European settlers in North America. If we believe historian of religion Jonathan Z. Smith, the problem of racial difference in the New World emerged from the Spanish encounter with Native Americans:

10

Introduction

It was neither Orientals nor Blacks, who had long been mapped on the old Greco-Roman and biblical taxonomy, that gave rise to the intellectual problematics of race. Rather, it was the unanticipated presence of native Americans.[23] *see* p. 151

There is a trajectory from sixteenth-century explorations to seventeenth- to nineteenth-century transatlantic slave trade to twentieth-century Asian American immigrations. Yet beyond the history of racism as experienced by discrete groups within the American social fabric, what is denied is the connection between the racialized class prejudice experienced by one group, Asian Americans, and its counterpart among another group, African Americans. Apart from forays into popular culture,[24] one finds few references to the parallel exclusion of blacks and Asians from white society.[25] An impassioned article by a South Korean American scholar, for instance, laments "the persistence of racial inequality and structural exclusion. Asian Americans must still contend with the discriminatory assumption that they are *not* Americans, and must face the question, 'where are you from'?"[26] Like African and Native Americans, Asian Americans have experienced stereotypical representation, along with racial prejudice and structural exclusion. All three groups, plus Hispanics, have felt the pressure to conform to Anglo norms, and it is that experience which has not only shaped their location in U.S. social history but also structured their relationship with each other.

In sum, to pursue a binary analysis or to rely on binary categories of Asian-American or black-American is to miss the sense in which Anglo unhyphenated still projects the fullest form of U.S. citizenship, placing Anglo Americans apart from and above all other groups, whether those groups are deemed to be others, outsiders, or minorities. At the outset of a new millennium the old prejudice lingers: all non-Anglos have yet to find the equal access, equal rights, equal hopes that mark the American dream.[27]

The option most often explored is to overleap class prejudice even when racial prejudice lingers. Bruce Lee and Tiger Woods may have made it, but the message of their success is not people of color unite and resist the oppressor; it is rather work hard so that you are less excluded than that other nameless minority—the Guptas or Singhs or Kims. To understand how popular culture reinforces rather than weakens or reduces stereotypical representation one need but glance at two Chinese American novels. Each attempts to engage critically the tension between inclusion and exclusion, but each also cannot avoid translating that tension into two others: the tension between success and failure, the tension between citizen and foreigner. In other words, to be included is to succeed—even a second-class citizen is a citizen. Both Lan Chang's *Hunger* and David Louie's *The Barbarians Are Coming* demonstrate how "the privileges of symbolic national citizenship and material socioeconomic success depend upon Asian American compliance with culturally racist narratives about Asians in America."[28]

Culturally racist narratives are etched in film as well as in literature. A powerful instance of stereotype reinforcement from popular culture appears in the 1992 Mira Nair movie *Mississippi Masala*. Though the movie's central plot revolves around an interracial romance between two minorities, a South Asian immigrant woman from Africa and an African American man from Mississippi, and though it offers oblique critiques of racism, it subtly reinforces both the power of Anglo normativity and also the compliance of South Asian Americans with those norms. When the woman's father questions the relationship, the challenged suitor explodes: "You and your folks can come down here from God knows where and be about as black as the ace of spades, and as soon as you get here you start acting white and treating us like we're your doormats." Reinforcing that perception is the reflection of an Indian motel owner on his own experience of racism. "I'm just a white person who stayed in the sun too long," he lamented, thus implying that his skin color was essentially light enough for him to be accepted by white Mississippians.[29]

In the face of durable institutions—from town house to White House, from classroom to workplace—that reflect the history of race/class inequity in the United States, and also the popular media, including Hollywood movies, that perpetuate rather than deflect that institutional bias, one needs to do more than advocate diversity or continue to debate about multiculturalism. One needs to have a rigorous rethinking of categories, replacing diversity with polyvalence, multicultural ideals with kaleidocultural ones. Polyvalence advocates cultural equivalence, not more variety in the collective rainbow or more seats at the common table. Kaleidoculture affirms that there is no cultural majority: all cultures, including mestizo or mixed cultures, should find equivalent symbolic and institutional space within the arc of twenty-first-century American public life, but until their representatives cease to be defined as minorities, they will remain confined by the pressure to conform, to adopt, to assimilate, to disintegrate.

Introduction

Sexism?

If the goal of polyvalent kaleidoculture is distant, it is because of racialized class prejudice and all that it embodies. Minorities will always be defined by both race and class, each reinforcing the stigma of being minority. There is more to the category *minority* than prejudgment about race and class differences; it is a word that denotes lesser in numbers but it also entails lesser in terms of access, power, and privilege in the public sphere. The word is entrenched in all discussion and analysis of contemporary social relations. I may not like what it means, yet I cannot avoid using it myself. My focus is Asian Americans and their religious/cultural worlds. I want to explore how one can think differently—at once more subtly and more positively—about Asian communities and other non-Asian communities in twenty-first-century America, but I cannot do so without using the word *minority*. Not just Asians but Latinos and Africans and Amerindians are American minorities because they are cast as such vis-à-vis the majority, which is also the dominant, Anglo community. It is never called the Anglo American majority because it is obvious that the American way is both Anglo and Protestant, while at the same time non-Anglo others are seen as independent minorities, whether Asian or Latino or African or Amerindian. Yet they are dependent on each other and not just on the relationship that each has with the dominant group—or so I want to argue in the pages that follow. Any long-term understanding of Asian Americans as a minority, in my view, will fail if it does not take into account their relationship to all three of the other minority groups who, along with the dominant Anglo group, are seen as defining the ethno-racial pentagon.

The ethno-racial pentagon? It is hardly a felicitous phrase, since the pentagon immediately connotes the Pentagon, a five-sided building that contains the headquarters of the U.S. military and projects U.S. political power throughout the globe. The ethno-racial pentagon, in its own way, is no less powerful than the military Pentagon.[30] The ethno-racial pentagon implies an equivalence among five groups that are far from equivalent. Each is defined by ethno-racial markings: Amerindian and African American are framed with Asian American as freestanding categories, while the Anglo category has a subset: Hispanic. To put it differently, it is called the ethno-racial pentagon instead of the racial pentagon because there is one ethnos, a group defined as like but not quite Anglos. These are Hispanics, meaning Latinos and Chicanos together, though one could argue that Latinos and Chicanos deserve to be separated, each with their own subcategory.[31] But then the same could be said for Asian Americans (where else in the world

13

are Pakistanis and Japanese regarded as statistically the same?) or Amerindians (tribes as diverse as the Cherokees and the Lumbini share little in common apart from the census designation) or African Americans (who include multiple Caribbean as well as African family trees but, and even more important, are mingled with Anglo-Americans far more than conventional wisdom or constructed categories admit).[32] In other words, almost all the "neat" rubrics defining minorities hide untidy subjects. None is strictly linear, all conceal multiracial histories.

The same could be said for the unmarked majority group: Anglo Americans. Consider the case of American Jewry. Why are they defined reflexively as part of the majority? Because, argues Hollinger, "multiculturalism [in the United States] has been a means of advancing not cultural diversity as such but several specific cultures popularly associated with groups who have suffered color-triggered discrimination."[33] In other words, Jews don't fit the model of color-triggered discrimination, since they are neither colored nor economically disadvantaged. The same could be said for Americans of German and Polish, Scottish and Welsh, descent. They are hardly identical as cultural groups, yet because none is disadvantaged as a group, all are combined under one category: white = Anglo = European American, for the purposes of the U.S. Census.[34]

There is more than a vast diversity cloaked within the ethno-racial pentagon. It is true that it rounds off squares, that it fits loose ends into a tight box, that it is procrustean, but above all, it projects the very racialized class prejudice that some of its defenders seek to remedy. Why, then, does it persist? Because it provides an administrative shorthand. First, it tags race as the key to wholesale notions of cultural difference, and then it provides socioeconomic entitlement for those marked as disadvantaged.

The history of the U.S. Census leaves little hope that the category "race" will ever be removed from this cornerstone of U.S. public policy.[35] Fixation on "race" reinforces popular perceptions that groups should be both typed and ranked by physical traits. How then can academic reflection on racialized practices help reduce them, or at least diminish their force? In chapter 1 I examine the work of two academics who have contributed to current debates about multiculturalism. One argues for religious pluralism, the other for civilizational purity, yet they both dismiss racialized differences as incidental, rather than central, to their own projects. They are not isolated voices; they represent an ill ease with race, or denial of its centrality, that pervades most studies of immigrant culture and Asian Americans. The analytic value of scholarly inquiry is reduced when predispositions amount to systemic biases among highly respected scholars.

Another way to move beyond the ethno-racial pentagon is to move beyond government, or at least beyond the state as the sole instrument of governance. In chapter 2 I argue that civil society is a critical category if we are to move beyond either state or community as competing alternative sites for citizenship. Civil society is not an autonomous realm. It competes not only with the state and ethnic communities but also with the family and the market. Yet civil society alone provides hope for individual initiative and collective planning among groups that advocate either critical distance from powerful institutions or active resistance to both their norms and their values.

Through the optic of civil society one can chart not just the lived experience of centuries but also the emergence of prejudice, the practice of typing, then stereotyping, and finally the critical role of modern media in both reflecting stereotypes and perpetuating them. The individual may appear to be free, but in fact she is shaped by the memory of a homeland, by the views that she carries across borders as well as the views that others have of her. There is at once the perception that the "foreign" group as a whole is marginalized, and also that individuals within the group share a double consciousness, a living between the world of bygone images, not all of them unsullied or hallowed, and another world of day-to-day interactions that also carry different norms and values. What characterizes the range of immigrant and native minorities is a sense that they are "outside" or "outcast" from the dominant group no matter what they do. The effort of this book is to elaborate on how out-groups in the United States have been marginalized by both race and class, and why both markers continue to elide in subtle but insidious new forms of prejudice.[36] At first blush, this distinctively American form of social exclusion may seem to have nothing to do with religion, since academic labor separates out religion, or religious studies, from the sociology of power relations, entailing as it does analysis of the social forms of hierarchy, prestige, and prejudice, yet neither Hindus nor Muslims, nor Buddhists, nor Sikhs can escape the elision of religious labels with race/class markers in twenty-first-century America. The benefit of civil society is to see how these connotations of religious identity are constructed by the state rather than being intrinsic to lived experience. They are neither timeless nor inevitable.

The state, moreover, operates within a framework of norm-setting institutions, one of which is the judicial system. It is too easy to assume that courts have an objective view of the interests of all plaintiffs, but notions of the Anglo-dominant center or core of U.S. society permeate legal reflection in general and discussion of immigrants in particular. Chapter 3 unmasks some of the strange turns that lawyers and judges have taken: their view of Asian immigrants at the turn of a new century/millennium includes assumptions about all immigrants from the past century that need to be challenged.

At the same time, it is crucial not to exaggerate the category of religion in thinking about immigrants. Not all immigrants are marked by religion as their dominant cultural difference. How does one account for the non-religious or the irreligious? This "hidden" aspect of the Asian immigrant experience is the topic of chapter 4, and because it also links immigrants to specific metropolitan centers, such as Los Angeles, Chicago, and New York, it raises the related question of media portrayal of immigrants. Even though "out" groups are out to the extent that they share cultural exclusion and economic discrimination, cultural citizenship is conferred by mainstream media as well as by historical precedent and bureaucratic fiat. It is the role of media that becomes at once more crucial and more problematic when minority groups are imaged or imagined through group profiles. Even though many Asian Americans are also working-class Americans, they are too often represented in media as spiritual lodestones. Asian gurus appeal, above all, to that aging segment of upper-middle-class Americans known as baby boomers. To correct this distorted reading of Asian Americans, chapter 5 explores the contours of a generic cultural indulgence that might be best labeled "hypervisualization."

Running through my analysis of racialized class prejudice is attention to the other element that, along with race, frames almost all American religious experience, including that of Asian American immigrants. That element is fundamentalism. Far from being peripheral to American culture, fundamentalism lies at its core. Fundamentalism has become axiomatic to contemporary American religiosity. It has become axiomatic because fundamentalists have defined the agenda even as they have protested that they are the ones excluded from the benefits of modernity. The politics of religion is identified with the fundamentalist voices, heard loud in America and abroad since the 1980s, channeled through visual as well as print media. What has not been heard is the echo of these same voices in the very agenda set by scholarly work.[37]

Introduction

The politics of religion has precluded attention to other expressions of religion in the public sphere. Religion can and does exist apart from the state. Equally, religion can and does exist apart from the family. And what comes between the state and the family if not civil society? Yet civil society has been downplayed in studies of American religion because civil society is seen as compromised by political structures and market forces. Contaminated by both Wall Street and Washington, civil society ceases to be viable as a third space, one subject to influences from the state and the market yet not fully determined by either. It is precisely this liminal, variable role of civil society that must be recuperated from the fundamentalist rhetoric about American religion.

Because civil society helps us to grasp the social expression of religious groups in general and immigrant religious groups in particular, the long shadow of fundamentalism must itself be revisited in terms of civil society. The necessary first step is to see the contours of a cultural fundamentalism that etches the Anglo-Protestant ethos. Henry May described it as Progressive Patriotic Protestantism (PPP).[38] The key element here is Protestant; there is no love of country without a Protestant accent, just as there is no progress without Patriotic Protestants. Each word in this trio is linked to, and interdependent with, the others. While Progressive Patriotic Protestantism may have its equivalent in other religious traditions and in other parts of the globe, what concerns me in thinking about Asian Americans is their relationship to PPP in the United States.[39] The basic reflex is to understand that PPP describes more than religion. It is the religious reflex writ large in civil society. It is civic virtue that is Protestant even when it has no creed. It is Protestant even when the creed is Catholic or Mormon or Jewish.

The literary critic Harold Bloom, himself a devout skeptic, was correct to speak of the American Religion and to distance it from Christian belief: "There are indeed millions of Christians in the United States, but most Americans who think that they are Christians truly are something else, intensely religious but devout in the American Religion, a faith that is old among us, and that comes in many guises and disguises, and that overdetermines much of our national life."[40] Yet Bloom was wrong to diagnose fundamentalism as "the great curse of all American religion, and of all religion in this American century." Bloom was wrong because fundamentalism is more than "the shadow side of what is most spiritual and most valuable in the American Religion."[41] It is also close to the core of civic virtue.

17

The reflex to think of America with slogans, such as "In God We Trust," or "One Nation Under God," runs deep through the American psyche, as we have seen repeatedly since September 11, 2001. What is overdetermined is not the reflex but its use toward political or cultural ends that reserve God for only one race or one class, one gender or one generation. The Progressive Patriotic Protestant is, above all, the middle-class white heterosexual male, with his wife and family. The actual advances in women's liberation and professionalization have not changed either the reflex or the stereotype; they have only served to reinforce its fragility and the need for neoconservatives to advocate more stridently its centrality to "the American dream."[42] Contemporary scholarship and media reports alike demonstrate that Progressive Patriotic Protestantism still pervades the minds, and motivates the actions, of many Americans, not just those self-labeled, or labeled by others, as Anglo-Protestants.

Who are the central advocates of cultural fundamentalism? One might presume that they are Protestant preachers identified with the Religious Right, such as Jerry Falwell or Pat Robertson. Some are preachers, at least to the extent that cultural assumptions of America as above all a Christian—meaning an Anglo-Protestant, market-driven, warmongering—nation pervade religious as well as political rhetoric. But the central advocates of cultural fundamentalism are also academic voices, whether Anglo, such as Samuel Huntington, or African American, such as Stephen Carter, or South Asian, such as Dinesh D'Souza.[43] All advocate some pure space that is defined as homogeneous, a group that is at risk, a culture that is in dire need of defense by high-minded politicians and their well-heeled, largely conservative constituents.[44]

In what follows I want to emphasize not just the official ethno-racial pentagon but also the unofficial racialized blinders that limit the analytical value of even the most detailed inquiries into new patterns of global diaspora. Where do Asian immigrants to North America fit into the religion, race, and class hierarchy in the United States?[45] The religious studies scholar Aminah McCloud offers a purely theological explanation for Muslim difference. "For immigrants," she argues, "there is a monolithic Islam in the Muslim world which is normative, and the real experience of African-American Muslims should be rejected; they should aspire to effect something called 'orthodox' Islam."[46] Yet the underlying racialized class perceptions of immigrants cannot be ignored. Muslim immigrants do not simply pick and choose between different versions of Islam. To the extent that a variant or heterodox version of Islam exists, and is linked to African Americans, it becomes doubly tainted: it is both American (not Arab) and it is linked to the underclass, the underprivileged, the discriminated against, the oppressed. African American Muslims are not given equivalent billing in the menu of options for immigrant Asian Muslims. So vast is this gap between American ideals and the African American lived experience that one astute Asian observer laments "the process by which new immigrants have for over a century (mis)translated the black American presence into their own perplexed lives."[47]

The imperative is to see the Asian immigrant experience in the broader spectrum of minority social experience and minority political activism. This imperative becomes even more clear when we realize that the Civil Rights Act, which defined the 1960s for African Americans, coincided with the 1965 immigration act.[48] The full impact of both acts was not felt till the 1980s, when it became evident that "most of the people of the world on the move—immigrants, refugees, or asylees—were of dark color."[49] U.S. immigration policy, unlike that of West European nations, attempted to avoid racialized xenophobia, in part because of the civil rights movement. As Lawrence Fuchs once observed:

> The fact that Europe generally tightened its rules for immigration . . . in the 1980s at the same time that the US had become more open to diverse immigration could be explained mainly by the impact of the civil rights revolution, which led to the conclusion that it is wrong not only to abridge fundamental rights by race, religion, or nationality, but also wrong to base immigration policy on those considerations.[50]

Yet racialized class prejudice against "people of color" remained even when the practical result of the new immigration policy was to expand beyond all expectations the number of Asians and Latinos who came to work and live in the United States. The newest immigrants were not free to choose their own lifestyles. According to a respected policy analyst, it was not wise even for Caribbean immigrants to identify with African Americans, because the latter were viewed as both indifferent students and unambitious workers. "The stereotypes that shape the relationships between white Americans and either Asians or Latinos," notes Christopher Jencks, "have little in common with the stereotypes that shape relations between whites and blacks." In other words, even among stereotypes there is a rank ordering, and some stereotypes are definitely more favorable toward immigrants than others. For instance, continues Jencks, "white Americans are not surprised when an Asian student hands in a good paper or when a Mexican worker in California holds two arduous jobs." What this statement insinuates about African Americans is nothing short of racialized class prejudice at its worst. It is evident that in each example the dominant figure—the teacher and the employer—are both Anglo and upper class, yet their stereotypical judgment is not qualified with irony or critique; it is merely reported as common sense. Of course, we are led to believe, a white teacher would not expect a good paper from an African American student; he would be surprised. Of course, it is implied, a white employer would not expect industrious behavior from an African American employee. And so the Asian student, and the Mexican worker, should be "pleased" that both are positively stereotyped while their African American minority counterpart is not!

And the realm where this racialized class prejudice runs deepest is marriage, or more precisely, racial intermarriage. Jencks's hyperbole extends to the white/black rift at the altar rail: "Intermarriage rates suggest that the social distance between whites and blacks is also far greater than that between whites and either Asians or Latinos." Using statistics to bolster his claims, Jencks declares: "Only 6 percent of married black men and 3 percent of married black women had a non-black spouse in 1998." The Asian case is starkly different: "While almost all Asian immigrants marry other Asians, a third of their children and over half their grandchildren marry non-Asians. The figures for Latinos are almost identical."[51]

So deep is this racialized class prejudice that it affects others who observe, analyze, then describe how American immigrants, regardless of their religious practices, are restricted in their social choices. *American Medina* is a pioneering study of Sunni Muslim immigrants to Chicago. Its Danish author analyzes intergenerational as well as professional cross sections of the diverse immigrant community in greater metropolitan Chicago. While it does not highlight the intrinsic racialization of choices by immigrant Muslims, the extrinsic racialization is evident. There is, for instance, the contest over language, dress code, mosque space between Arabs and South Asians, but these issues pale next to the inter-Muslim racial values that separate African Americans from South Asians. Consider an especially powerful local preacher, an African American convert to *multiculturalism doesn't address race, class, power.*

Islam in the Chicago area. He focuses on Islam as the solution to the social gap between white and black America. Why? Because, observes the Danish scholar, this young preacher "formulates Islam according to an African American experience that still, by the late 1990s, is placed at the bottom end of the social scale."[52] There is no qualification or critique of the assumption that to be African American is to occupy the lowest rung in a nominally classless society that is rife with class, and also race/class, assumptions. Similarly, an Egyptian researcher, in examining a Houston mosque/Islamic center, discusses relations between its Arab and Pakistani members. Then, turning to African Americans, she offers the stark observation that "immigrant Muslims choose to identify themselves with whites rather than blacks . . . [since] the children of Arab and Pakistani immigrants rarely marry African Americans."[53] In other words, the barrier between all immigrant Muslims and the largest group of American converts, African Americans, remains high, as it does for other Asian groups defined by religion, whether they be Hindu or Buddhist or Sikh.

Because racialized class prejudice persists, it needs to be included in any assessment of American religion or American society, and precisely because it has been so routinely neglected or presumed as "self-evident," it informs the chief theoretical contribution of this book. My intent is to frame notions of cultural citizenship and cultural fundamentalism on a continuum that includes both immigrants and nonimmigrants, Asian, African, and Anglo-Americans. At the same time, I want to acknowledge, and preserve, the internal diversity of the very groups who are put in conversation with each other as though they were "obviously" different from all others when often they are also different from each other. Cultural fundamentalism presupposes the unquestioned centrality of Anglo culture, while multiculturalism seems to oppose it. Yet, all too often the advocates of multiculturalism frame difference in terms of static, essentialized notions of culture/religion that freeze persons into a textualized, abstract norm that makes them but one part of a neat, lapidary mosaic. Multiculturalism at its worst allows neither for internal difference nor for multiple strategies nor for multiple speaking positions—especially, second- and third-generation immigrants are never the same in all circumstances and should not be treated as though they are.

Even more problematic is the failure of multiculturalists to address hierarchies of race, class, and power. The multicultural label not only disguises and manipulates difference, it also starkly raises the question of who decides who gets what benefits. If we do not accept black, brown, red, yellow, and white as self-evident, then "why should the tax monies of a democratic nation state go toward the project of encouraging individual citizens to remain culturally in the color-coded [and class-tilted] enclosures into which they were born?"[54] The answer is, They should not, and also these enclosures must be critiqued time and again, until dominant institutions—not just the government and the courts and the academy but also the media—promote class and color as markers of dignified difference, markers that invite engagement and respect rather than prejudice and discrimination. That may be a goal as utopian as it is distant, but to entertain anything less as a goal is to accept and also perpetuate racialized class prejudice.

In short, my approach in the chapters that follow is critical and comparative; it is equally interpolating and integrative. I am critical of racialized class prejudice even while acknowledging that it is a stubborn virus in the American social body. I compare many perspectives on race, on religion, and also on minority Americans, especially but not solely Asian Americans. I interpolate disparate views from polyvalent sections of the cultural kaleidoscope called twenty-first-century American religion, yet at the same time I try, whenever possible, to make sense of how irreducibly different subgroups engage each other, even at angles, even obliquely, even fleetingly. The continuous, imaginative engagement of Asian with non-Asian Americans—and vice versa—remains the best hope for a vibrant civil society. Though the United States can never be free of race or class or religious preferences, these preferences, to the greatest extent possible, should be acknowledged rather than presumed. To acknowledge is to challenge, to challenge is to change, and through gradual change future generations may yet hope to reduce the burdens of a too violent past and a still troubled present.

CHAPTER 1

American Religion as Commodity Culture

American cultural studies . . . have been so preoccupied with our early inferiority complex vis-a-vis Western Europe, our frontier mentalities, our regional diversities, our shifting democratic consensus, and recently our racialized and gendered hybridities that we have overlooked the underlying American relation of markets to religion. . . . The dominant U.S. ideology of individualism . . . may be rooted in the often ignored relation of capitalist markets to religious sentiments.
— Cornel West, foreword to *One Nation Under God?*[1]

Over the past three decades, Asian American studies has . . . taken up a number of subjects, including gender issues, diasporic perspectives, interdisciplinary cultural studies, and comparative racial analysis. *Amidst the growth and maturity of Asian American studies, however, religion and religious experience continues to suffer from relative neglect* [emphasis added].

David Yoo, "Racial Spirits"[2]

Framing Narrative: The Tale of Two Professors

Let us accept the challenge of the first epigraph. Let us assume that all religion, not just religious sentiments, is related to markets, and that the relationship of religion to capital can best be examined through a cultural studies approach. How then do we pursue the question in the second epigraph, how do we put a market face onto racialized hybridities, combining Asian with Latino and also African Americans?[3]

This is the challenge of religion and culture in twenty-first-century

America, but it must first be addressed by reviewing the multiculturalist project. As David Hollinger has convincingly shown, it is multiculturalism that supplants all other shibboleths in describing the current flux of American society. Only after seeing the hopes and the limits of multiculturalism as presented by two of its most ardent analysts—one an advocate, the other a critic—might we hope to imagine beyond it a complex hybridity, one that I call the polyvalent kaleidoculture of a future America.

How did the multiculturalist project implode? It is a plot with many academic protagonists. Ironically, two of them come from the same university: Diana Eck and Samuel Huntington. Both are Anglo-Protestant professors at Harvard, yet they represent opposite tangents of the multiculturalist project. In their labor they project seemingly incommensurate approaches to American culture. She is a religion professor identified with religious pluralism, while he is a political science professor highlighting religion not as the basis for tolerance but as the catalyst for conflict.

Let us begin with the religion professor, Diana Eck.

In fall 1998 on the campus of Wellesley College a group gathered to consider pluralism in late twentieth-century America. The topic of the weekend symposium was "Education as Transformation." Its participants attempted to explore how religious pluralism and spirituality are—or should be—integral to higher education. More than two hundred persons coming from twenty-seven colleges and universities addressed a single question: How can the modern university "facilitate the formation of multi-constituency dialogue teams (including presidents, faculty, students, administrators, religious life advisors, alumni and trustees) on college and university campuses nation-wide"?[4]

The event included opportunities for Buddhist meditation, for Protestant Christian worship, for a Roman Catholic mass, for a multifaith celebration. What would a multifaith celebration be? Well, at Wellesley it featured American Indian, Sikh and Hindu, Muslim, Jewish, and also Bahai voices. Representatives from these traditions offered spiritual invocations and performed ritual acts for the Wellesley conferees. Among the worship leaders were religious folk as diverse as their names: Abu-Rabi, Drowning Bear, Khalsa, Rambachan, Leammle, and Buddha Bob, aka Robert Thurman, the Jey Tsong Khapa Professor of Indo-Tibetan Studies at Columbia University, and, of course, Uma's father!

Beyond meditations and workshops, there were featured speakers at the Wellesley gathering. Eck's plenary address was titled "From Religious Diversity to Religious Pluralism." A Methodist by background and a specialist in Hinduism, she argued that the major challenge for late twentieth-century Americans was to move from religious diversity, now a ground-level fact, to religious pluralism, a future prospect. As welcome as diversity was, it would not—indeed, it could not—be effective, in her view, unless those who advocated diversity also embraced difference. How? By listening to others, by dialoguing with others, by expanding their own worldview to include the others' difference.

About the same time as the Wellesley conference was taking place, else-where in the United States, at another university, Samuel Huntington, the proponent of religion as the basis for cultural conflict, was also giving a ple-nary address. Before an audience of three hundred students, professors, administrators, and local visitors, he was arguing that America now faced a moment of decisive crisis. The present crisis grew out of an earlier crisis, the Cold War. Though the Cold War had ended in 1989, it stoked still another crisis, the one now confronting us globally. It was a crisis of postnationalism, a crisis in which not nation-states but civilizations were warring with each other. While the USA may have vanquished Ronald Reagan's "evil empire," the former Soviet Union, since 1989 we Americans have had to face an even more formidable foe. The new enemy consists of a coalition of disenchanted marginal players in late twentieth-century global politics and capitalist sweep-stakes. They are the have-nots, or the have-not-enoughs, of the new world order. These have-not-enoughs are motivated by deep civilizational reflexes, reflexes defined above all by religion. While Western civilization was built on Judeo-Christian ideals, abetted by Greek philosophy and Enlightenment rationalism, the non-Western civilizations are neither Christian nor Greek nor rational. They are not defined or guided by a group of freethinking, unfet-tered individuals. Instead, the dominant elites in these other, non-Western civilizations are obscurantists limited by religious slogans. Post-1989, with the failure of communism, it is these religiously antagonistic reflexes that have come to characterize the political life of failed nation-state experiments from Eastern Europe to Latin America, throughout Africa and Asia.

Having established the global profile of religiously based conflict, Hunt-ington then specifies the most dangerous of these slogans. They are the slo-gans defined as Islamic and Confucian. The Islamic slogan sees the West as the advocate of special privilege for materialism and Zionism, rendering invis-ible both Muslim egalitarianism and Palestinian irridentism. On a parallel track, the Confucian slogan sees the West as the advocate of equality over hierarchy, of democracy over authoritarianism, of the West over the East.

Regions, according to Huntington, reflect their dominant religious outlook. While North Africa, the Middle East, and West Asia are the domain
of the Islamic slogan, East Asia, especially China, remains the domain of
the Confucian slogan. Separately, the regions motivated by Islamic and
Confucian shibboleths are dangerous, but combined they could become
lethal, posing a major threat to world peace, as also to Euro-American pros-
perity, in the twenty-first century. The military-industrial complex must be
prepared, defense spending must be increased, especially in view of the
possibility that Confucian China could provide Islamic Pakistan with the
nuclear know-how to destroy Hindu India.

This prediction was first advanced by Huntington in 1993. In summer
1998 nuclear testing in both Hindu India and Islamic Pakistan seemed to
validate Huntington's grim analysis as also his catastrophic prediction. Or
did they? By fall 2001 neither side had resorted to more than saber rattling,
despite the intense pressure felt on both by the American war waged in
Afghanistan after September 11, 2001. The half-century problem of competing and incommensurate claims to the mountainous region of Kashmir
persists, yet leaders in both nations have refrained from resorting to the
nuclear option. For the moment, they are more concerned about the enormous American military presence in their region than about their own
divergent civilizational outlooks.

Neither Eck the ardent dialogue advocate nor Huntington the die-hard
cold warrior has examined the religion-culture link at the heart of each of
their projects. What, then, are we to make of religion when it elicits such
opposite futures?! From one angle, religion is seen as cross-cultural dialogue. It bodes an irenic future constructed by individuals willing to
expand their worldview and to accommodate different neighbors. From
the opposite angle, religion is seen as the backbone of rival civilizations. It
goads political actors to advocate religious loyalties as shibboleths of separation and antagonism. It stokes alliances of convenience and provokes war
that threatens to engulf all humankind.

Religion as Culture

The Tale of Two Professors illustrates the goal of this chapter: to link religion to culture, without reducing either to an invariant particularity. Neither Eck nor Huntington acknowledges the link because it renders prob-

lematic their own investment in keeping the two separate. The need for this link becomes more evident if one skips from defining religion, itself difficult, to defining culture, nearly impossible. Immanuel Wallerstein has aptly underscored how culture became the ideological battleground for the modern world-system, at the same time that culture itself is a subject of mystifying complexity in the twenty-first century. There are two uses of culture, observes Wallerstein: though incommensurate and non-equivalent, they are often confused with each other. The first is culture as a broadbrush distinction of one group from another; it isolates and emphasizes certain traits or characteristics that are said to pertain to one group but not to others. (Germans are not like French are not like British.) Let us call this Culture One. The second is culture as an intramural yardstick, distinguishing some members of a particular culture from others of that same culture. (Berliners are not like Bavarians, Marseilles is not Paris, Manchester will never be London!) Depending on location, German or French or British culture will be seen differently by capital city urbanities than by their rural counterparts; moreover, what appeals to different groups may have as much to do with class and gender, race and education, as with location. Let us call this Culture Two.[5]

The move to define culture then parallels the just deferred move to define religion. Whatever religion is, it is also, like culture, etched by concentric but not overlapping circles. The first is a notion of religion as whole and universal and timeless: call it Christianity, Buddhism, Islam, call it goddess worship, shamanism, magic. Each term presupposes an internal order and an external other; sameness and difference are accounted for without being contextualized, but even when they are contextualized, it is often with reference to geographic signifiers that describe rather than interpret or explain: Christianity Western, Buddhism Eastern, Islam Middle Eastern, etc. Let us call this Religion One. There is also religion internally differentiated—Christians who are urban sophisticates versus Christians who are rural preliterates, Muslims from Djakarta versus those from Dakar, upper-caste Hindus from Bombay versus lower-caste Hindus from Bengal, and so on. Let us call this Religion Two.

Nowhere is the fragile contingency, and the analytical necessity, of generalizing about culture/religion more problematic than in trying to trace North American indebtedness to, and separation from, West European antecedents. Are Americans still burdened with an inferiority complex vis-à-vis Western Europe, as Cornel West suggests? It was to separate the two that the sociologist Will Herberg prized religion over culture, claiming that those who argued for cultural, rather than religious, pluralism as the defining badge of American social experience were either backward-looking romantics or shrewd opportunists or both.[6]

Yet the opening epigraph from Cornel West presupposes that the relationship between capital—that is, market-driven values—and American religion, whether expressed as religious sentiments or through religious structures, has been largely unacknowledged. This perhaps is due to the other stress in West's intervention: the accent on individualism, with individual religious beliefs and practices viewed as above all private, voluntary, and nonpolitical.

For West, one of the most forthright mediators between the academy and the public, between high culture and pop culture, between African American public intellectuals and their Anglo counterparts, the issues revolve around key points in the past: West Europe, frontier, region, democracy, and one key point from the present: our *recent* racialized and gendered hybridities.

The major question is the one that West defers: How do new hybridities, whether marked by expanded gender options or by racial mestizo/border crossing, relate to the old issues of West European superiority, the frontier mentality, regional difference, and democratic quarreling? Obviously they relate through the market, but they always and everywhere relate not just through gender and race but also through class and generational location. It is the need to accent the full array of time-specific and material markings, to pay attention to Culture Two, and Religion Two, that informs this chapter. Culture Two is always America at some time and some place, Religion Two is always someone's Christian, or Muslim, or Hindu, outlook shaped as much by race, gender, and class as by belief and practice.

The crucial issue is to acknowledge that one speaks not just from a particular time but also from a particular place. We cannot simply speak about religion, we must speak from a particular religion and, even more, from a particular place. Even if our register is a blank, that is, a secular disavowal of any religious commitment or orientation, practice or ritual, we must still say from which norms we are demurring when we say: "I have no religion; I live in Antartica." And the place from which we speak here is within the academy, trying to link religious studies to cultural studies. The specific place of the speaker is also crucial: I speak from within the North American academy, where the link between theology and religion is as natural as is the divide between religious studies and cultural studies. What follows is an exercise to move from the prescriptive, often triumphalist declarations of theology to the descriptive, ever cautionary, and always tentative observations of culture. Self-awareness of the extent to which all our reflections on religion and place are conditioned by our place and privilege can never be too great.

But self-awareness also induces wariness. Above all, it is of unspoken or unacknowledged assumptions that one must be most wary. Consider the assumption, implicit in the title of the edited volume for which West wrote the foreword, that we Americans are disposed to think that (a) there exists but one "true" nation, and (b) the basis of our national unity is its divine sanction: One Nation Under God. Especially in the aftermath of September 11, we have seen a profusion of bumper stickers that echo a divinely sanctioned oneness: UNITED WE STAND, GOD BLESS AMERICA, OUR HOME SWEET HOME.

This close link of homogeneous culture, religion, and nation long preceded September 11, 2001. It is etched in social science as well as popular culture. An authoritative article appearing in a major sociology journal as recently as 1995 claimed to demonstrate how there was a core American culture; not only was it core but it was defined in the Anglo-American period (pre-1880s) and has remained normative from then till now:

> This *American* culture and society—the shared characteristics that are substantially Anglo-*American* in their roots and which lie at the heart of what people have defined as essentially *American*—remain the measure for all others. No *ethnic* group has challenged that preeminence, nor is any likely to do so; some have contributed additional features to its profile, but none will supplant it.[7]

Yet beneath capitalist markets and beyond their influence, both evident and subtle, can we even presume to speak of One America, much less One Catchment of Religious Sentiments that might be labeled North American religion? The very question of One America has multiple political implications, but above all it has a cultural substrate. There can be no One America or One American Religion unless there is a common North American culture.

To nuance this set of related yet discrete questions—One America? One Culture? One Religion?—each of us must ask the questions from somewhere. But from where do we ask: Is there one America? Is there one American religion? Is there one American culture?

Let us ask the question of one or many North American religions/cultures from outside the United States. We face some curious choices. If we were Canadian and looking from Canada south, we might be skeptical: How can there be a single U.S. culture? Is not U.S. culture too diffuse to be singularized? Are there not too many ethno-racial groups? Are there not too many languages? And are there not too many religions? How can one presume to speak of "one United States culture"?

Or let us suppose we ask the question from across the Atlantic Ocean. If we situate ourselves in Europe and look back at America with European eyes, might we not ask: Isn't American culture too young, too recent, to be labeled *a* culture? Should we not instead talk about a larger Euro-American or a still larger Western culture, of which North America, and the USA, are but one subset?

The European perspective would focus on immigrants. While immigrants are not native-born, who else but immigrants lends credibility to the idea of an American culture? European immigration to Canada and to the United States dates back to the sixteenth century, and it is these immigrants who infuse American space with difference, a European difference transplanted to the New World. Subsequent immigrants from Africa and Asia also influenced North American culture, its norms and values, its variations and continuities, but at least till the middle of the current century, the burden of proving "American exceptionalism" depended on tracing European traditions. It was from European antecedents, along with African and Asian contributions, that one could frame the case for a distinctly American culture. It remains true till today that defenders of the American way of life are Progressive Protestant Patriots. Protestants by temperament if not by creed and practice, the core Anglo-Americans define the USA as the space that not only inherits but also epitomizes the best of European culture. To be patriotic, in their view, is to embrace American territorial space, to defend it, to enlarge it, to make it progress at all levels.

While I myself prefer the Canadian to the European model of U.S. collective identity, it is the European or Euro-American model that pervades the so-called culture wars.[8] By this approach, there is no singular, separate American culture, but rather a common Euro-American or Western culture of which North America—the USA and Canada (though not Mexico, because of its Latino distinctiveness)—is a mere subset.

Critiques of Eck and Huntington

Despite their contrastive uses of religion, Eck and Huntington share a fixation on religion as the answer to the problems of contemporary American social and foreign policy alike. Not religion linked to race or to class or to some location, but religion as the universal abstract. Religion One, not Religion Two, informs the cultural project of both the dialogue advocate at Wellesley and the cold warrior at large.

The multiple critiques of each project reflect flaws in design, ready-made assumptions that are never qualified, revisited, or revised. Eck's legacy as a religious pluralist is twofold: the CD-ROM *On Common Ground: World Religions in America* and the book narrating her experience while making that CD-ROM, *The New Religious America*. Since it is the CD-ROM that exemplifies her approach, we will focus on its achievements and limits. Part of the limits are intrinsic to the medium of choice: every CD must have access points that evoke rather than expand or explain complex topics. *On Common Ground* includes three horizontal bands, each of which is marked by several buttons. The first band, "the New Religious Landscape," lists eighteen places as if they are inclusive. The second band, "America's Many Religions," lists fifteen religions as if they are consensual. The third band, "Encountering Religious Diversity," lists conflicts as if they are exhaustive. None fulfills the advance billing of the topic labels, even though each advances the surface knowledge of Asian religious communities and their growth in the United States since 1965.[9] The individual buttons fail at two levels: first, they serve more as parking lots than as patchwork quilts—groups cobbled together under one rubric that in reality have little to do with each other; and second, the nonreligious or ethnic marking of particular groups may be as strong an identifier as the religious, yet because each is subsumed under "religion" it is also reduced in importance.

This is not a trivial point of interpretation; it is a fundamental challenge to the framework of data collection, analysis, and presentation that *On Common Ground* offers. Consider, for instance, the insight of Peter Kivisto. A sociologist concerned with immigrant studies, Kivisto laments the fact that we know much more about Korean immigrants, mostly Protestant, than we do about Filipino Catholics. Is that attributable to a Protestant bias in ethnic studies, or rather to the fact that there are more Korean than Filipino social scientists in the United States? Kivisto argues that it is the latter imbalance that is decisive, that it produces the more sustained attention that one finds to Korean religion in general and to Korean evangelical churches in particular.[10] Yet if one reviews *On Common Ground* it is impossible to imagine this discrepancy in academic labor, much less its consequences for the study of immigrant religious life.

The same lack of analytical depth informs the issue of interreligious violence and its manifestations in late twentieth-century America. In summarizing the major points of *On Common Ground*, Eck gives an example of contemporary racism in the United States. It is a terrible story of an Indian immigrant who was beaten to death in 1987 by New Jersey Anglo assailants shouting, "Hindu, Hindu!" "They conflated race, religion and culture in one cry of hatred," muses Eck,[11] yet the strongest element in that assault was surely race, combined with class. This was not an Indian computer engineer who was murdered but a low-income laborer who fell victim to racialized prejudice. The key question is, Whence this racialized class prejudice? That is the necessary query to all immigrant experience, including religion, and it needs to be foregrounded rather than backgrounded or collapsed into other explanatory referents. As one South Asian scholar has noted, "The indigestible fact of working-class and lower-middle-class South Asian Americans, who are not considered bearers of Indian mysticism or avatars of Indo-chic, is precisely the unassimilable contradiction with which we must grapple."[12]

Yet for Eck, neither the 1987 episode nor the 1998 sequel episode in Queens when an Indo-Trinidadian man was beaten senseless by three white males is evidence of persistent racialized class prejudice. All such episodes, in her view, are but dark moments on the way to light. The light will be marked by religious dialogue. Racism in the American public square will be countered, then replaced by interreligious dialogue.

The same rapt rush to dialogue, and the neglect of racist/class judgments, erases genuine interracial dialogue in *On Common Ground*. Seldom are Asian or African Americans depicted in conversation with one another; instead they are grouped with Anglo Americans. So disturbing is the hegemonic white texture of *On Common Ground* that it evoked passionate protest from my colleague, Charles H. Long, when he first saw excerpts from its sections on Islam. An African American historian of religion noted for his engagement with the need for contextual markers, Professor Long exclaimed, "Every button should have an asterisk next to it:

Black Folk Excluded." Pressed to elaborate, he said, "The only black voices or faces are in tandem with whites. Where are Malcolm and Martin, i.e., where are the persons within the African American Muslim community who shaped Malcolm X, or those within the African American churches who brought Martin L. King Jr. to prominence? A program that only shows black folk and brown folk talking to white folk reinforces the very Anglo conformity that it is supposed to be challenging."[13]

Also omitted from consideration in Eck's taxonomy of eighteen/fifteen are the extremes that deny the viability of either external pluralism or internal diversity—that is to say, malleable religious dispositions, as the preferred future for American society. On the one hand, the Religious Right will continue to act as a *major* spoiler among Protestant Christians, not only rejecting Mormons and Roman Catholics as beyond the pale of salvation but also condemning all non-Christians to perdition. Even before September 11, Jerry Falwell had suggested that President Bush's program for faith-based social initiatives should exclude Muslims, but after September 11 Franklin Graham, the son and heir designate of evangelist Billy Graham, went still further. "We're not attacking Islam," he observed in October, "but Islam has attacked us. The God of Islam is not the same God. He's not the son of God of the Christian or Judaeo-Christian faith. It's a different God, and I believe it is a very evil and wicked religion."[14]

Paralleling Graham's Christian exclusiveness are parochial reflexes among Asian/African immigrants. What to many are heartfelt connections to homeland, to culture, and to history may be seen by cosmopolitan pluralists as nationalisms in new guise, ethno-religious nationalisms that stir immigrants and make them feel as though they remain "in-between," neither fully American nor fully disconnected from their countries of origin.

To survey immigrant religions accurately, one must map the limits of their potential engagement in a common American public space. Even though neither Christian exclusivists nor Asian recidivists will enter that space, their very presence near it reduces the access and the influence of other Asians, even Christian Asians, if one is to project a broader, more accurate picture of immigrant America.

Finally, there must be a way to address the "no-religioners," perhaps under a fourth band titled "Accounting for the Non-religious or Culturally Agnostic." Many are the Asian immigrants, whether Muslim or Hindu, Buddhist or Sikh, for whom "religion" is too marked as an institutional identity that requires public allegiance. Whether labeled "no-religioners" or "cultural agnostics," these Asian immigrants, mostly socioeconomic elites, are thoroughly American and professedly modern in that they care about neither monism nor pluralism nor, for that matter, about any religious practice or outlook.[15]

Despite the multiple critiques that Eck's project evokes, there are even more severe critiques to be leveled at Huntington's thesis as it is presented in his *Foreign Policy* article "The Coming Clash of Civilizations?" (1993) and then in its book-length sequel, *The Clash of Civilizations and the Remaking of World Order* (1996). Edward Said has etched its flaws at the level of inter-civilization awareness.[16] The most evident are also the most damaging. Huntington cites civilizations as though they are fixed containers of norms and values, loyalties and dispositions. While Huntington does acknowledge other factors besides religion that shape civilizational profiles, he presupposes that nation-states are influenced, above all, by civilizational/religious interests. He discounts the significance of pragmatic or ideological considerations that may have little to do with either the long sweep of history or the deep reflex of religion. Instead, Huntington marks entire regions by singular civilizational motivations, thus ignoring the internal diversity that characterizes Asia and Africa as much as it does Europe and North America. In this sense, his political scientific project parallels that of V. S. Naipaul: on the one hand, to laud the unique benefits conferred by Western civilization and on the other, to excoriate those who challenge or limit its benefits, especially Muslims.[17]

Yet in response to numerous critiques of his wholesale homogenization of culture as unitary religious outlook, Huntington has narrowed his gaze still further. In a major article that appeared after the civilizational debate, Huntington reverts to his earlier advocacy of internal cultural homogeneity. Religion, once the capstone of his argument, now disappears. As he charts nostalgically the move from Anglo to Euro to multicultural American identities, he casts almost the entire burden of a possible future political denouement (read: anarchy, loss of global power, internal fragmentation or balkanization) onto multiculturalism. Could there be a worse fate for the United States than to follow the post-1989 path of the USSR? No, certainly not, according to Huntington, and yet nothing less than that is our collective fate, he predicts, should the winds of multiculturalism continue to blow unchecked: "If multiculturalism prevails," he warns, "and if the consensus on liberal democracy disintegrates, the United States could join the Soviet Union on the ash heap of history."[18] The old fear, a polyglot, piebald citizenry, will lead to a fragmented, incoherent public profile. The only faith that can spare the USA such a dire fate is unreflexive Anglo-conformity, the cultural project advocated by Progressive Protestant Patriots.

Disciplinary Differences and the Future of American Religion(s)

Less evident than either their common invocation of Religion One or their differences in measuring its impact are the divergent disciplinary interests that separate Eck from Huntington. Beyond the limits of each, it is their disciplinary perspectives that shape their approach to North American religion and religions. Huntington, harking back to a tradition of social scientists from de Tocqueville to Bellah, argues for a single American disposition that is coded as cultural-religious. His motto is, One Nation Forever Under One God. Eck, going back to a tradition that embraces theologians and philosophers, linguists and historians of religion—all within the humanities—argues for a multiple American outlook that announces pluralism, or one nation newly re-formed under many gods, and even a few goddesses.

The division between humanities and social sciences is seminal. While humanists remain wedded to historical or foundational texts, social scientists sift through contemporary, empirical data. The different nature of their labor renders problematic any consensual academic approach to key issues or key terms,[19] and none is more portentous than the contrasting valuation of culture and also religion.

How, then, do we cross without ignoring the disciplinary divide? In my view, humanists must take account of, and relate to, social scientific methods and studies, but at the same time social scientists cannot ignore the particularist, which is also the historically specified, dimension of their subject; they must attend to human subjects in context, and not advance context-less data to confirm models of change or, in Huntington's case, conflict. In short, both humanists and social scientists have to pay more attention to the conflation between Religion One and Religion Two, and for immigrant religions that would mean a CD-ROM far different from *On Common Ground*, one informed by more internally comparative and sociologically sophisticated micro-studies of particular communities, such as Helen R. Ebaugh and Janet S. Chafetz recently did for Houston.[20]

On the debate about North American religion(s), my stance is to choose

Religion Two. Even though it is impossible to guess what will be the protean shape of American society/religion in five, ten, or twenty years, I think it is possible to conjecture that generational shifts, like technological innovations, will outstrip our imagination. Consider with what speed we have already moved from the nation-state to civil society to the information age as wholesale categories. The implications of this shift in analytical variables are global, with Southeast Asia providing an example of their pervasive power. The Malaysian government, hoping to stave off excesses of millenarian expectation, regularly invokes 2020 vision. While the metaphor lumbers, the point is apt: if we sight a point enough beyond our own era from which to reflect on current issues and arguments, we may yet say some things that are not evident today but are still worth saying about the future of North American religion(s).

The first is that religion will not lose its hold on the popular imagination. While it may change in its particulars, it will continue to refract in multiple ways that have as much to do with ideology as with spirituality. Social scientists who once predicted the end of religion with the advent of secularization are now reinventing religion. Neither they nor humanists can ignore religion, but at the same time they cannot simplistically invoke religious claims. Both academic research and foreign policy agendas require sustained, nuanced, and particularized accounts of religious actors and groups, norms, values, and interests. Religion Two must finally prevail, or religion ceases to have any explanatory value.

The second point about religion in the future is that the religion that will matter most in North America, at least in public discourse about religion, will continue to be Protestant Christian, a version of Religion One. Despite the advance in social sciences and the humanities since the 1950s, no one has yet refuted the basic contention in Will Herberg's groundbreaking book, *Protestant-Catholic-Jew*, first published in 1955. Though he exaggerates the role of Protestantism and often omits contradictory data,[21] Herberg's recurrent argument remains salient almost half a century after it was first advanced. America, for Herberg, is a consensus-seeking society, with a strong religious catalyst driving the nature of the consensus sought. America, meaning the USA, has blended both Catholics and Jews into some version of Protestant American religious belief and practice. Though not quite the civil religion so dear to Bellah and other Parsonian sociologists, it is still more akin to American notions of polity (separation of church and state, along with patriotic fervor) and society (freedom over equality, support for voluntary groups) and economy (frontier capitalism, with creativity and wealth equally prized) than to any set of globally consonant norms and values. It is these American "Protestant" norms that I epitomize as Progressive Protestant Patriot, referring to Henry May[22] but also referring back to Will Herberg. To the extent that they pervade all American believers, they separate them from both pre- and non-American notions of polity, society, and economy.

And what is the outcome of Americanization? As Herberg declared, the outcome is that American Jews have more in common with American Protestants than they do with European Jews, that American Catholics have more in common with their Protestant and Jewish compatriots than they do with Catholics in Ireland or Italy, Poland, or Brazil, that even American Protestants do not look like their counterparts in Ireland, Scotland, Britain, or Germany.[23] Why should we not then conjecture that American Muslims will have more in common with American Protestants, Catholics, and Jews than with Saudi or Egyptian, Afghani, or Malay Muslims, and will not the same conjecture apply to American Hindus and Buddhists, Sikhs and Jains?

The result, alas, is to have this complex process summarized in a single phrase that has become now a metaphor for the distinct American process of assimilation: the melting pot. The melting pot originated before Herberg, in a 1908 play of that name. Later it was transformed by the philosopher Horace Kallen into a notion of cultural pluralism that had more to do with religious than with ethno-racial diversity, though the two remained intertwined. In Herberg's deft analysis it makes religion out to be the vanguard of cultural norms, and religious pluralism, limited to Protestant-Catholic-Jew, becomes the divining rod by which one can measure all subsequent indices of solidarity, or dissidence, in the collective outlook of public America.

Yet the current post-1965 emergence of a polyglot, polyvalent USA presents a different profile than either Herberg imagined or Huntington feared. In thinking about a U.S. collective identity that is no longer modeled after Europe and eschews European antecedents, I refuse to identify one place with one race or one culture or one religion (as did Kant implicitly when he saw the Americas as the location of red barbarians, Asia as the site of yellow polytheists, Africa as the continent of black magicians, and Europe as the bastion of white Protestants).[24] Instead, I see not multiculturalism but multiple grids on particular cultural formations as the preferred option. What we face in the twenty-first century is a kaleidoscope of cultural perspectives. I prefer to call this new crystallization of disparate groups a kaleidoculture. It is the opposite of the Progressive Protestant Patriot, or Huntingtonian, view of America; instead of a monoculture diversified and refracted, as the term *multiculturalism* implies, kaleidoculture is a piebald, pluralist profusion of different accents, profiles, outlooks, and, yes, religions. Does it have a center? No, but it does have a common focus, the collective commitment to preserve multiple approaches to the changing circumstances and opportunities of twenty-first-century America. In the words of contemporary anthropologists, we are best served by multiple grids, each helping us to represent variations within and between specific places and their cultural/religious options. Above all, multiple grids reflect race/class markers that are at once bounded and elastic. In tandem with gender/sexuality markers, race/class markers constitute the same place and the same culture as a different grid for persons who otherwise would appear to share the same religious preferences and to be pursuing similar religious practices. And the observer? It matters a lot that the observer, or critic, is located in multiple fields of power that distance her or him from the same subjects with whom he is empathetically linked.[25] I cannot escape my own boundedness as an Anglo male elite, who is also a university professor with Christian commitments, a lifelong engagement with Islam, and an exuberant attachment to South Asia. Everything that I think or say or write projects that idiosyncratic grid onto my own academic and personal labor.

While no one, least of all the scholar, can escape the ethno-racial pentagon, one can burrow within its conceptual corridors to find a more creative, and more liberatory, space. The ethno-racial pentagon,[26] for instance, is not solely an invention of the U.S. Census Bureau or an imposition of the U.S. Congress or a caricature of Hollywood movie moguls. As noted above, the ethno-racial pentagon is a marker for collective identity that lures both those privileged and those less privileged to think in terms of hierarchy, or citizenship ranking. "All may be created equal," yet most experience inequality within the parameters of social norms, options, and, above all, access to resources.

They also experience hierarchy within the modern university, even the most progressive university, even the University of California at Berkeley. Since 1989 Berkeley has had a multicultural requirement. Before graduation every student must take one course that deepens her or his awareness of U.S. diversity. "The curriculum is designed to study comparatively—and we underline ' comparatively'—five groups, which we have identified as African American, Asian American, Latino, American Indian, and European immigrant groups. . . . Berkeley offers approximately 125 courses that fulfill this requirement, fielded by faculty in almost twenty different departments."[27] At stake is more than the comparative study of these groups. As Wallerstein observed about cultural blindness, these groups cannot be constructed as wholesale in their difference when, in fact, it is the hierarchical privilege of European immigrant groups in general and the Anglo-American overclass in particular that requires the construction of an ethno-racial pentagon that appears to be neutral when it is actually lopsided and asymmetric in its five parts.

A preferential pyramid rather than a fictive and deceptive pentagon would be a better way to describe the interracial mixture of groups in not just California but all of twenty-first-century urban America. Latinos join Asians and Native Americans as subgroups less privileged than Anglo Americans, though not as underprivileged as African Americans. It is this contest for the middle ground that links both Latinos and Asian Americans in an ongoing struggle for recognition. It is a politics of recognition, in Renato Rosaldo's terms, that grips Latino (and, I would argue, Asian) Americans. It is a politics that assumes inequality at the same that it advocates cultural citizenship. Cultural citizenship goes beyond a green card or voting rights; it claims cultural difference, and also religious loyalty, as badges of distinction, not marks of discrimination. Yet it also acknowledges that the very terms in which this contest for cultural citizenship has been framed means that all victories are partial, all gains subject to reversal.

It is against this background that the claims for multiculturalism have to be assessed. On the one hand, they are lauded through agents of religious dialogue as a genuine advance toward an America remade on a rainbow model but still having its same core principles. On the other hand, they are challenged, even rejected, because they are thought to undercut the Anglo-American ideals of a Protestantism that is at once Progressive and Patriotic. Not just Anglophiles but Progressive Protestant Patriots are at the heart of the battle for a revived cultural fundamentalism in twenty-first-century America, a battle waged even more fiercely in the aftermath of September 11, 2001 by those who feel that *all* immigrants, not just Arab Muslim immigrants, challenge the social fabric of a piebald twenty-first-century America.

Fortunately, the past is not always our best guide to the future. However difficult and challenging the task, we must face the difficulty, and we must accept the challenge, of moving from projection to prediction.[28] If I merely project on the basis of past and current developments what will continue for the next twenty to twenty-five years, I am extolling the immovable weight of history. I am assuming that the future will be shaped by the past, both distant and immediate. (Even when I acknowledge multiple pasts for disparate groups with contrasting views of the future, I am still wedded to the notion of some "secure" past.) But if instead I try to predict, especially if I try to predict what will be the impact of continued immigration to the United States from both Asia and the "other" America, I have to take a risk.

My risk is also a wager. I will wager that two major shifts will take place. My first prediction/wager is that internal rivalry will continue at many levels. One kind of rivalry will be between different groups of immigrants seeking the same equivalent of the good life in similar locations, such as Vietnamese and Latinos in California, or African Americans and Asian Americans in suburban Chicago.[29] Even when these groups are extremely violent, as they already have been in some instances, they will have less to do with religious affiliations than with racialized class prejudice. But at the same time, we will also witness rivalry within groups, often across generational lines, as younger persons or second-and third- generation Asian Americans or Hispanic Americans, embrace a broader spectrum of immigrant and non-immigrant American life than did their parents or grandparents.

Lawrence Levine, perhaps the most wry and most seasoned of cultural historians still practicing his trade, rejects the melting pot or the common ground or shared-table image, despite the fact that he embraces the pluralist vision and accents its religious tone. Levine recalls another historian, Marcus Hansen, who back in 1938 noted that the attachment to religion skips a generation in the immigrant experience. "While the second generation may welcome the host country's norms and values and assimilate them as his own, what the son wishes to forget the grandson wishes to remember."[30] Yet what grandchildren remember may not be what their grandparents believed and practiced as religion. Not only sons but also daughters will want to pursue religious practices, and to participate in religious ceremonies, that have familiar names and distant echoes of authenticity. But they will be repackaged in new forms. Though it may be Religion One—Hinduism or Islam or Buddhism or Sikhism, it will be projected in cyberspace as well as in actual temples or mosques, and it will include chat room exchanges with persons of wildly variant perspectives who might never meet face-to-face or, precisely because of the Internet, may someday not just meet face-to-face but marry.

While neither the Internet nor intermarriage is a stable component of the future, together they will increasingly mark American culture in general and Asian American religions in particular as Work in Progress. The progress will include Protestant Patriotic Progress; it will embrace even those cultural fundamentalists who want to exclude others unlike themselves. Twenty-first-century America will be a time/place of exuberance as well as excoriation. It will be a time/place worth marking in its religious template. Along with social and political polyvalence, there will also be religious and cultural polyvalence. Polyvalent kaleidoculture will become most evident in major metropolitan areas, but it will also emerge elsewhere.[31]

My second prediction, again echoing Levine in its optimism, is a suggestion that we are not doomed but blessed to repeat our experience of immigration. While the 1965 immigration law has fostered multiple, often unexpected and surprising changes in the texture of American society, the current generation — whether the older boomers or the younger Generation Xers — is less unique than it imagines. "Diversity, pluralism, and multiculturalism have been present throughout our history," Levine reminds us, "and have acted not merely as the germs of friction and division but as the lines of continuity, the sources for the creation of an indigenous culture, and the roots of a distinctive American identity." But what are lines of continuity? And what is the indigenous culture being created? How, and to what extent, is it distinctly American? These are all questions to be addressed below, but even in their initial formulation, they are questions that mark hope not despair, cooperation not contestation, as emblematic of America's future. The blessing is that the future is unclear, that it has yet to be written, that despite the fear of aliens and immigrants, "every previous generation of Americans has been incorrect in its fears and its certainties because every previous generation — and our own as well — has understood only very imperfectly the phenomena of immigration and assimilation."[32]

Racialized Class Prejudice and Polyvalent Kaleidoculture

None of us has understood the complex process of immigration and assimilation, even when we are academics, even when we make that inquiry part of our life's labor. The most basic of all points is to note that assimilation began not with immigration but with the presence of Otherness, first in the form of the Native Americans or Amerindians, who were reduced and forgotten, and then in the form of African Americans, whose numbers increased throughout the nineteenth century and whose presence could not be forgotten in the twentieth. Assimilation was defined as racialized precisely because of the African American presence. The European immigrants were a challenge to Anglo-American norms, but one that could be redefined as "whiteness." As Toni Morrison observed in *Playing in the Dark,* "though Italians, Germans, French and Jews saw each other as distinct and separate in Europe, they became countrymen in the U.S. through the creation of a social identity that came to be called whiteness. Such a creation was impossible without the existence of its opposite, its other, blackness, those who were defined as not being white."[33] In other words, assimilation to whiteness was possible for European others, but not for African others.

What, then, does assimilation mean in twenty-first-century America? It means, first of all, to recognize that "race, precisely because it has been so central to U.S. identity, has polarized the grammar of U.S. political culture into two extremes: white and black."[34] To be genuinely assimilated one must go beyond the simplistic dyad—black/white—that blinds Americans to other hues, yet it is not a simple, linear step. One cannot take it without first acknowledging the flip side of double consciousness.[35] Not only do Asian and Hispanic immigrants know that they are not "fully" American because they are not Anglos, but they are also socialized, soon after their arrival here, to identify themselves in terms of a spectrum of values that places white at the top and black at the bottom. The internalized perception of race must be acknowledged, if it is to be combated and reduced, since it is even more invidious, and more durable, than its bureaucratic counterpart, the U.S. Census division of all Americans into four categories—Indian, African, Asian, and Anglo, with Hispanic an ethnic subset of the last. This racialized taxonomy of public identity will continue to affect immigrant identity, including religious practice, yet it is neither self-evident nor invincible. African is not the opposite of Anglo, even when members of the other groups, Amerindian, African American, and Asian American, relate to the bi-polar, black/white cultural divide as if it were natural, as if its force were irreversible.

Among those who have ignored the negative, deleterious effect of cultural bipolarism is Samuel Huntington. He identifies space with culture fully and unqualifiedly: the West stands for Anglo-American preeminence, the Rest stands for threats to that preeminence from within and beyond the U.S. border. (As one of my students noted, Huntington's motto seems to translate white as the West and the best, while black becomes the beast and the least!) From that presumptive grid of power, Huntington has to be alarmed at the prospect of thousands of new dark-skinned "aliens" coming to both Europe and the United States as immigrants. For Huntington, as for others like him, there is no distinct American culture but only American culture as a subset of European, which is also Anglo or white, culture. Therefore what happens in Europe affects what happens in the United States, and vice versa. The West and the Rest are his favorite dyadic opposites. In addressing "The West and the Rest: Intercivilizational Issues," Huntington expresses alarm about immigration over there and right here in the same breath. There is no ocean separating the USA from Western Europe when it comes to recognition of the common problem of non-white, religiously other, aliens: just as the influx of migrants of non-European origin has brought a high number of Muslims to Europe, so it has brought many, too many, Mexicans to the United States.

In both cases, for Huntington, the need is to preserve conformity to Anglo-Protestant norms or what Levine calls Anglo-conformity. The biggest problem is the distance between the norms of the newest immigrants and the norms defining Anglo-conformity. To the new faiths, Huntington raises an old fear. It is fear couched in racialized terms. It is not only Huntington's fear but the fear of a host of others who listen to Rush Limbaugh and support Gary Bauer for political office. It is fear of the loss of Anglocentrism. And like all fears, it has a specific location that marks its current genesis. For Huntington it is that the Anglo conquests to the south in the nineteenth century will be reversed by the immigration conquests to the north in the twenty-first century. "The results of American military expansion in the 19th century," he warns, "could be threatened and possibly reversed by Mexican demographic expansion in the 21st century."[36] In other words, they will reverse on our soil the Anglo-norms that we had imposed on them; internal Latino-norms will confront, and weaken or distort, the Anglo-norms at the heart of Western civilization. Anglocentrism, and with it Western civilization, will be doomed.

Huntington's lament would not be significant were it his alone, but he stands among a host of those who fear the new faiths as harbingers of the old fears. The solidarity of civil religion that binds Americans is threatened by too much difference. Pluralism, rather than a hope, becomes itself a fear. "Pluralism comes at a cost," warns a prominent legal scholar, echoing Huntington's concern.

> It dilutes the concept of 'citizen,' making it difficult to identify what being an 'American' is all about. If there is to be a common core of tradition and affection, it must emerge *indirectly*, from what Rawls might call the 'overlapping consensus' of different traditions, rather than through conscious inculcation of a public ideology or a civil religion. It is for this reason that many thoughtful Americans fear that the pluralist approach will exacerbate an already dangerous balkanization of American public life.[37]

To speak of the "balkanization of American public life" at the turn of the century, while memories of the Yugoslav/Bosnian catastrophe remain vivid for American readers, is to suggest a dystopia even more grim than Huntington's. It makes all the more necessary a critical evaluation of the options offered by Huntington and Eck. In the battle between hegemonic pluralism (Eck) and cultural fundamentalism (Huntington), I would prefer the former over the latter. Eck is, after all, a grounded humanist with a broad ecumenical agenda while Huntington is a provincial patriot parading as a New Age cold warrior. Yet theirs is finally another pseudo-dyad, a false contest ignoring the real contestants. The real contestants are those immigrants, along with marginalized or alien others, who seek not a place at the table of Anglo-conformity nor assimilation into a melting pot Anglo-culture but rather life on their own terms within a participatory democracy. That democracy also remains a work in progress. It is a democracy still to be achieved that will replace Progressive Protestant Patriotism with patriotism marked both by openness toward religious "others" and by the disposition to make minimal resources available to the newly enfranchised as well as to previously disenfranchised Americans.

In my view, neither the alarmist predictions of Huntington nor the dialogic preferences of Eck will prevail. Neither will dominate the religious scene of mid-twenty-first-century America. Instead, there will be many varieties of family life and spiritual expression. Hybrid and creole, polyphonous and piebald, they will permeate our imagination far more than the fixed-container traditions of their ancestors. Side by side with these new forms of solidarity and different from them, there will exist transnational religious loyalties. They will create allegiances, less benign and pacific than the experiments of Asian, African and Caribbean Americans. The "new" forms of North American religion will prevail only through generational change, nor will they prevail without verbal opposition or physical violence. Yet their end result will be a kaleidoculture, a porous container of fungible subgroups of Americans, all polyvalent, neither minority nor majority, just American.

In the aftermath of September 11, it is even more important, though also much harder, to remain optimistic about a polyvalent kaleidoculture in the twenty-first-century United States. Arab Americans, and Asian Americans who seem to resemble Arab Muslims or who are elided with them, have been targeted as possible suspects. Even when they cannot be directly linked to the crimes of September 11, law enforcement officials, following the lead of Attorney General John Ashcroft, suspect them of future crimes that may be planned but not yet carried out. It is a draconian policy, which the public in general seems to support, though responsible media have provided alternative, resistant perspectives.[38]

Alas, public backlash against the Asian Muslim Other will be slow to subside, even if foreign wars, in Afghanistan and elsewhere, are waged successfully. In fact, the very persistence of a propaganda war in tandem with a military campaign overseas ensures that a percentage of "patriotic" Americans will find unwitting accomplices at home to scapegoat as fifth column supporters of the foreign enemy. These perceptions are not only suspect; they also cut against the other American instinct, to trust that freedom of expression, including religious worship and loyalty, can be, and must be, maintained as part of the American dream. September 11 may have deferred, even complicated, Asian Muslim participation in a polyvalent kaleidoculture, but it remains a dream delayed, not erased.

CHAPTER 2

Civil Society and Immigrants

However admirable the idea of civil society is as a political slogan we should have serious doubts as to its efficacy as a concrete model for social and political practice. . . . It reflects not only a particular stage of historical development in the West but the particular conditions that obtained there and not necessarily in other parts of the world.

—Adam Seligman, *The Idea of Civil Society*[1]

In all times and places civil society alone has the inherent power to change usage, custom, and itself. Civil society is the space which creative individuals open between tradition and the state or the priest and the prince. While the priest and the prince, whenever they rule together, are the enemies of civil society, civil society can combine religion with politics and so provide a more dynamic, if less stable, system of governance than a state-established religion or a religion-based state.

—J. P. S. Uberoi, *Religion, Civil Society, and the State*[2]

It is difficult to trace any version of the American dream without invoking civil society, yet fewer categories of social analysis are less stable than civil society. Almost every student of contemporary global events must decide on her or his evaluation of both the history and the relevance of civil society. For me in the current chapter the central question is, <u>Will the newest immigrants to North America become critical cosmopolitans through the venues</u>

This chapter is a much-revised version of a paper given at the Emile Bustani Middle East Seminar at MIT on April 13, 1999. I am indebted to Professor Philip S. Khoury, chair of the Bustani Seminar and professor of history and dean of the School of Humanities and Social Science at MIT, for the invitation both to address the Bustani Seminar and to engage other attendees at a reception/dinner with conversation that matched the marvelous fare of the MIT faculty club.

of civil society, or will they instead perpetuate a racialized class prejudice through transnational circuits, including the World Wide Web? This question does not take civil society for granted but also does not dismiss its viability. What it requires, above all, is a more radical application of civil society to the analytic gaze of Asian American life than has so far been evident.

Civil society has a long history in West European, then North American, social thought. It provides, along with the state and political society, three sites from which to project a coherent vision of social order that both grants individual rights and acknowledges collective duties. Civil society implies control without preempting freedom. It becomes a core element for the liberal democratic order and its socioeconomic counterpart, industrial capitalism.

To the extent that immigrants choose to come to the United States, it is, in part, because they accept the dominant notion that the private and public realms, individual hopes and institutional norms mesh without collapsing. The political order is not limited to the state, nor are the actions of social groups monitored or prompted from a praetorian center. But how do these assumptions actually play out in the real lives of immigrants, and can their actual experience in the United States be separated from that of twenty-first-century citizens living elsewhere on the globe?

And then what happens if one includes religion—religious institutions and also spiritual practices—in the public square and adds religion to debates about civil society? What difference does it make for the independent or autonomous role of groups of immigrant Muslims in Chicago or immigrant Hindus in Pennsylvania? These are the questions that we will explore in two framing narratives before coming back to the question of, Why civil society?

As in the previous chapter, this chapter has a framing narrative. Like the framing narrative in chapter 1, it is a doublet; it consists of two stories, one of a Muslim, the other of a Hindu. Both are shaped by their location in the United States, even as they, in turn, reshape the kaleidoculture of America through their own polyvalent experience of its options and limits.

Framing Narrative, Part 1: A Muslim Story

It was March 1997. The previous month two Muslim youths had been killed in a gang fight on the South Side of Chicago. An E-mail had been posted in the chat room of the Muslim Students Association of the University of Chicago (*MSA-Chicago Net*). It was posted by a young Palestinian Muslim, Hussein, who was himself linked to a local community outreach group—IMAN (acronym for Inner-City Muslim Action Network that also means, in Arabic, "faith"), and since Hussein often attended local MSA meetings to project the views of IMAN, namely, to offer Islamic solutions to the social difficulties faced by inner-city families, both his name and his message were familiar to other members of the chat room. "The deadly life for youths growing up in America's inner-cities can only be solved by Islam," Hussein asserted, then added, "but this means Muslims everywhere must work towards this end. It is in this spirit that we invite all Muslims in the Chicago land area to a planning meeting for an event entitled 'Taking It to the Streets.' Taking it to the Streets will be an all day type Islamic festival held in the heart of a diverse community on the Southwest Side of Chicago. . . . We need everyone to be involved in some way or another, so bring yourself and several friends to the planning meeting this Sunday." The festival's subtitle underscored its inclusive and collective nature: "Nurturing Unity, Revitalization, and Success."

Successive E-mails reinforced both the urgency of the moment and the need to have other Muslims get involved. College students, some of them African Americans, and many of them already volunteers in IMAN, did attend the festival, which took place on June 21, 1997. At the event there were food tents, game booths, a job fair, a health clinic, and also free legal counseling. Here and there signboards announced: "Do you know that Islam is the fastest growing religion in America?" "Did you know that only 15% of Muslims are Arabs?" There was also a *da'wa* (or proselytization) booth, which distributed pamphlets from a local group known as the Institute of Islamic Information and Education (III&E). At one moment in the daylong gathering, Hussein mounted a platform in the middle of Marquette Park and proclaimed: "Islam encompasses many cultures. That is what we celebrate and mark here. In a moment when you see us pray together, you will see African Americans, Latinos, Arabs and Indo-Pakistanis standing side-by-side." And when the event concluded, a sequel E-mail announced that one of its major objectives had been achieved: "We have been able to bring Muslims of diverse ethnic and racial backgrounds together to strengthen bonds of sister/brotherhood in a community where Islam is generally associated with a particular ethnic background (by both Muslims and non-Muslims)."

While Hussein advocated ethnic diversity and interracial harmony as hallmarks of universal Islam, there were other signs that it remained a goal to be achieved rather than a reality to be celebrated in late twentieth-century America. Despite flyers and mosque announcements in Arab and Indo-Pakistani neighborhoods of Greater Chicago, few Arab or South Asian volunteers joined with others till near the end. And at least one South Asian Muslim from the suburbs criticized the inner-city Muslims for their "bad example." He suggested that to identify with the festival would be to risk "a negative judgment from non-Muslim neighbors and colleagues, challenging the suburban claim to Islam as fulfilling the requirements of the American middle-class ideal: a well-defined family structure, a respectful husband and a devoted wife, and straightforward business/religious morals."[3]

Among the groups that supported the IMAN festival in 1997 was the III&E. It is part of the story of new Muslim organizations in the USA. It was founded in 1985 by an Indo-Pakistani immigrant to the United States, Amir Ali, and his wife, Mary, a convert from Roman Catholicism. Amir Ali, a biochemist by training, had lived in the USA since 1962, but did not establish III&E till his return from a period of employment in Saudi Arabia. He claimed independence from any foreign influence, yet three Saudis, including a member of the Council of Shura (Consultation), Dr. Abdullah Naseef, sat on his eight-person board of trustees in the mid-1990s. In 1987 Amir Ali launched a twenty-five-year project, the goal of which was to reach the entire U.S. population by 2012. Specifically, III&E hoped to remove misinformation about Islam and Muslims, to present true teachings of Islam, to help indigenous Americans who revert or convert to Islam, and to recruit Muslims for da'wa or proselytization work. The first goal was the most difficult because ignorance was abetted by groups openly hostile to Islam and Muslims: "atheists, secularists, agnostics, Zionists, Fundamentalist Christians and all those who have an agenda against Muslims, the world over." Reflecting on the racialized nature of American society, Amir Ali saw Muslims as located in a special, lower class because of religion. "In America," he lamented, "it appears that the value of life of Jewish and white Americans is the highest, the blacks and the Spanish speaking take the next far lower rung, whereas American Muslims, irrespective of their nature or racial origin, have no value at all."

But the problem of valorizing Islam and projecting its correct image in public was compounded, according to him, by the residual ignorance of immigrant Muslims. Instead of correct knowledge of universal Islam, immigrants were bound by local notions of cultural Islam. "The immigrant community," in Amir Ali's view, "is so ignorant about their duties and what Islam is that they don't know what to do. They think that their own culture is Islam." And because of this foundational ignorance some immigrants even turn away from the primary sources of revelation, the Qur'an and the Sunnah, and instead place faith in pseudo-Islamic leaders, such as Sufi masters or Qadiyanis, also known as Ahmadis, and of course, Farrakhanis, that is, members of the Nation of Islam who acknowledge Louis Farrakhan as their leader.[4]

Framing Narrative, Part 2: A Hindu Story

Like the III&E, the Vishwa Hindu Parishad (VHP) of America has only come into being in the USA since 1965. It began holding meetings in 1970, then became formally organized in 1974. It publishes literature on the Hindu way of life, it arranges seminars and lecture tours for visiting spiritual luminaries, it provides family counseling modeled on a Hindu outlook, and it funds social service projects in India. On one level it seems like an immigrant community for immigrants only: its network of contacts and affiliations extends to other Indian religious and social organizations in the USA, and its board members are often prominent in them.

Yet on another level the VHP is highly politicized: it wants to influence both politics at home and non-Indians in the United States. On politics in India, the VHP promotes temple societies, language, regional and professional networks, as well as India associations, which have links to the subcontinent. They often organize around specific causes and direct not just attention but also funds to these same causes. The most prominent was the Ayodhya Mandir/Babri Masjid conflict of the early 1990s. It arose from rival claims by Muslim and Hindu groups in India to original ownership of a specific holy site in North India. The logic of the VHP was simple: the mosque was built on a destroyed temple marking the birthplace of the Hindu god Ram, therefore the mosque had to be destroyed and a new temple dedicated to Ram built on the same site. For that purpose bricks were brought from all over India, and after the VHP mobilized a large-scale assault to destroy the mosque in December 1992, a Hindu temple was built in its stead. Along the way, riots occurred in major Indian cities, with thousands of people left dead by the tensions and hostilities generated by this action. It was, in short, both politically volatile and religiously marked as a Hindu/Muslim divide. During the movement to rebuild the temple, local groups throughout India organized events to dedicate specific bricks that devotees would then bring to the Ayodhya site to be part of the new temple. The VHP in America also organized groups in thirty-one cities. Bricks were ritually sanctified at local meetings, then sent to Ayodhya to be part of the new Ram temple. With the bricks also went funds, large sums of U.S. dollars, that became part of the financial support for the Ayodhya restoration movement in India.

At the same time as VHP strengthened the political ties of immigrants to India, at least one elder VHP member took the stance that it could help Hindu values permeate the larger U.S. society. Like ISKCON, or the Krishna Consciousness Movement, VHP advocated a kind of cultural syncretism that, in his view, would appeal to the intellectuals (read: Anglo, upper middle class) of America. Since VHP had some 3,800 cultural organizations in the U.S. by the year 2000, and since the preponderance of its members were professional Indians, they could continue to influence others, especially if they were able to unify efforts with like-minded U.S.-based Hindu groups. Unification among Hindu Americans thus became a major priority.

It was with the goal of furthering unification that VHP of America convened a Dharma Sanad, or World Parliament of Religions, in rural Pennsylvania in November 1998. The event brought together thirty Hindu teachers or swamis, along with two hundred community leaders, to develop a code of conduct for Indian immigrants to North America. The chief speaker, Ashok Singhal, was the leader of the Ayodhya restoration movement in India, and he saw the threat in America to be not unlike the threat in India: the rising tide of Muslim influence. If temple restoration was the preferred tactic abroad, the preferred tactic in the United States was to prevent exogamy. Up to 30 or 40 percent of Hindu girls were said to be marrying non-Hindu men. Cultural regeneration became "a task of Hindu men saving their women from Muslim men, thereby demarcating the character and limits of the VHP's American project. The absence of an ostensible interest in wider political issues could render it a relatively non-controversial presence in the U.S. At the same time, defining its mission as one of protecting the Hindu patriarchal family enabled the stigmatizing of the non-Hindu, crucially the Muslim male, thus reinforcing the VHP's emphasis on Hindu identity."[5]

The Scope of Civil Society

Neither of these framing stories is complete. They omit other groups, both Muslim and Hindu, that operate within the circuit of civil society throughout the major urban centers of the USA, but two prior questions haunt any discussion of their interrelatedness or their wider impact. Fundamental to civil society discourse, these questions need to be addressed and answered before one can analyze the data of particular associations, whether Muslim or Hindu, Christian or Buddhist:

Must contemporary civil society include religious groups?
Is it only in the West that civil society extols individual rights?

We seem to have answered the first question YES merely by the examples we have given. But ours is not the sole answer. Can religious institutions contribute to creating, then maintaining civil society? The answer, at least for most Enlightenment theorists, was NO. To be sure, insofar as religious groups constitute private associations and insofar as religious professionals educate citizens in civic-mindedness or civic virtue, churches—as also synagogues and mosques—might assist in the civil society project, but only as a secondary aspect of their existence. Even de Tocqueville and Montesquieu, both of them major advocates of civil society as a hedge against tyranny, underscored guilds and unions as more efficacious exponents of civic virtue than churches. And the valuation of those from the left was still more dismissive of religious groups as agents of change or challenge to the existing order: For Marx, civil society represented a direct expression of bourgeois values inscribing class privilege and economic exploitation, while for Gramsci the function of civil society was more indirect than direct: It provided a fig leaf, a cultural phalanx that guaranteed ideological hegemony for the ruling classes. Insofar as religion mattered, it mattered merely as an institutional ally of schools and voluntary associations, channeling like-minded, privileged persons to imagine that they were resisting even as they were being co-opted.

Neither the fall of the Berlin Wall nor the redemocratization of parts of Eastern Europe changed the Enlightenment prejudice against religion. Since 1990 civil society has been lauded as the major force protecting individuals against the intrusive, unbounded power of the state, and it is civil libertarians who are said to provide a buffer against autocratic rule or human exploitation! Yet the gain for civil society continues to include religion only through the back door. It is not a signposted back door, and it is also a door that seems to be half shut as well as half open. It comes from the concept of public sphere, originating from the German social theorist Jurgen Habermas, at least in its most recent incarnation, and it requires the application of a Habermasian discursive model of the public sphere to both civil society and religion. The first stage of the argument is to recognize political life as framed by three units: the state, political society, and civil society. The second stage is to acknowledge that for many societies, not just for Western Europe and North America but also for Southern and Eastern Europe as also for Latin America, there is a modern form of public religion that may intervene in civil society, or rather in the public sphere of civil society. Examples abound from both the Catholic Church and evangelical, or fundamentalist, branches of Protestant Christianity, but they all tend to reinforce the notions that (a) there are consensually accepted universal principles that are both modern in origin and public in expression and (b) these public articulations of religion through civil society have been best achieved in the West.[6]

At its narrowest, the argument lauds the West as the sole carrier of these principles through the vehicle of civil society (with or without the cooperation of state and/or political society). From a variety of disciplines and from several scholarly perspectives, the argument has been made that only among the advanced states of Western Europe and North America can one find the social resources and also the collective will to create, sustain, and articulate civil society.

Typically the argument is made in terms of the need for individual choice and also for affirming individual rights. The stark emphasis on the priority of the individual over the collective is never questioned as a good; it is simply presumed, and then upheld as the basis for asserting the Western "difference" in social modeling. The entire history of Western philosophical reflection on civil society, from Aristotle to Derrida, we are told, demonstrates that only the Greeks and their successors were preoccupied with civil society; it is these protectors of the individual who have made of civil society a necessary buffer between the individual and any totalitarian state, between the individual and any public ideology, since totalitarian states and public ideologies alike deny the possibility of individual choice, the prospect of freedom of thought.[7] In the first of our epigraphs for this chapter, civil society is also said to appear only in certain societies and under certain historical conditions. Elsewhere the author specifies the indispensable condition for civil society: It is the individual, for "the very pluralism that so many in the West identify with the idea of civil society," claims Seligman, "rests on an almost Durkheimian idea of the individual as infused with moral and transcendental attributes, which is lacking in the East."[8]

Lacking the autonomous individual, the East also lacks civil society. Civil society remains the pride of the West, which is to say, Western Europe and North America. Closely allied to it is the concept of citizen, also said to be uniquely Western but tied as much to the formation of cities as to the persons who inhabit them. It was the grandfather of modern sociology, Max Weber, who argued: "Only in the Occident is found the concept of citizen (*civis Romanus, citoyen, bourgeois*) because only in the Occident again are there cities in the specific sense."[9]

And crucial to the autonomous individual, who as urban resident becomes responsible citizen, is the role of capitalism. Civil society is linked as both catalyst and beneficiary to the expansion of modern-day capitalism, above all, by ensuring the right to private property and the right to commercial expansion that is limited only by the need to respect others' rights to the same benefits. If citizenship is the first cognate for civil society, then civility is its second, so that civil society becomes defined by three elements: civic life (including political parties outside the state), citizenship (meaning full rights and responsibilities), and civility in interaction. Nor is it static. Civil society effects change through legitimate process, through a liberalization process that carves out a larger and larger realm for civic non-state activity and for civil rights.[10]

Real civil society was absent from the twentieth century, according to most political pundits, till its final decade. Civil society came into public view only after the end of the Cold War, that is, since the 1990s. If there was one event that triggered attention to civil society, it was the velvet revolution in Czechoslovakia, led by a poet, Vaclav Havel. Relying on neither the mechanisms of the Communist state nor the structures of traditional groups, including the Catholic Church, the Czech revolution seemed to be fostered by informal associations and voluntary networks. Were they linked only to Eastern Europe or did they exist elsewhere also? It was the hope of civil libertarians that civil society existed latently in all societies and that its latent potential could be conjured to produce other transitions to docile forms of capitalist democracy.

But the Czech experiment with civil society proved bumpy, and neighboring states—Yugoslavia, Bosnia, and Croatia—fell into a war that was anything but civil. The utopian potential for civil society seemed more limited at the end of the century than it had a mere decade earlier. Countries conditioned to socialist planning, it seemed, may not be able to adopt democratic institutions or to embrace global capitalism without a transition period.

The biggest challenge to civil libertarians was, and remains, the ex–Soviet Union. Russia today, according to an eminent historian, is "a poor power trying to modernize in the real world after the failure of its caricature modernization in the surreal world of Soviet Socialism." Russia, he argues, "must first become rich if she wishes again to be powerful." While this may take a long time, he still predicts that it is possible, but only through private property and the market, so one must hope that "the predominance of private property and the market . . . will in the long run produce the same effects in Russia that they have everywhere in the contemporary world: the formation of a civil society and a pluralistic culture."[11]

Private property . . . the market . . . a civil society . . . a pluralistic culture. It is the familiar teleological mantra of neoliberalism. It holds the key to both national reconstruction and global competitiveness. Private property, not only for Russians but also for all others, remains the sine qua non of a competitive market. Private property accents the autonomy of individual members within market economies, at the same time that it projects the logic of market forces to produce a civil society as also a pluralistic culture, within and beyond specific nation-states, large and small, East and West![12]

Premodern Civil Society

There is a different approach to civil society that accents not its market-driven, late-capitalist features, epitomized in Western Europe and North America, but instead its medieval occurrence on a global pattern. It harks back to the great empires, stretching from the Mediterranean to the Pacific, that marked the world system before the rise of European commercial, then colonial expansion. Noting the prevalence of religious pluralism in the premodern world, historian William McNeill reckons that urban centers, in particular, had embraced a form of "permanent poly-ethnicity," allowing a series of religiously defined communities to exist side by side.

In other words, religious communities were seen as conciliatory components of viable civil societies rather than as sources of mutual alienation, distrust and conflict. What evolved in the nineteenth and twentieth centuries, in effect, were two contrasting notions of civility. According to one, which characterized most nation-states in nineteenth-century Europe, the preferred path to religious and ethnic civility was homogenization and assimilation. But there remained the lingering examples, and the collective memory, of multinational empires, where permanent poly-ethnicity, at least in urban spaces, was an acceptable, even commendable, alternative.[13]

McNeill's analysis is a healthy reminder that civil society is linked, above all, to civility, that civility depends on institutionalized pluralism, and that the nascent West had neither a monopoly on civility nor the only model for a civil society.[14]

Yet both the premodern pluralist model and the modern liberal capitalist model of civil society presume a certain kind of state. Both presume that the state is unitary, but with limited powers. They also presume that pluralism—whether defined by religious or commercial or elective affinities—is invariably good, at once welcoming difference and promoting tolerance. Further, they presume that there exists a kind of social contract about what counts as good.

But can those conditions pertain elsewhere than in Western Europe and North America? After all, it is the institutions, associations, and networks of European and North American civil society that are said to "operate in a pluralistically, continuously contested public space or public civic realm, a zone between the state and private sectors. Distinct from either the coercive and bureaucratic functions of the state public sector or profit-seeking private sector businesses . . . civil society represents a third, non-governmental, non-profit, voluntary sector of modern society."[15]

Civil Society, Islam, and Sikhism

While it would seem that civil society is limited to Western Europe and North America, the case of Turkey suggests otherwise. Indeed, the modern Turkish state provides a valuable test case of civil society as geographically itinerant. Modern Turkey, projecting Kemalist ideology from the 1920s on, defined itself negatively in relation to the Islamic past. All that was deemed lacking or detrimental to a unified and modern Turkish nation was derived from the cosmopolitanism of the Ottoman Empire. The Republican leaders were the catalysts for a new state, at once secular and rational, but this very project meant that the Kemalist elite "sought to perpetuate its guardianship whilst limiting both political participation and the autonomy of civil society."[16] In other words, the Turkish state from the mid-1920s to the mid-1980s defined itself not only against its Islamic past but also against ethnic and religious groups whom it deemed to be "outsiders," recalcitrants or impediments to its own modernizing ideology. It was, in fact, civil society that was repressed though not eliminated, and it was civil society that had a religious as well as an ethnic and cultural component. In trying to explain what has been happening in Turkey, especially since the mid-1980s, commentators have referred to civil society in order to account for nonpolitical initiatives that were neither fundamentalist nor traditionalist in origin yet highlighted aspects of Turkish identity and values that many Turks felt had been excluded from Kemalist ideology. Turkish civil libertarians demanded ethnic homogeneity, they asked for recuperation of Ottoman symbols and successes, and they also asked for a healthier, broadened role of Islamic beliefs and practices.

The role of Islam is especially complex. The Islamic culture of modern-day Turkey is "ordinary," in Raymond Williams's sense of that term. It has to do with the everyday and the routine. It has to do not only with affirming Islam as the last and best religion but with looking at Islam as "a strong presence in civil society, where religious foundations (*vakifs*) provide support in education, housing and health for those let down by the inadequate social services of the state," and also where Muslim thinkers offer thoughtful and imaginative responses to the structural problems and difficulties of change in Turkish society.[17] This is not to say that there are not doctrinaire Muslim leaders in present-day Turkey, but there are also others, including a group of Muslim engineers, who are both modern and inclusive in outlook. Since the 1980s they have engaged questions of democracy. They have pursued the conditions of plural democracy. They have welcomed the benefit of civil society, even as they seek a form of modernity that acknowledges local cultural identities and accommodates specifically Turkish social structures.

If the Turkish case allows us to see how civil society does more than promote Western exceptionalism, it also qualifies Michael Walzer's presumptive claim that "the state itself is unlike all other associations in that it both frames civil society and occupies space within it." In its framing capacity, argues Walzer, the state "fixes the boundary conditions and the basic rule of all associational activity."[18] For Walzer, as for Durkheim earlier, the state becomes the moral gatekeeper, which "must be present in all spheres of social life and make itself felt. . . . It must even permeate all those second-ary groups of family, trade and professional association, Church, regional arenas and so on."[19] The Turkish case suggests otherwise: Islamic demo-cratic initiatives directed to the post-1980 state were neither anticipated by, nor framed within, the Kemalist model of modern Turkey, yet they remain a major factor in the maelstrom of Turkish politics.

Beyond Turkey, can we further demonstrate that civil society includes attention to religious actors, organizations, and issues? Yes, and again with an example from Muslim Asia, but from Southeast rather than Central Asia. The example comes from Indonesia, where religion is central to civil society. Without the intervention of civic groups, including religious organizations, into political space the revolution that toppled Sukarno and brought an elected government to Indonesia would never have occurred in 1998. The lesson is clear: Whatever dreams will motivate Muslim societies, the civil option will be among them. In modern day Indonesia, "the civil option may promote *public* religion, but distanced from the coercive machinery of state. It strides proudly into the public arena but insists that its message is clearest when its bearers guard their independence. Religious voices must be ready to balance and critique the state and the market, rather than give both a greater measure of social power. Here is a religious reformation that works with, rather than against, the pluralizing realities of our age."[20]

Nor do Turkey and Indonesia exhaust the potential for civil society in contemporary Muslim nations. Senegal is yet another Muslim society that fits the model of civil society, offering an alternative to the state that is also its competitor, rather than its co-opted other face. Senegal? In West Africa, with barely ten million inhabitants and no oil resources, Senegal receives sparse attention in most studies of globalization and change. Yet Senegal boasts a vital civil society, in part resulting from its history as a majority Muslim state in which Sufi orders have played, and continue to play, a cru-cial role. The Sufi pattern has shaped a religiously based civil society, one in which a mode of social organization vis-à-vis the state is tilted toward the societal side of state-society relations. How is this possible? Because Sufi

leaders, or marabouts, have expanded their networks of master-client relations through the colonial and now the independence period of Sene-
galese history.

While numerous scholars, as we have seen, underscore how important
it is to have a well-developed civil society in order to make political society
function on a pluralist basis and to avoid authoritarian state structures, it
has also been assumed that where civil society does emerge and become
strengthened, as it has post-1989 in parts of the Eastern Europe and the
ex–Soviet Union, it is "modern" institutions that have led to its expansion.
Unions, trade groups, voluntary associations—all these are acceptable and
predictable sites for the emergence of civil society. Yet in Senegal it is religious, not secular, organizations that have fulfilled the role of civil society,
providing a third way beyond the state and political society. In Senegal, it
is institutional brotherhoods, or Sufi orders, that have shown the capacity
both to aggregate interests and to project sufficient solidarity, with the result
that they require the state to engage them in the interest of collective governance. At the same time leaders of the major orders have developed flexible responses to state actions that range from the confrontational to the
dissociative. They confirm the general principle that religion as an element
and religious communities as groups are integral to the worldwide pattern
of civil society, not just in Western Europe and North America but also in
Asia and in Africa.[21]

There is still another religious group that merits inclusion in studies of
civil society: the Sikhs. A detailed semiotic examination of Sikh history
reveals how inherently polysemic is the notion of civil society. It stretches
back at least to the sixteenth century and includes the formation of Sikh
collective identity in distinction from prevalent notions of political loyalty
(Mughal/Muslim) and social hierarchy (Hindu). In effect, civil society can
reflect newly formed notions of identity that rival traditional authorities,
both political and religious. In terms of exemplary types, the arbiter of civil
society is neither the priest nor the prince but the martyr, or at least the
would-be martyr, that is, the resistant, creative individual who imagines a
space beyond inherited political and religious parameters and is willing to
fight to the death to achieve this ideal. This approach is epitomized in the
second of the two epigraphs with which I began this chapter. Some might
dismiss the credibility of its author, J. P. S. Uberoi, since his narrative might
seem to be unduly self-justifying: He writes as a Sikh academic who wants
to affirm a collective past that allows "strength in diversity" and thereby

invokes civil society merely to separate himself from the twin hegemonic forces of his own past, one Hindu, the other Muslim.

Such a preemptive dismissal of Uberoi is, however, not justified. His analytical honesty allows him to criticize Sikhs as well as others. He practices rather than merely invokes double consciousness and redoubled criticism. Through Uberoi's recapitulation of the origins and intentions of Sikhism, one could imagine civil society as formative even before it was theorized by Western Enlightenment scholars, from Montesquieu to Derrida. One could also begin to see how its global expanse could include Sufi brotherhoods, Buddhist monks, and Sikh reformers as well as Christian missionaries.[22] Still more important, one can see how groups who come to the United States as Asian immigrants, including Sikh immigrants, could bring with them notions of a third space that does not merely mirror Western theory or American norms but rather projects their own values, private and public, individual and collective.

Civil Society and the High-Tech Era

What the immigrants confront no less than the citizens of the state where they hope to relocate is technicalism. For in the high-tech era, civil society has to confront the market as well as the state, if it is to continue to have relevance during the next phase of global history.[23] And civil society must also have a religious face if it is to combat the excesses of both political and commercial elites, those who occupy the top rung of the global/local hierarchies of power that have not been eliminated since the end of the Cold War or the advent of the Internet. ✳

But herein lies a major problem for religion. The state, even the democratic state, even the democratic American state, protected by the First Amendment clause separating church from state, cannot be exempt from having religious preferences. The temptation is to create a state-sponsored religious ethos that backs away from the seeming moral anarchy of laissez-faire religious competition and in its stead offers a civic religion. A civic religion of the right would ensure order, but it would also enforce hegemony and worse: It would demonize or deride internal others. The most vulnerable to its dictates would be recent immigrants, formed through the polyvalent nodes of alternative religious/ethnic structures. Hispanic immigrants are Abrahamic but not Anglo-Saxon, while Asian immigrants, except for the large Christian subset from East/Southeast Asia,[24] are neither Abrahamic nor Anglo-Saxon.

How can the Internet strengthen civil society to encourage new networks of resistance to stereotyping? Can persistent racialized prejudice be opposed through cyberspace? It is too early to tell, but it may not be too early to explore another prospect: that civil society will elide into cyber society. Even though the Internet has been popularly used for less than a decade, we may already be witnessing the rapid shift from a state-civil society model to an all-pervasive information society. Whether we call it the Info Age or the Cyber Century, high-tech connectivity has become integral to the twenty-first century, and radical technological shifts will envelop both the state and its adjuncts, including civil society, not just in Western Europe and North America but also in major metropolitan centers of Latin America, Africa, and Asia.

More than thirty years ago the world historian Marshall Hodgson warned that the speed and scope of technicalism would overwhelm not only Orientals but also Occidentals: Both the West and the East, according to Hodgson, would be transformed by "the expectation of continuous innovation" and its often unintended consequences.[25] More recently, the urban sociologist Manuel Castells has tried to theorize the unexpected advent of the computer and also to assess its long-term social impact. Looking at what Hodgson termed the latest phase in global history, Castells calls it the Information Age.[26] Castells traces how computer-driven telecommunications have intensified global interactions at the same time that they have created innumerable networks that reconfigure indeterminate, atomized groups of individuals into new virtual communities. What is emerging, in Castells's view, is a global network society. A global network society? Yes, a globally diffuse heteronomic network of equivalent nodes where simultaneous flows of space define a circuit of electronic impulses that articulate social as well as economic reality.[27]

But there is a dark side to the Information Age, and the shadows as well as the light of cyberspace concern Castells. Informational politics, in his view, renders the state less powerful in its supervisory, regulatory, and disciplinary force. While most conservatives would welcome that shift, informational politics also reduces the protective and redistributive functions of the state, which most liberals would not applaud. In other words, the Information Age inherently favors an elitist status quo. What we face, laments Castells, are "the black holes of informational capitalism," which give rise to social exclusion and therefore "the fourth world." The benefits of the Information Age, far from being distributive and universal, portend a global economy that is at once mercurial and criminal, its outcome less a New World Order than a prolonged experience of "New World Disorder."

Central to Castells's argument is the role of world cities, and world cities as the sites of immigrant experience. It is, above all, urban location that defines the current diasporas of the post-Vietnam and now post–Cold War eras, in both North America and Western Europe. Yet the urban accent does not itself alleviate the inequities of Info Age structures. Some immigrants—the highly educated and professional upper classes—benefit, while others—manual laborers, semiskilled workers, and service-sector employees—do not. Indeed, the pernicious effect of "cyber-segmentations," according to a prominent sociologist, will be the increasingly disparate and unfair distribution of economic wealth, social benefits, and life options. Unbridled capitalism and unexamined patriarchy may have conspired to produce not new frontiers of hope or freedom but rather cyber-fantasies that, at least for the marginalized, amount to global obscenities.[28]

Cyber Society and Asian Americans

Precisely how do the technical shifts now so evident from the Internet further marginalize the newest immigrants as cybercitizens? Cybercitizens? Yes, the term is not mine but Arjun Appadurai's. Writing in 1996, Appadurai observed that global developments had produced new crises about the meaning of citizenship:

Many proposals [he observed] are circulating for new kinds of public spheres, third spaces, virtual communities, transnations, and diasporic networks. The results are surely contradictory. It may be that *cybercitizenship* draws some into a more tolerant and accessible public realm. But it also seems to drive others further into the recesses of the private and the market. Alas, nation-states . . . [have failed] to produce convincing fantasies of the commensurability of its citizens . . . [but until] transnations attain more flesh and bone, cities may still be the most important sites in which we experience the crises of national membership and through which we may rethink citizenship.[29]

Appadurai places hope for cybercitizenship not in nations but in cities. Sassia Sasken, another prominent social theorist, defines globalization as above all the hyperlinkage of global cities through international nodes that constitute a new transterritorial "center" of global economic activity.[30] Yet neither Appadurai nor Sassen specifies the particular groups of immigrants who participate in this system from the margins even while seeking citizenship on new terms. They are generalized as intractable foreign immigrants rather than model minorities who will become docile netizens.[31] Civil society drops out of the discourse, except insofar as it is inflected through the international human rights agenda, and specific groups only reappear in endnotes or summary conclusions.

While it may be true that "the encounter between Islam [or Hinduism or Buddhism or Sikhism] and the transnational technologies of communication is as multifaceted as the religion itself,"[32] information technologies remain inherently conservative. They reinforce global capitalist structures and asymmetries, without auguring a new or revisionist notion of civil society. What we are likely to see is the further marginalization of the already marginal. Euro-American elites, together with their Asian and African and Arab counterparts, will continue to project interests and promote options via the Internet. Yet most of their energies will be directed to nonpolitical goals; neither a new civil society abroad nor a reconstituted civil society at home is high on their list, and to the extent that the undervalued become less visible as also less empowered, we may yet see not a socially transforming revolution but rather racialized class prejudice reinscribed.

An example of how perilous is the path to equity via cyberspace comes from the two communities with which we began this chapter. Despite the pitfalls of civil society, and despite the inequities of cyber society, the two together promote the best hope for Muslim and Hindu religious groups to function in twenty-first-century America. Rejecting the worst excesses of Anglo-conformity, both the Institute of Islamic Information and Education (III&E) and the Vishwa Hindu Parishad (VHP) argue for cultural citizenship on their own terms. III&E limits the fractiousness of different Muslim groups under the umbrella of its call for "orthodox" Islam, while VHP uses transnational circuits to advocate Hindu neoconservatism in the USA as well as in India.

Yet neither III&E nor VHP is exempt from the criterion of nonpartisanship that Uberoi stated with enunciative logic as pivotal for civil society. Civil society must, above all, be civil, according to Uberoi, and exponents of civic associations must conjoin religion with politics as equivalent and competitive nodes of authority. Ruled out by this standard is either a state-established religion or a religion-based state, where competition is replaced by complicity and the same priorities are advocated through different structures, one political, one religious. By this criterion, both III&E and VHP are compromised. They are compromised through their tacit networks of support. III&E accepts the Kingdom of Saudi Arabia as the preferable form of Islamic governance. Saudi Arabia is not a democratic but a theocratic state, a tribal monarchy where all variant forms of Islam and all non-Muslims are precluded from the public square. III&E benefits from a religion-based state and inherently advocates Sunni Islam as a state-established monopolistic religion. VHP has a similar stance: its American leaders advocate the Republic of India as a model. Their long-range hope is to rid India of its "uncomfortable" minorities—above all, Muslims but also Sikhs and Christians. At the same time, they uphold a caste system that punishes those deemed "untouchable" or lower class. Their strategy is no less undemocratic or antipluralist than that of III&E, even though their religious profile, and global networks, are entirely opposite.

In short, the umbrella of civil society exposes rather than excuses the deficits of immigrant civic associations that occupy a niche in twenty-first-century America. Though they embrace freedom of religion as freedom to pursue their own religious practices and social strategies, they do not replace prejudice with tolerance. They prejudge internal as well as external others; prejudice remains prejudice, even when it is projected as a long distance form of racialized class and/or sectarian prejudice.

This chapter has related Asian immigrants to civil society in order to bridge the private and the public, the family and the state. But we have also linked Asian immigrants to earlier networks of avowedly religious actors. From Turkey and Indonesia to Senegal and India, religious actors have formed far-flung networks, crossed vast distances, and pursued collective well-being within but also against state structures. Religious actors may not have been the initial exponents of civil society, but they were central to its continued appeal and influence throughout the twentieth century.

Of equal importance, we have indicated that civil society was global before it was theorized as Western and secular. Civil society was both regional and transnational, even as it was marked by religion. Civil society formed a third space, conforming to neither the state nor society. And finally, we have seen that in today's late capitalist pattern of global exchange, the nexus of commercial and cultural networks runs through major metropolitan centers. To the extent that civil society can function, it must rely on these networks at the same time that it resists the forces making them seamless extensions of bourgeois power, reinforcing the gap between the poor, the weak, the immigrant, and Anglo-cosmopolitan elites.

Attention to civil society indicates that there can be no productive analysis of immigrants, including immigrant religious experience, unless one pays attention to global capital formations and their shift. What Cornel West speculated as a future desideratum in 1999 appears to have already happened: the social message of *Mississippi Masala* is that racialized class prejudice between Asians and Africans did not begin in the USA. The site for tense relations between South Asians and African Americans in the 1990s had its preamble in Kenya during the early twentieth century; it was the needs of British capital in Kenya that brought Indian merchants to that part of Africa, and then the postindependence disruption of Kenya that propelled them from Africa to America. Without understanding both economic production and political change on a global scale, one misses the deeper dynamics of what appears as just another interracial romance gone awry in rural Mississippi.

Again, we are helped by thinking in terms of Culture Two rather than Culture One. One must scan multiple localized sites rather than projecting single space-culture containers. Only then can we begin to understand the intricate relationship of economics to politics to civil society to religion. One must begin with the logic of global capital. As one cultural critic has observed, "The need for cheap labor, semi-skilled labor, technicians, and particularly skilled workers is not simply produced by the country of immigration [i.e., the host country], but that need itself is the product of the globalization of national economies."[33] And with the movement of labor often come shifts in political power, which also influence the trajectories of culture/religion through the third space of civil society. Civil society becomes the carrier, at once necessary and unpredictable, for polyvalent cultural citizenship, often with demands for religious autonomy.

American versions of civic associations are not less vulnerable to the subversion of democratic principles because they are based in the USA; each needs to be understood and evaluated on a close reading of general criteria that keep state and religion in tension with one another, at no time more necessary than post–September 11. Since the horror of September 11,

2001, it is pivotal to maintain the space between church (temple/mosque) and state. The frequent invocations of "In God We Trust" or "God Bless America" carry the message that only faith can sustain genuine patriotism; yet the implicit message is that only those with the "right" faith can fight those enemies who have targeted us because of their "wrong" faith. Wrapping religion in the flag not only undermines a polyvalent patriotism, it also makes the God of all humankind and all history into a partisan for one group and its political/strategic objectives.

Finally, we have seen that cyberspace needs to be understood as an extension of civil society. While the technological revolution has changed both the scope and the speed of global communication, cyberspace still retains the contrasts, even as it reveals the contradictions, of civil society. Technoculture is both centripetal and centrifugal, drawing all forces to virtual nodes that are interconnected one with the other at the same time that they provide sites of opposition to "virtual" political and commercial elites. Digital culture, like civil society of which it is a part, will continue to reflect the status quo, yet not without vistas of resistance and alternative sites of network formation.[34]

CHAPTER 3

New Immigrants as Pariahs

The emancipated Jew [like the immigrant] became a cultural hybrid, a man living and sharing intimately in the cultural life and traditions of two distinct peoples; never quite willing to break, even if he were permitted to do so, with his past and his traditions, and not quite accepted, *because of racial prejudice*, in the new society in which he now sought a place. He was a man on the margin of two cultures and two societies, which never completely interpenetrated and fused.

—Robert Park, *Race and Culture*[1]

The repressive ideological apparatus of immigration law [is reinforced by] the popular perceptions of "foreigners" and "aliens."

—Akhil Gupta and James Ferguson, *Culture, Power, Place*[2]

Framing Narrative

Ramesh was a South Asian graduate student who pursued his degree in engineering at an American university. Short of funds, he saved money by rooming with an American radical, who also happened to be a graduate student but in history. Alexander studied revolutions. He did not refrain from talking about them with his new roommate, even late into the night, even after Ramesh had gone to bed and was trying to go to sleep.

Much of Alexander's oratory bounced off Ramesh's half-asleep brain, but from time to time a few sentences made an impression and stuck in his memory.

"You must view yourself as free and equal," Alexander said.

"Equal to whom?"

"To those around you who consider you less than equal."

"Me? Less than equal?"

"No! Not you, stupid. The oppressed person. Oppression could be social, religious, foreign, traditional."

"Who oppressed me?"

"No! No! Not you! An imaginary oppressed person must first see himself as the equal of his oppressors. The idea of equality will ultimately sow seeds of freedom and revolution in his mind. The idea is the first step."

Later, Ramesh graduated, got a job, applied for a green card, and became an American citizen. He then went home to India for a visit and also to pick a bride. Rani, his future bride, had to pay a dowry, or rather her parents did. But since their means were modest, the dowry wiped out their savings. Ramesh generously tried to waive the dowry, but *his* parents insisted. The dowry was paid, and though Ramesh later repaid the entire amount to Rani's parents, the bitterness lingered. It tainted the life of the newlyweds; it made Rani feel less happy about both her married life and life in America, far away from her aging parents.

Sometime later Ramesh told Rani of his conversations with Alexander.

"Makes sense," she said, looking very earnest.

"Really! You mean you understand?" Rani's reaction amazed Ramesh.

"Yes, I do. I am an oppressed person, socially and traditionally. That's why my parents had to come up with a dowry."

Ramesh had a good job, but it did not last. He had to relocate several times. When he was laid off, he went to job fairs looking for new employment. Eventually his persistence paid off. After numerous failed interviews, he won a very competitive job. He got the good news by phone. Hanging up the receiver, he bounded up to Rani and exclaimed, "Rani, I got the job. The others didn't."

"I told you you are as good as any of them," Rani responded nonchalantly and continued to fold the laundry.

"Maybe . . . possibly . . . they needed a minority candidate," Ramesh muttered.

Rani stopped folding. "Ramesh," she said as her eyes scanned Ramesh's face, "you may have the job and the knowledge and the qualifications, but you are not free and equal."

"What do you mean?" Ramesh asked.[3]

My Immigrant Past

I, too, have an immigrant background but my life's trajectory could not be more different from Ramesh's. I come from a European/Hungarian, not a South Asian/Indian immigrant family. I have traveled to many parts of the world, but I have always returned to the USA, and I have had the good fortune to hold a continuous job at one university through my whole professional career. The prejudgment of status that first Ramesh's wife and then Ramesh experienced are beyond what most Euro-American immigrants need fear. They are beyond what I could have imagined; they are far removed from my own life experience.

In retrospect, the journey of my immigrant family to America seems marked more by nostalgia and hope than by ambiguity and doubt. At the turn of the last century, exactly in 1900, my German-Hungarian father came to the United States with his father, a tailor, and they settled in Buffalo, New York, eventually saving enough funds to bring over his mother (my paternal grandmother) and two other brothers. Later the family expanded to include sisters—eight in all—and two more brothers, my father being the oldest of thirteen siblings. Though I never heard Hungarian or German spoken at home, except on Thanksgivings when we all gathered at my grandparents' home, I did learn German at school, and I also learned to love the strudel and shoofly pie that my Aunt Lil, my father's youngest sister and my favorite aunt, used to make, as she said, with "a recipe from the old country."[4]

Immigration was never discussed in my family. It remained inchoate through most of my life in New Jersey, Connecticut, Massachusetts, and, most recently, North Carolina. It was as though we had always been Americans and that our American identity subsumed and erased all others.

In this chapter I want to address the legal challenges facing the new Americans who were not as fortunate as my father. Immigration since 1965 has been a process that has steadily shifted numbers and names, even as it has raised not only political but also legal issues in American public life on the cusp of a new millennium.

Labels and Categories

When I speak about new immigrants, I want to speak inclusively because it is my contention that to look only at one subset is to miss the issues that face all, or nearly all, immigrants from beyond Europe. I am concerned in this chapter, and the next, about the representation—popular as well as academic—of the most recent immigrants to the United States from Africa and Asia, but also from Latin America, during the past three decades. Though the newest immigrants are a huge, sprawling, internally diverse group, it is often the case that for U.S. census takers, as also for legislators, for journalists, and, alas, for many academics, they are viewed as one group, labeled immigrants or Asian/Hispanic immigrants, or just non-Americans.

Why this should be the case requires a view of what the French historian Fernand Braudel called *la longue durée*. For American history, *la longue durée* is an easy affair. It casts a net over a mere 150 years, as it conjures the contradictoriness of immigration during the period from the mid-nineteenth century till now. The immigrant experience is, above all, projected through the image of the Asian American. In *Immigrant Acts*, the cultural theorist Lisa Lowe, through her own engagement with East Asian Americans in San Diego, has epitomized the problematic status of Asians in the United States who become Asian Americans.

> In the last century and a half the American *citizen* has been defined over against the Asian *immigrant*, legally, economically, and culturally. These definitions have cast Asian immigrants both as persons and populations to be integrated into the national political sphere and the contradictory, confusing, unintelligible elements to be marginalized and returned to their alien origins. "Asia" has always been a complex site on which the manifold anxieties of the U.S. nation-state have been figured: such anxieties have figured Asian countries as exotic, barbaric and alien, and Asian laborers immigrating to the United States from the 19th century onward as a "yellow peril" threatening to displace white European immigrants.[5]

What Lowe highlights is the extremely racialized view of Asians harbored by many white European immigrants. Despite their own economic hardships, my grandfather and Anglo others were homogenized into the

U.S. Census. They were lumped together with the dominant majority or the mainstream, which is to say, "white, middle-class, native-born Americans."[6] But what of Native Americans and African Americans? Not only the U.S. Census but also Lowe's analysis overlooks the prior racialization of both of those groups, and also the state-level social ordering of all American citizens into the ethno-racial pentagon, especially after 1977.[7]

Why 1977? Because 1977 marked the culmination of bureaucratic responses to the unexpected non-European influx of immigrants after passage of the 1965 Hart-Celler Act. By the 1970s the new wave of Asian and Latino immigration had become too large to ignore. The previous white-black dichotomy was expanded to a white-black-Hispanic-Asian formula, with American Indians as the fifth race.[8] And in 1977 the Office of Management and Budget (OMB), the oversight agency for the Census Bureau, specified the exact shape of this new ethno-racial pentagon. It consisted of five mutually exclusive categories: (1) American Native and Alaskan Native (North America only), (2) Asian and Pacific Islander, with Asia beginning in Pakistan and going West, (3) Black, to include all persons of African descent, though excluding North Africa at some unspecified line of demarcation, (4) Hispanic, to include all Spaniards, descendants of Spaniards, and Spanish-speaking people, while (5) White was reserved for the original people of Europe, North Africa, and the Middle East up to the Pakistan border.

What these new categories, with their porous and woolly boundaries, ignore is the spectrum of linguistic, cultural, and ethnic difference intrinsic to American social history. Hybrids or mulattoes cannot be independently recognized. They have to be categorized as one or the other, a distinction so variable that in the early 1980s a Louisiana woman who had lived her whole life thinking she was "white" had to go to court to sue for a reclassification as "white" after the Louisiana Bureau of Vital Statistics registered her as "black"! It was not the color of her skin but the content of her genetic bank, insofar as it could be identified, that determined who she was! Eventually she lost her suit and was permanently reclassified as "black." Her case, far from being isolated, raises a crucial point vis-à-vis the law: Racial discourse and racial politics, like race discrimination and race violence, depend on categories that are neither consensual nor scientific; instead, they are governmental responses imposed for contradictory purposes, on the one hand to maintain a monitoring of racial "purity," and on the other to remedy perceived sociopolitical needs for disadvantaged races.[9]

South Asians as a Subset of Asian Americans

It is all the more important, then, when talking about Asian Americans to retrieve agency for the very people marginalized by using a single, blanket category such as "Asian" or "Asian American." My concern for most of my academic life has been with South Asia, with that vast terrain beneath the Hindu Kush mountain range that is known historically as the Indian subcontinent but today is called South Asia or Indo-Pak (for those who choose to ignore Bangladesh and Sri Lanka as well as Bhutan, Nepal, and Afghanistan). Yet they encompass a staggering diversity, made more complicated to address in the United States because of the constant confusion of South Asia with Southeast Asia, resulting from the long shadow of the Vietnam War. When I think of South Asia, and when I speak to American students of South Asian realities, I must begin by tracing the trajectory, both the motives and emotions and the displacements and relocations, of South Asians who have come to the United States. They constitute a diaspora within the larger Asian diaspora. Their distinctive experience demands its own analysis.

And that analytical task becomes still more challenging when we look at numbers. Why? Because demographic numbers, even of legal, registered immigrants from the Asian subcontinent, vary. The rate of growth is the most astonishing, if elusive, datum. Most observers agree that as of 1965 only 50,000 Asian Indians resided in the United States, but the 1990 U.S. Census showed that the South Asian Americans numbered almost 900,000, and the likely figure by 2000 must have exceeded 1.25 million.[10]

The South Asian subset of recent immigrants is numerically small. Despite its rapid percentage increase, it falls well below the large-scale pattern of immigration to the USA involving South Americans as well as East and Southeast Asians since 1965. For the thirty-year period from 1960 to 1990, there were 13.5 million legal immigrants to the this country. Of that number, more than two-thirds, or 10 million, came from Latin America and Asia combined. Yet this counts only legal immigrants, with the number of illegal immigrants from, e.g., Mexico, numbering at least another 2–3 million. At the same time, within Asia we find a dramatic breakdown, with East Asians (Chinese and Koreans) numbering almost 1.5 million and Filipinos alone accounting for slightly less than 1 million, while all South Asians represent but 900,000 in official census figures.[11]

New Immigrants as Pariahs

One would like to focus immediately on the need to differentiate internally among South Asian immigrants, between Pakistanis, Indians, and Bangladeshis, between skilled workers, semiskilled workers, and students, and so on. But it is a huge problem to look at any subset of Asian Americans when *all* immigrants, Asian and Hispanic, South Asian and Southeast or East Asian, are depicted in terms that flatten internal cultural differences and lift up socioeconomic variables. The situation has become still more acute now that the year 2000 census takers have introduced even more comprehensive race and ancestry questions to complicate the notion of ethnographic identity in the United States. How are they/we to gauge American social mobility/diversity? Can any computer-generated projections be substituted for actual head counts in arriving at figures for that roughly 10 percent of the American population who happen to be either immigrants or inner-city dwellers or both?

Let me be clear: the right of center, conservative, Anglo-dominant group that controlled the rhetoric of 1980s America still shapes the approach to socioeconomic issues in public forums. Nowhere is this more evident than in the debate about immigration that occupies many national journals. It is easy to pillory archconservatives such as Peter Brimelow, the *Forbes* and *National Review* editor, when he bristles at how the new immigrants threaten "the racial hegemony of white Americans"[12] or Herrnstein and Murray when they lament that Latino and black immigration has lowered American intelligence and provided new beneficiaries for the already oversubscribed welfare system,[13] or the Sloan Foundation demographer Michael Teitelbaum when he calls for a State Department coordination of oversight on global population and refugee issues so that we can curb the outmigration from poor countries that would contribute to "destructive economic and political developments in the USA."[14]

Even were we to dismiss outright all the above, we would still have to contend with those on the other side of the political spectrum in the knowledge class who echo the refrain of neoconservatives on immigration issues. Hence we find the South Asian economist Jagdish Bhagwati, now teaching at Columbia University, urging the liberal embrace of the lowest of the low, "the sub-subaltern," as the test case of American democracy. Though that strategy may be liberally laudable, Bhagwati pursues it in terms that inscribe racialized categories every bit as firmly as do his opponents to the right. Bhagwati seems to reverse the economic argument of conservatives. While he agrees with them that we should reduce illegal immigrants, he argues in the same breath that we ought to admit *all* immigrants regardless of their education level or skill base. He frames his case in terms of two hypothetical candidates.

> Suppose we had only one place for an immigrant [he asks], and could give it either to a rich doctor from India or to an impoverished peasant from Haiti. Suppose you are to vote entirely on the basis of whom you wish to assist and not a whit on which immigrant will do you good. Which would you choose? I have little doubt [he asserts,] that the average American would choose the impoverished peasant."[15]

Bhagwati, of course, can speak against the Indian doctor and for the Haitian peasant because he is himself of upper-class Indian origin and therefore has benefited from a double process of class formation and relative privilege. In the first instance, there is the colonial history of class formation in South Asia. It produced an indigenous class with the education, talents, and opportunities of the British colonial elite, and persons from this privileged though still subordinate group were then able to participate in the first Asian diasporas, diasporas that went east to Malaysia and Singapore, or west to Ghana and Kenya or South Africa.[16] Descendants of these early subcontinental salariat, as they are sometimes called, eventually migrated again in the late twentieth century, either to Britain or to the USA, as many Americans, immigrant and non-immigrant, now know because of the movie *Mississippi Masala*. And it is the presence of these South Asians as both immigrants and also spokespersons on behalf of other immigrants that makes the current debate about immigration and law at once so freighted and so complex.

The Legal "Fiction" of Immigrants as Pariahs

Nowhere has the intricacy of issues and actors in the current immigration debates been more thoroughly displayed than in two end-of-the century publications, one from the *Boston Review* (October–November 1998) and the other from *Social Text* (Fall 1998). Both give feature-story status to immigrant (re)location and its consequences, political and social, legal and economic, but never cultural or religious. It was not the first time that the

New Immigrants as Pariahs

Boston Review had raised the issue of immigrant challenges to Anglo-American norms. It had, for instance, published Martha Nussbaum's controversial essay "Patriotism and Cosmopolitanism" in 1995, in which Nussbaum argued that cosmopolitanism could be achieved by educating all Americans as "citizens of the world," presuming that there was a bounded character to the community of citizens labeled "American" and further presuming that one could reach a consensus on how all Americans collectively should view other, non-Americans.[17]

The issue lingers: what does it mean to be both citizen and American without being anti- some other region or worldview, race or class that is deemed non-American? The issue lingers and then is redeployed in Owen Fiss's provocatively titled essay "The Immigrant as Pariah" in the Fall 1998 issue of the *Boston Review*. I devote attention to this matter because it touches Asian Americans as well as other new Americans, and also because it is impossible to project cultural/religious options for Asian Americans beyond the arguments raised by Fiss. Moreover, Fiss does not write in a vacuum: The *Boston Review* includes eleven responses to Fiss's arguments, along with his rejoinder to these same respondents.

Fiss is arguing against the notion that the immigrant is, or should be regarded as, pariah. Yet what characterizes both his arguments and his rejoinders, in part because of the heavily social scientific or juridical weighting of the contributors, is an emphasis on the lowest common denominator. The markers are both race and class specific. Recurrently, the immigrants singled out are illegal, lower class and nonwhite. Hence, Myron Wiener, in his response, calls attention to "Mexican, Chinese, and Thai illegal immigrants in sweatshops and in servitude, forced to pay back traffickers, and lacking the legal means to protect themselves against unscrupulous employers."[18] Other national cohorts, most of them legal immigrants, are not cited by country of origin, nor do scholars from these same countries identify their own stake in the arguments they advance. Jagdish Bhagwati, earlier mentioned, is South Asian, professional, and Hindu, while Muzaffar Chishti, another of the respondents to Fiss, happens to be also South Asian and professional, but Muslim.

Instead, Fiss wagers that one can argue, on principle, that *no* immigrants should become pariahs, while still acknowledging that in practice court decisions, like legislative acts, reflect popular prejudice. Illegal immigrants who are poor and unskilled as well as brown, yellow, or black suffer, in his words,

77

from the degradation that all people of color suffer in the United States. But race seems to be only an aggravating factor, not essential to the harm. Even if the illegal immigrants were not from Mexico, or Asia, or Africa but from Canada, or Ireland, or even a number of North European countries, the danger would exist that these people—not defined by race or even national origin, but by their legislative or cultural designation as immigrants—would be isolated from the dominant groups in society and treated as inferior. They would become the new underclass.[19]

What is degrading about this debate is its backdoor retrieval of race as "not essential to the harm," yet instrumental to the harm that is caused, but even more odious is the obliteration of attention to "the dominant groups in society." Who are they? And how are they defined? We need to return to the crucial, recurrent question: "From where do I speak?" In the case of Mr. Fiss, he speaks as a Yale Law School professor, and he speaks from the so-called mainstream, the white, middle-class, native-born American.

The South Asian Difference

What is needed, in the press as in academia, is a more balanced debate on the latest wave of immigration, set against the history of racialized prejudice that still pervades the USA. I would like to offer two new directions—one topical, the other methodological. The first is attention, both comparative and critical, to the South Asian difference, especially because of the culturally significant number of Indians, but also Pakistanis, Bangladeshis, and Afghanis who, despite their comparatively smaller numbers vis-à-vis those of other Asians, still contribute to popular perceptions of the latest wave of immigrants. The other is attention to the humanities, including cultural anthropology, as a disciplinary perspective bringing culture into conversation with economics and politics, allowing for religious experience as part of the dynamics of culture but also looking to the specific local contexts of religious experience rather than general assumptions about sociohistorical trends.

The South Asian difference is significant, in the first instance, because South Asians still must resist the lure of instrumentalist strategies that lump South Asians within an Asian American panethnicity defined largely by

East and Southeast Asians who minimize but more often ignore South Asians altogether. Yen Le Espiritu, in her oft cited monograph, assumes that pan-Asian solidarity for advocacy of common sociopolitical goals trumps primordialist concerns for cultural continuity or religious expression. She advocates a single strategy for erasing racial prejudice and ensuring social cohesion in twenty-first-century North America: "interpersonal pan-Asian ethnicity," or cross-racial marriages. Such marriages, and only such marriages, in her view, will provide the long-term solution to subgroup ethnic difference. One may applaud her personal skill at projecting her own circumstance, as a Vietnamese American married to a Filipino American, onto a broadscale national agenda, yet I still find it necessary to insist on my prior question: where are the South Asians, absent alike from the pages and the politics of her study?[20] And how do the lifelines and social options of South Asian Americans compare with those of African Americans, or Hispanic Americans, equally missing from her pages?[21]

The South Asian difference also allows a close view of multiple differences within the diverse South Asian subset of the current Asian American population. There are, for instance, two waves of immigrants, each of which produced its own profile—with both problems and prospects that relate to but are not identical to each other.

The first wave, like other immigrant waves, dates from 1965. It cannot be too strongly stressed how the 1965 U.S. Immigration and Naturalization Act has become more than a benchmark statistic for talking about new immigrants. The act, ironically but appropriately situated in the midst of the most intensive American war in Asia (Vietnam, 1963–1975), reversed decades of discrimination and initiated preferential admission of Asian immigrants even while American troops remained locked in combat with other Asians, many of them countrymen of the newly admitted immigrants.[22] The 1965 act stressed two criteria: "family reunification" and "occupational preference." While it was assumed that the first criterion would serve to replicate the then current racial-ethnic profile of the USA, the second was intended to strengthen the U.S. labor force by "welcoming members of the professions with exceptional ability and workers in occupations in which laborers were in short supply."[23]

During the first two decades (1966–1986), most of the South Asian immigrants came under the occupational preference rubric. Whether Muslim or Hindu, Jain or Sikh, Buddhist or Christian, they were highly educated professional people who had been part of the British professional classes, beneficiaries of the transnational system set in place by the British, and they could therefore choose to migrate, either to the USA or to Canada or to Great Britain.

At the same time, many chose to continue to maintain close ties with their countries and subcommunities of origin. They may have subscribed to the myth of return, but for them it was just that, a myth of return; they were—and are—committed to remaining in the USA.[24]

There has also been a second wave of immigrants, however, mostly those who came from South Asia since 1986. They represent a much lower percentage in managerial and professional jobs, a much lower median income, and a much higher unemployment rate. They are not the "model minorities" that those of the first wave are thought to be. They came under the criterion of "family reunification," and many arrived at a time when the U.S. economy was in recession. A subsequent U.S. immigration act, in 1990, prioritized even more than the 1965 act a preference for highly skilled immigrants from India (and Asia generally) at the expense of unemployed immigrants (parents and spouses of citizens) as well as unskilled workers. The 1990 act also helped spur increases in the Bangladeshi, Pakistani, and Sri Lankan populations.[25]

How then does one wrestle through a nuanced argument about shifts within the South Asian immigrant community? What to call them? Are the newest immigrants "mere" immigrants, or are they exiles? Do they see themselves as prospective citizens, even as Anglo Americans consider them to be diasporic aliens? Each of these questions presupposes a still more central question. Indeed, it is the crucial question: How does relocation affect cultural identity and also religious boundaries?

Race—and Class—*Do Matter*

One must begin by bracketing together the official and unofficial biases against immigrants. We have traced the official bias to the infamous ethno-racial pentagon: since 1980 the U.S. Census divides all citizens into five "equivalent" categories: African American, Asian American, Euro-American, Indigenous, and Latino.[26] Unofficially, the categories are far from equivalent: The privileged group remains Euro-American or Anglo-American. Some purists still gloss Euro-American as Anglo-American, echoing the nostalgic devolution of American culture as initially Anglo-American

(1789–1861), and then Euro-American (1875–1957). Only since 1972 has American culture devolved, or declined, into a mold that is neither Anglo- nor Euro-American. It is not even "American," strictly speaking; it is instead "multicultural." The multicultural phase is, of course, anathema to Anglo- purists, and it is within their taxonomy of decline from Anglo to Euro to multicultural America that we have to frame the unofficial bias against Asian Americans. For it has been during the past three decades, the so- called multicultural phase, that the Asian American category has taken on new meaning. It remains an "ethno-racial bloc," which, while hardly admitting of internal homogeneity or consensus, is still seen as distinct from, and also at odds with, the hegemonic Euro-American bloc.[27]

I alluded to the unofficial bias when summarizing Fiss's jaded piece in the *Boston Review*. But Fiss shares with other proponents of liberal-style mul- ticulturalism the view that race, while it needs to be acknowledged as signif- icant, is finally unimportant. One of the slipperiest of such liberal multicul- turalist advocates surely is Robert Bellah. Citing the African American philosopher and public intellectual K. Anthony Appiah as his source, Bellah argued in his 1997 American Academy of Religion plenary address that Amer- ica is unique because it boasts "an exceptionally powerful institutional order," expressed through education, the state, and popular media. Together these institutions, in Bellah's view, forge a resilient common culture that goes back to colonial Protestant prophets, the ideological pioneers who foresaw that beyond individualism and economic greed there was a "second lan- guage" of collective solidarity and national consensus. Bellah pretends to be a wavering prophet, on the one hand warning that the second language is now under threat, while on the other hand hoping for the rescue of this pre- carious second language through the familiar nodes, "churches, other reli- gious and civic organizations, even nooks and crannies in the universities."[28]

Even were we to agree with Bellah that the greatest need facing the United States today is to rearticulate a "second language" of collective sol- idarity and national consensus, the actual role of African Americans in the past or South and East Asians, along with African Americans, in the pres- ent is far from clear. Bellah may allude to "churches" as sources of hope, but where are the mosques, the temples, the *gurudwaras*? Are they pre- sumed, under the broad rhetorical sweep of "other religious and civic organizations"? Can the new South Asian Muslim Americans, for instance, find their voice unless they, along with similar groups, are specified and detailed beyond the presuppositions of a largely abstract and covertly

Christian "second language"? Unless the newest Muslim Americans are identified by both region and religion, do not they, too, risk becoming religious as well as political pariahs?

While I want to expose Bellah's problematic assumptions, I also want to dispel his dystopic projections. I would like to perform this double feat by looking at that subgroup of South Asian immigrants who self-identify as Muslim. How has living in the United States shaped their self-understanding as religious subjects? What has been the response of indigenous Americans, specifically African American Muslims, to their presence? These questions feed into a larger question that connects relocation to memory and to cultural identity: Is there an American Islam, and if so, who are the American Muslims?

South Asian Muslims resemble Ramesh, the Hindu engineer, with whom we began this chapter. Let us suppose that Ramesh has an American counterpart named Ahmad. Both he and Ahmad as South Asian Americans remain connected to their countries of origin, whether India or Pakistan or Bangladesh. They remain connected through what Benedict Anderson calls "long-distance nationalism"[29]; their memories and also their experiences, and probably also their cross-generational family ties, link them to the Asian subcontinent. But at the same time, they must come to terms with an American Islam that is shaped not by Hindu or Sikh others but by Muslim others—in this case, African American Muslims who are other because they too claim to be equal participants in an American Muslim collective or *ummah*.

To date, only one American scholar, a South Asian cultural anthropologist, has looked at the actual circumstances of these newly arrived immigrants beyond a single neighborhood or a major city. Karen Leonard argues that the magnet of American culture is homogenizing for Muslims, as for others; it flattens out other "non-American" cultural traits, whether ethnic, linguistic, or religious or all three. At the same time, the North American context forges an American Muslim community that is as much American as it is Muslim in its defining features.[30]

And one of the major aspects of the Americanizing process is the census apparatus that forces South Asians, like other Asians, to choose their ethnic/racial identity. For much of this century, Asian was elided with white, or Anglo. Now, since 1970, Asian has become a separate category on the census, compelling Asians to think of themselves as distinct from both Anglo and African Americans, while framing in their own minds a new value preference that is at once racially and class based: Anglos remain the preferred upper class, Africans the marginalized underclass.[31]

Leonard's analysis echoes the familiar theme of "Mainstreaming Muslims." One recent book title frames the theme as a question: *Muslims on the Americanization Path?*[32] The coeditors claim objectivity, yet the question already stipulates its answer: Second-generation immigrants—in this case, South Asian Muslim immigrants—will not cling to the "ethnic" manifestations of their collective identity as defined in previous generations and also in their countries of origin. Instead, they will assimilate, losing their sharp Muslim edge as they adopt a rounded American identity. As one of the authors asserted more than a decade ago: "Over the generations a process is evidenced by which Islam is identified to accord with the basic tenets of American civil religion, leading to a deemphasis of its distinctive features."[33]

Let us suppose that American Islam will become yet another variant of "American civil religion." But was there ever an American civil religion that did not also have internal fissures, gaps, and aporia that said as much about the kaleidoscope of American culture as civil religion says about its homogeneity?

While applauding Leonard's close ethnographic analysis, I want to distance myself from conclusions that seem to echo the Progressive Protestant Patriot rather than the wary participant observer. Islam Americanized ignores not only the diversity that persists across generations in both the indigenous and the immigrant Muslim communities but also the major fault line that separates South Asian from African American cultural norms.

This fault line, internal to the American Muslim community, has been clearly identified by the preeminent African Muslim scholar, Ali Mazrui.[34] Mazrui identifies it as a racial, rather than a racialized class, prejudice, but he sees it as fundamental to the American Muslim future. Even though other scholars have ignored this same fault line,[35] it is impossible to project the future of an American Muslim community without noting differences that may persist or may attenuate, but in either case remain distinctive markers of that community and not of other non-American Muslim or non-Muslim American religious communities. It underscores the persistence of cultural disparities, despite creedal and ritual sympathies, between indigenous African American and immigrant, largely South Asian, Muslim communities.

The major impediment to collective solidarity among Muslims remains internalized racial prejudice. It is not mere happenstance that while discursive analyses simply ignore the social distance between different Mus-

lim groups that mirrors the larger societal profile placing African Americans at the lowest step of the ethno-racial pentagon, almost all narrative
accounts of the American Muslim experience not only acknowledge but
also stress the reciprocal tension between Asian and African American
Muslims. Racialized class prejudice runs deep, even in the face of a universal religious ethos that eschews race as a marker of worth, even among
American Muslims in the twenty-first century.

In the aftermath of September 11, 2001, it becomes all the more important
to highlight racialized class prejudice without granting it overriding importance. The crucial strategy is to explore and problematize the nature of
racialized class prejudice, while also holding out long-term hope that the
newest wave of South Asian Muslim immigrants can move beyond its vise-
like grip on their imaginations and also their social experience. To the
extent that they accept the value constraints of the late capitalist global
order, they will be able to forge their own hybrid identity, at once Asian and
American, Muslim and "secular," through a variety of institutions. All these
institutions will emerge through civil society, not through the state. Some,
like III&E, will be influenced by foreign governments, but they will continue to explore a third track beyond domestic or foreign restrictions. Some
will be linked to "traditional" religion, such as local mosques and cultural
associations, but others will make use of nontraditional forums, including
cyberspace, that link them to their countries of origin but also to co-religionists of all nationalities. In so doing, South Asian Muslims may yet avoid
the twin minefields of social conflict with African American Muslims and
ideological complicity with ethno-nationalists from their countries of origin.[36] But they will not do so soon or easily.

Marc Bloch once cited as an Arab proverb "Persons are shaped by their
generation more than by their forefathers." Robert Park was less sanguine
about the malleability of persons. Park observed that personhood is first of
all a kind of public mask: "We come into the world as individuals, achieve
character, and become persons."[37] All immigrants, including the newest
South Asian Muslim immigrants to the United States, hope to become better persons, yet they cannot become better if they are tainted by racialized
class prejudice. That prejudice continues to flourish. More than seventy
years ago, Robert Park mused that "the immigrant who settles in a foreign
community, meets with discrimination and prejudice because he is identified with a race or nationality [or religion] which is regarded by the native

peoples [*sic*] as inferior—inferior mainly because different. The stranger, though he may be accepted as a utility, is rejected as a citizen, a neighbor, and 'a social equal.' A social equal, as ordinarily defined in America, is one that you will be willing to have your daughter marry."[38]

Park's words ring true today, for even were Asian Americans to overcome prejudice from their non-Asian neighbors, prejudice linked to persistent Anglo-Protestant norms, they would still have to overcome its internalized reflex: Many Asian Americans—not just South Asian Americans but also East and Southeast Asian Americans—assume that a hierarchy of value and status defines who they are as well as how others see them. The major criteria for negative discrimination combine race with class, projecting racialized class prejudice *among* Asian Americans as well as between them and non-Asian Americans.

A poignant example of racialized class prejudice appears among American Buddhists. It was largely ignored until bell hooks, a black feminist Buddhist, brought attention to the problem in 1992. She decried the fact that black Buddhists were virtually absent from any discussion of either immigrant Buddhists or American converts to Buddhism. Her lament sparked a debate that led *Tricycle: The Buddhist Review* to devote a special issue to "Dharma, Diversity, and Race" in 1994. The genie was let out of the bottle, as many Asian and American Buddhists came forward with their own tales of how cultural preconceptions influenced Buddhist practice rather than the reverse. One well-known American Buddhist, Rick Fields, even went so far as to confess that Anglo-American Buddhists like himself had refashioned Buddhism in their own image.[39] A major Buddhist scholar, Jan Nattier, theorized the emergence of two strata of Buddhists in North America since 1965.[40] One she labeled Elite Buddhists. These were American converts to Buddhism whose class origins and racial location projected an implicit American hierarchy of values. Elite Buddhists contrasted with Immigrant or Ethnic Buddhists, those Buddhists whose interests and needs did not conform to the interests or needs of their elite co-religionists. The two lived in different worlds, remote from each other, within the arc of what outsiders called "American Buddhism."

Contrary to the homogeneous picture projected by Diana Eck and also by many Buddhist spokespersons, there were competing social strata that also marked American Buddhism. Like American Muslims but also American Baptists, American Buddhists found their local, congregational identity shaped by social preferences reflecting deep-seated ethnic and class differences. These differences clashed with universal ideals, for Buddhists as for Baptists as for Muslims.

Ethnographic studies of particular Buddhist communities in the United States, notably Southern California, have confirmed the picture of an ethnically fractured American Buddhist community. The major Taiwanese Buddhist temple near Los Angeles, for instance, attempts to project a post-1965 Chinese American identity. It is a splendid architectural structure with myriad programs and achievements, yet it remains beset by an internal ethnic contradiction: The ideal of Buddhism as a non-ethnic, social truth is projected by a predominantly Chinese American membership. Anglo converts, though encouraged and welcomed, remain a fractional minority.[41]

Los Angeles, in fact, has become a critical test case for nearly all attempts to chart a pan-ethnic American future. Yet two East Asian American sociologists have challenged the notion that Asian immigrants to Los Angeles aggregate as a "model minority." Their conclusion may be extended to the nationwide status of Asian Americans at the outset of the twenty-first century: "Asian Americans still have a long way to go before they reach full socioeconomic, legal, political [and religious] equality in this country."[42] Whatever the strategy pursued to attain full equality, it will retain a glass ceiling: racialized class prejudice. Racialized class prejudice will persist, and it will be limited only to the extent that it is recognized, confronted, and opposed in religious as well as political forums.

If no immigrant Asian community is spared the impact of racialized class prejudice, then how does it affect particular communities? The case of Iranian Americans is instructive, and since there is no city where their population has increased more rapidly since 1965 than Los Angeles, the next chapter will focus on the Irangelinos, as Iranian Americans from L.A. sometimes call themselves. Neither East nor Southeast nor East Asian, Iranians, like Arab Americans, are *West* Asians, and their relationship to the USA includes a special set of memories and experiences. Irangelinos reflect a tension between their country of origin and their country of location, between homeland and host nation. Cultural citizenship via civil society is the preferred route for Iranians, as for other immigrants, Asian and non-Asian, but the challenges are always local, the options always complex. For Irangelinos these challenges can best be traced through the experience of a fictive Iranian Muslim immigrant to Los Angeles, and so it is the journey west of Ali Rizwani that will occupy us in the next chapter.

CHAPTER 4

Religious Options for
Urban Immigrants

Made You Mine, America
America
in the poems of Walt Whitman
Langston Hughes
Allen Ginsberg
the songs of Woody Guthrie
and Joan Baez
I made you mine.
. . . .
Loving
your children
daughters
sons
mothers
fathers
grandmothers
grandfathers
hating your aggression
you aligned yourself with the worst
of my kind
exiled my George Washington—
Dr. Mohammad Mosaddeq—
helped Saddam bomb my birthplace
destroy the school of my childhood
. . . .
Now I lay claim
to your Bill of Rights
and Declaration of Independence.
I came to you
. . . .

with a suitcase of clothes
and books . . .
Hafez
Rumi
Shakespeare
Nima
Forugh
and a small Qur'an . . .
my grandmother's gift . . .
—Ali Zarrin[1]

Despite the importance of religion as a social variable, the U.S. Census has never included a question on religion because of the high premium placed on the separation of church and state.
—Barry Kosmin and Seymour Lachman, *One Nation Under God*[2]

The central issue of this chapter concerns immigrant religious practices: are immigrant religious practices best understood as an extension of prior religious preferences or as a double engagement with both urban location and class/status markings? Answering this question is complicated, not just because the new Asian American communities are so new but also because the religious outlook of their members is undisclosed in the U.S. Census figures.

The long arm of institutional religion may not stretch beyond the first generation of immigrants to the United States, but it also may vary even within that first generation. Consider the case of Iranians in Los Angeles. We know that in two decades, from 1970 to 1990, the Iranian population in Greater L.A. increased from 20,000 to 100,000,[3] but we do not know how many of that group self-identify as Shi'i Muslims, especially since many are refugees from a religious revolution that was avowedly Shi'i.

The major question to ask is, against the model of assimilation, how does one construct a model of internal difference that recognizes both universal citizen rights, including the right to be *non*-religious, and ad hoc religious practices, reflecting individual idiosyncrasies? No norms or rights can be gauged without attention to two states, one theocratic and Muslim,

88

the Islamic Republic of Iran, the other secular and Anglo-Protestant, the USA. Civil society may be a critical third space between them, but does it function as transnational civil society? Can transnational civil society project a spectrum of norms and values? What are the religious as well as cultural parameters for immigrants, such as Iranian Americans, who view themselves as citizens between two countries? Do they bridge two incommensurate political/social structures through transnational civil society?

In a provocative book titled *Transnational Religion and Fading Nation-States*,[4] two political scientists, Suzanne Rudolph and James Piscatori, argue that transnational civil society holds the key to understanding the efforts of individuals to negotiate state/society relations across national boundaries. Transnational civil society, in their view, is above all characterized by transnational religious movements, and it is immigrants who are often the agents of transnational religious movements. When they are, we must attend to two forces that are at work simultaneously: Mobility and invisibility. It is the recent mobility of huge numbers of migrant workers that has led to what Benedict Anderson calls long distance nationalism,[5] while it is the invisibility of the motives and motivations, the sensibilities and emotions, of these same migrants that has led to theses of hybridity or creolism—that is, to the presumption that immigrants themselves always carry baggage and either assimilate or confront a uniform American context during their relocation in "the New World."

Nowhere is this presumption more wholesale than in the attribution of religious belief/practice/loyalty/institutional affiliation. Precisely because the U.S. Census precludes any notation of religious preference, all attempts to measure religious outlook and commitment are suspect, and yet one needs to account for even latent religious sensibilities, as evidenced in the first epigraph. The Iranian immigrant brings with him in his "suitcase" copies of traditional poets, Hafez and Rumi, but also modern poets, Nima and Forugh, along with Shakespeare. There is also a copy of the Qur'an. All are the gifts of his grandmother, or perhaps just the Qur'an, but in either case attachment to Islamic scripture is part of the baggage that he brings with him to America.

How, then, does transnational civil society embrace transnational religious movements? It must recognize that religion is always at some level part of the public sphere, that it counts as collective ideology as much as it does private devotion, and that for Iranians, even secular Iranians, the distinction is not as sharply etched as it is for older Americans conscious of church-state issues.

In the account that follows, I want to trace the dilemmas that Iranian immigrants face by looking at a single Iranian immigrant, whom I will call Ali Rizwani. Here is Ali's story.

Framing Narrative

I left my home country after a religious revolution. I had not been fond of the secular government; it was run by one man and his family and his friends; it benefited only a limited number of people, mostly in the capital city; and so, like many of my countrymen, I had favored a change in government, even a revolution, but not this revolution.

My father had often talked proudly of the first Iranian revolution, a revolution for democracy and justice. It had happened in 1905, at the beginning of this century. It was a revolution which his father, my grandfather, had supported, even though he was just a young man. He had been a *madrasah* or theological student. Though devoutly religious, he also favored a constitution. That revolution was called the Constitutional Revolution, and it brought Iran not only into the twentieth century but into the modern world. I never understood why that revolution failed, or why the Iranian experiment with democracy that brought Mohammed Mossadegh to power as prime minister in the early 1950s also failed.

I had never been much concerned with either politics or religion. My hero was Ahmad Kasravi. Kasravi, like my grandfather, had trained as a religious scholar, but he was also a modern empirical thinker. He loved science, and he had been impressed by Halley's comet. He, too, supported the Iranian revolution, and later when he gave up a religious career and became a journalist, he wrote against traditional ideas and in favor of democracy; he especially loved public debate and did much to encourage it during the hard times of the 1930s and early 1940s. He was killed by a religious fanatic in 1943, but many people of my generation still regard him as one of the true Iranian heroes of the twentieth century.

Alas, the revolution of 1979 was not like the 1905 revolution, and the person who came to power was not a skeptic and a constitutionalist like Kasravi, but a firm believer who wanted clergy to run the government. Khomeini returned from Paris to Tehran, but he brought nothing French with him. Instead, he helped religious people like himself come to power. They forced others to accept religious laws and dictates as public norms. I mean, everyone had to be pious, whether men wearing beards or women covering their bodies and hair, and young hooligans served as thought police, checking cars for women who were not covered or couples who might be holding hands. And work also became harder and harder to find, especially profitable work, with the major positions in education or industry or even the army going to those who supported the new regime and its religious leaders.

I was among the lucky. I, together with my family, was able to bribe officials to get a work exit permit, and then to bribe border officials to allow me to leave the country overland with more goods than would normally be permitted. But where to go?

The best place was the USA because other people from my country who had gone there even before the revolution spoke of the prevalent mood of nonconformity: No one family, no one culture, and no one religion was forced on all Americans, and besides it was a huge country, with many cities, not just a dominant capital city, and of all the cities that my friends who had left before praised, none was praised more than Los Angeles. It was the home of Hollywood, with all the liberty for different values that Hollywood suggested to those of us in my country who had seen Bogart and Monroe, Grant and Haywood. It was also the home to many immigrants from Latin America, especially Mexico but also countries further to the south like El Salvador, Nicaragua, and Guatemala. It was a city with many communities and neighborhoods, and the neighborhood where my friends lived, and of which they had sent me pictures, looked almost uncrowded with its clean sidewalks lined with trees and houses set back from the road, side by side, none more than two or three stories high.

And so, my family and I, taking advantage of the 1965 Immigration and Naturalization Act, migrated to the USA and to L.A., where we settled in one of those neighborhoods with manicured homes and tidy walks and other people who looked like us. Work was not always easy to find, but it was available. I had a strong network of friends, family, and community. I had the freedom to do what I wanted, go where I wanted, and to find God, or not find God, in my life.

The Iranian Context

What does the westward journey of Ali Rizwani, and other Iranian immigrants like him, tell us about transnational religion and also about nation-states that seem either burdened or threatened by religious actors on the move? States may seem burdened by those who come from beyond their borders, if they are the host country and worry about assimilation or uniformity as national priorities. They may be threatened by those who have left but continue to exert influence, if they are an autocratic or theocratic state where alternative views are neither welcome nor tolerated.

But to presume that the Islamic Republic of Iran is indeed both an autocratic and a theocratic state is to answer preemptively a question that still puzzles many Iranians. Was the Iranian revolution of 1978–1979 a transformative revolution? For many it was. It was a major revolution of the twentieth century, comparable to the Bolshevik revolution of 1917. Whether a Third World revolution or an Iranian-Shi'i or both, it may prove to be less long-lasting than the Bolshevik revolution, but it was at least a revolution.

To Iranians like Ali Rizwani and his cohort, however, this revolution was not their first revolution. That distinction belonged to the Constitutional Revolution of 1905–1911, and in many ways that earlier revolution prefigured the events of 1978–1979. It, too, was a revolution against the Shah, though he was then a Qajar rather than a Pahlavi Shah. It, too, was sparked by a protest against foreign (then British, now American) influence, involving tobacco rather than oil. It also had the support of at least some segments of the Iranian clergy. However, the principal agenda for that revolution was strikingly different: Its advocates insisted above all on the implementation of a uniquely Western democratic instrument, namely, a constitution. Hence the name the 'Constitutional Revolution." It was that revolution with which Ahmad Kasravi so strongly identified through the experience of his grandfather, and it remains true till today that the Constitutional Revolution etched symbolically the entrance of Iran both into the modern world and into the circle of modern polities marked by participatory democracy.

As firm and positive as is collective memory of the Constitutional Revolution, dim and splintered is the memory of another Iranian revolution, the failed "White" Revolution heralded by the late Shah in January 1963. As its name suggests, it was intended to be a revolution without violence, one that would modernize Iran's economy (especially the agricultural sector) during the remainder of the twentieth century. The White Revolution failed, yet its deeper aspiration, to modernize Iran and make it a country that would benefit from the global economic system, is one that many middle-class Iranians such as Ali Rizwani had hoped to see continued by the Islamic Republic of Iran.

But the very middle class who were supposed to engineer a full-scale economic revolution in Iran left the country after the 1978–1979 revolution, not just because that revolution brought an ancient cleric back from Paris to rule in Tehran but also because that ancient cleric, the Ayatollah Khomeini, was drawn into a protracted war with neighboring Iraq that lasted almost ten years and drained the economy and the manpower of both countries.

To understand how immigrants like Ali Rizwani relate to their home country, one must note that neither the mode of political representation nor the sources of income have changed in the nearly twenty years of the Islamic Republic of Iran. Though the state has been called an Islamic republic, it does not function as a democracy. There is a single party *majlis* (parliament), with courts, mosques, schools, and land law operating under a hierarchically monitored state ideology as rigid as that which prevailed before 1978. The income that allows the new government to function domestically and also to prosecute its foreign policy continues to derive from the export-oriented segment of the economy. Since the fall of the Shah, oil revenues as a percentage of total foreign exchange revenues have actually increased; they now constitute 80 percent of Iran's export earnings, while non-oil-related exports have continued to decline.[6]

In the past twenty years, new revolutionary institutions have been established, but many of them shadow institutions remaining from the ancient regime, with only the personnel circulating. Particularly at the provincial level, where there is great disparity between the less- and more-developed provinces, almost the same procedures are followed today as were in place twenty years ago. The court system has not been reorganized. In the absence of the Islamic Retribution Bill (ratified in 1981 but not yet enacted), individual revolutionary courts and firing squads acting as neighborhood committees continue to operate. On the crucial issue of land reform, little has been done since the time of the Shah.

Khomeini died in July 1989, but a viable policy on social change remains paralyzed by the same forces that were at work during his lifetime. Rather than focusing on ideological claims that continue to stress how the Islamic Republic is an agent for social justice acting on behalf of the dispossessed, one must look closely at the class distinctions that stymie the Islamic revolution and its present leadership. The first, and crucial, point to note is the absence of cross-class rivalries. It is not different classes but different factions within the same class, the middle class, that rival each other. They compete because they subscribe to different types of economic policy and development strategy. When they debate, they debate as members of the same social class, arguing, in effect, about how their class relates to those beneath them, i.e., the vast majority of Iranians.

Among the three middle-class groups that continue to vie with one another for the mantle of leadership in post-Khomeini revolutionary Iran, one is conservative, another is radical, and a third is centrist-pragmatist. The conservatives control the armed forces and the clergy but the centrist-pragmatists, with some support from radicals, have dominated urban politics since Khomeini's death, and with the election, then reelection of Khatami to the Presidency in the late 1990s, they have become the group most likely to determine the future course of events in Iran. They have not yet succeeded in transforming factionalism into full-scale participatory democracy. That remains a distant goal in the Islamic Republic of Iran, but even short of that ideal, if the three factions could succeed in cooperating to the extent that they ensure enough political stability and social security to cause a sustained upturn in the economy, they may institutionalize the Islamic Revolution. However, it will be a revolution with a small *r*, rather than a capital *R*, one that allows Iran to survive as a modern-day theocracy with a mixed socioeconomic policy, at the same time that problems of ethnic and religious minorities persist. It is difficult to see how immigrants like Ali Rizwani will find a way back to Iran except as visitors who long for ties with their relatives and countrymen, their language and culture, their "roots." Instead, they will become more like the poet Ali Zarrin, embracing the Declaration of Independence and the Bill of Rights while continuing to read Hafez and remember the Qur'an.

What remains true of Iranian immigrants in Los Angeles and elsewhere is that their attachment to their home country remains just that, an attachment to the past, not a strategy for return. As was noted about South Asian immigrants, while they "retain collective memories of their homelands and often organize themselves in the USA on that basis, many have recognized that the 'myth of return' is indeed a myth."[7]

The No Religion Option

Yet in a very major sense, the Iranian immigrants to the USA since 1979 are not like their South Asian counterparts or like other immigrant groups.

Most Iranians who have immigrated to this country in the past twenty years exhibit what Kosmin and Lachman call "the no religion" preference.[8] That is, they choose to distance themselves from any affiliation with institutional religion, specifically, with Shi'i Islam, the lodestone of the Islamic Republic of Iran.

In this sense, Iranian Shi'is contrast not just with other Muslims but also with other Asian minorities in the USA, especially the Sikhs. Sikh Americans are an interesting group to compare with Iranian Americans because they, like the latter, have both benefited and suffered from European colonial influence throughout West and South Asia, yet unlike Iranian Americans, they have retained a firm religious identity even during a multistaged experience of diaspora.

Within the sprawling diversity of the Asian subcontinent, Sikhs seem very small. Limited to the Republic of India, Sikhs can claim but 16 million in a population that exceeds 900 million: their numbers are not only fewer than those of Hindus (more than 600 million) but also fewer than those of Muslims (more than 140 million). Yet Indian Sikhs are a hardy minority. Like Iranian Shi'is, they often migrate abroad, and also like them, they almost always prefer to live in cities. Sikhs are internationally engaged as traders, middlemen, and entrepreneurs in a wide range of communicative, technological, and electronic industries. But most Sikhs continue to dwell in a single region of South Asia, the agricultural heartland of present-day North India, the Punjab. Sikhs are Punjabis, by ethnic background, by linguistic preference, and by cultural outlook.

Most are also deeply religious in their private and public profile. They trace their ancestry back to a North Indian protest movement whose heroes were saintly warriors known as *gurus*. Two of these gurus, Guru Nanak and Guru Gobind Singh, dwarf others in the historical and, even more, the symbolic force that they have imparted to current Sikh perceptions of collective identity. While Guru Nanak is lauded as an apostle of ecumenical engagement, Guru Gobind Singh is heralded as the exemplar of communitarian separatism, demanding loyalty to the insider-group against all others. The ideal Sikh community, according to Guru Gobind Singh, is the *khalsa*. But aspirations of the *khalsa* have been thwarted by political developments: after gaining independence from the British, Hindu nationalists have denied Sikhs the benefit of the only territorial patrimony they ever claimed, the Punjab.

The period since 1947 has been especially bitter for those Sikh agriculturalists who migrated to eastern Punjab from western Punjab (which became Pakistan), joining their destiny to the newly independent, secular state of India. Told to subordinate their interests to Indian national identity, they were not granted the same measure of autonomy as Hindus in adjacent Kashmir. Neither in 1947 nor in the decades immediately after did Sikhs get either a separate state or its psychological equivalent. In 1961 Tara Singh coined the rhetorical query: "The Hindus got Hindustan, the Muslims got Pakistan, what did the Sikhs get?"[9] Five years later the Sikhs got a positive answer, or so it seemed, to this query, for in 1966 the Sikh leader, Sant Fateh Singh, threatened to fast until death if his group's demands for a separate state were not granted by the government of India.

The result was a compromise: The former state of Punjab was divided into two states, one Haryana with a Hindu majority, the other truncated Punjab with a Sikh majority. Sikh Punjab proved to be elusive, however, since Sikhs did not constitute a decisive majority and their demographic margin slipped to barely 52 percent by the early 1980s. Also there continued to be rural-urban demographic disparities, with Hindus maintaining their plurality in the major cities of the Punjab. Even the unprecedented increase in Punjabi wheat production during the late 1970s did not benefit all Sikhs, nor did it translate into greater political power, either at the national level or in the jockeying for influence at the principal *gurudwara* sites.

It was in response to these circumstances of alienation and distrust that during the 1970s one subgroup of Sikh cultivators, the Bhindranwale Jat, began to call in increasingly strident tones for spiritual restoration. The Bhindranwale Jat never spoke for the majority of Punjabi Sikhs, and many other Sikhs openly opposed its leadership. But the Indian government chose to ignore the potential danger of intra-Sikh factionalism; some have even argued that government officials tipped their influence toward the underdog Sant Bhindranwale, presuming they could always outmaneuver or outlast him.

The result of that fatal miscalculation, whether deliberate neglect or malevolent intervention, was a bloody moment of state-sponsored terrorism: In 1984 the Indian Army in a massive assault, code-named Operation Bluestar, overwhelmed Sant Bhindranwale and his supporters at the holiest of holy Sikh shrines in Amritsar. Thousands were killed, among them Sant Bhindranwale; at the same time irreparable damage was done to the major structures of the Amritsar complex. The outrage of Sikhs was not quelled till Indira Gandhi, who had ordered Operation Bluestar, was herself assassinated by Sikh bodyguards in November 1984. Her death triggered further carnage, as revenge-minded Hindu nationalist gangs assaulted Sikh neighborhoods. In less than four days, more than 2,000 Sikhs were killed in Delhi alone, most through random acts of mob violence that also led to the damage or destruction of more than 400 Sikh temples (*gurudwaras*). Also victimized were the 50,000-plus Sikhs who, fearing for their lives, migrated from different parts of India to their Punjab homeland: They sought, though seldom found, refuge from further acts of Hindu nationalist violence.

As a result of Operation Bluestar and the chain of events it unleashed, the agitation for a separate Sikh nation that the effort intended to quell actually increased. It persists till the present day. Sant Bhindranwale became a martyr, a lightning rod for all the longings of Sikh separatists. At the same time, dissent from the nonseparatist position was less and less tolerated, especially after the major accommodationist, Sant Harchand Singh Longowal, was himself assassinated in 1985.

Yet this checkered history of resistance politics has not prevented Sikhs from migrating overseas and participating in multiple cultures through an expanded network of professional and personal contacts. Sikhs have become prosperous but also loyal citizens in many urban centers of late twentieth- and now early twenty-first-century North America. If we were to have a Sikh equivalent to Ali Rizwani, it might be a woman, a Sikh woman in her mid-twenties. Let us call her Ranjeet Singh, and let us imagine that she has completed her education in India with a joint degree in both business and Internet technology. Many of her friends and family have immigrated abroad, and now her parents are encouraging her to follow them, but first she must get married. Instead of following convention and asking a close relative to arrange her marriage, she seeks a suitable male partner via one of the many Internet Sikh-only marriage lists. Whom does she seek as her ideal mate? Another young adult Sikh with a career in law, medicine, or business. Like her, he must be kind and sincere, affectionate and loyal, honest and humble and sensitive. He should also be physically attractive, but above all, he must be able to negotiate Eastern and Western cultures. That means watching feature-length films, whether in English, Hindi, or Punjabi, listening to all kinds of music, not only Hindi and Punjabi but also classical, jazz, and hip-hop, and it also means going to the *gurudwara* at least once a week.

In practice, one could imagine Ranjeet negotiating, and even forfeiting some of these criteria, for instance, the expectation of listening to hip-hop on a regular basis, if the future spouse was too conventional in his music taste, but it is unlikely that she would bend very far on the requirement to attend the *gurudwara* on a weekly basis. It is the center of Sikh spiritual life abroad. *Gurudwaras* abound in all major urban centers of the USA and Canada; they also dot the landscape in many smaller regional cities. The link to tradition, to culture, to family is forged, and maintained, through the *gurudwara*; absent other links to Punjabi and the Punjab *gurudwaras* provide a home away from home, and are critical to Sikh immigrant identity in Western Europe as well as North America.

By contrast, Iranian immigrants to the USA see religion as but one among several markers of their distinctive American identity. In Los Angeles not all Iranians are Muslims nor are all observant. Ali Rizwani's cohort includes Jews and Bahais, Zoroastrians and Parsees, as well as some Armenian and Assyrian Christians. "The Muslims form the largest group," according to one observer, "but interestingly, when taken together, Iranian minorities here outnumber Muslims, who form 98 percent of the population in Iran. In exile the Muslim majority finds itself, for the first time, to be a minority."[10]

Nor has minority status in urban L.A. led Iranian Muslim immigrants to be more devout as Muslims. According to an authoritative study, only 2 percent of L.A.'s Iranian Muslims said that they were religiously observant![11] One might infer that they were secular before coming to the USA, or that opposition to the Islamic Republic of Iran has led them to distance themselves from all profession of Islam, or one might argue that they are responding to what Kosmin and Lachman call "the frontier mentality," in which no religious preference can be as valid as belonging to a church (or synagogue or mosque or parallel community).

Yet the major lesson to be derived from this look at the Iranian community of L.A., with a brief glance at recent Sikh immigrants, is that nonreligion or irreligion remains an American option. To pursue or profess no religion can as likely be the choice of some immigrants to the United States as to adopt a new religious identity or reinforce a traditional loyalty. It is only by looking at discrete groups of those who emigrate to the United States and considering their status as transient or liminal that we can presume to accept, or prefer to challenge, the thesis that immigrants are uprooted, that they leave so much behind in their home country that on relocation the one cultural anchor is religion, that religious practice for immigrants, as for converts, becomes more intense, that they define themselves as the "true" believers.

How to mutate into religious categories the experience of Iranian immigrants like Ali? How does one translate the religious identity of an Ali or Fatimah, who might well declare, "I'm an atheist but I still consider myself a Muslim"? What does that mean? The ritual practice of Islam may not be observed, even the basic creed may seem moot, yet engagement with the language, the food, and the lifestyle, the values, the norms, and the outlook of Iranian culture is so deep, and the interstitial impact of Islam on that culture so great, that one cannot simply say, "I don't believe, or I don't pray."[12]

That reflex has informed many of the Asian immigrants to the USA since 1965 — how many is difficult to say because most of the literature focuses on what religious practices immigrants *do* pursue, whether it is the CD-ROM *On Common Ground* or the special edition of the *Amerasia Journal* dedicated to Asian American religious concerns[13] or an edited volume such as *Gatherings in Diaspora: Religious Communities and the New Immigration*.[14] What must be resisted is the notion of a single, fixed identity, or the impossible choice between two equally rigid, uncompromising sites of identity. Almost all recent studies of Asian and other immigrants stress how limiting is the notion of a single ethnic/religious identity. One can be hybrid or mestizo not only to the outer gaze but also to the inner eye: One can intermarry or choose different genealogies, but one can also adopt a different persona on different occasions for different goals.

White Skins, Black Masks was Frantz Fanon's clarion cry about the process of internal colonization, and he demonstrated how inextricable was any strategy of liberation from the structure of oppression against which the colonized were reacting. In the context of Asian immigration to the United States on the cusp of a new century, one can also find individuals and groups who protest against structures, and they find variant voices, not a single voice, and many modes of behavior, not one, to encompass the nature of their claim both to join and to resist the host society. These reflexes are not dissimilar from those of Native Americans or African Americans, though they may vary in form and intensity. They require engagement rather than neglect, respect rather than fear, from Anglo others.

Iranian Americans as a New Model Minority

While acknowledging the benefit of focusing on religious identity as a primary marker, I also want to call attention to what is too often omitted from consideration: the possibility of accommodation by neither maintaining long distance nationalism nor intensifying religiosity as psychological adjustments to dislocation, but rather by forging new cultural links that reflect class and status markings as much as political or religious aspirations.[15]

Consider Ali Rizwani's fellow Iranians in L.A. Crucial to their life after 1978 is the potential to pursue new lifestyles in the American West that transform them into Anglo-Iranians. They come here not as the poor and downtrodden but rather as the affluent, the educated, the professionally skilled. In short, despite the troubled recent history of Iran, the Iranian immigrants to the USA possess attributes that combine to make them "a model minority," middle- or upper-middle-class urban Americans linked to the American dream. They are Anglo-Iranians, as much a part of the consumer capitalist, bourgeois culture of twenty-first-century America as are native-born Americans, or South Asian immigrants. They not only fit the assimilationist model, they seem to confirm its universal applicability.

The group(s) with whom the Iranians contrast most vividly are Mexican Americans and Latinos. It is extraordinary that the lucid and insightful study of the Iranian American anthropologist Hamid Naficy begins with a dream narrative, recounted in letter form. He writes about Mexican American grave diggers, whose poverty for him personifies the social tension of modern-day America:

> those who lowered the coffin into the grave . . . are Mexican-Americans. Through teary eyes I see before me the increasing social inequality of the United States: a class of poor, Third World immigrants carrying out the most menial task of a class of affluent European immigrants. . . . [I also see] Los Angeles becoming a "world city," itself composed of a series of interlocking small Third World communities: Taiwanese, Vietnamese, Filipino, Iranian, Korean, Arab, Ethiopian, Chinese, Mexican.[16]

What is so extraordinary about this vision narrative is the glossing of the Mexicans and Mexican Americans as the poor and the dispossessed in the dystopic capitalist system of twenty-first-century America. It is extraordinary on the one hand because Iranian Americans are as likely to use Mexican American grave diggers as their European neighbors, but even more extraordinary because it does not take into account the heightened prominence of Latinos in California generally and in L.A. particularly. If the total population of Los Angeles County in 1990 was 12 million, then fully one-quarter were Latinos, with more than 75 percent of them being of Mexican origin.[17] In other words, while there are Mexican American grave diggers in L.A., there are also Mexican American entrepreneurs and businessmen, doctors and lawyers, even anthropologists and television programmers! One of the ongoing issues that coalesces the diverse Mexican American community of L.A. is cultural citizenship, or how best to be represented in the economic, political, and cultural restructuring of Los Angeles, which will either transform or marginalize their children and their children's children.[18]

Perhaps even more astonishing, given the convergence of geographical location and historical experience, is the omission of any reference to South Asians in Naficy's otherwise commendable study. South Asian immigrants — Muslim and Hindu and Sikh and Parsee — mirror Iranian immigrants not only in their internal diversity but also in the gifts that they bring to the United States: education, professionalism, wealth.

Even though Naficy praises the high profile of Iranian immigrants, it remains true that "those born in India have the highest median household income, family income and per capita income of any foreign-born group in the 1990 Census."[19] And why? Because "of the total Indian-American population of just under one million, 48 percent are professionals, engineers or in managerial positions and include as many as 35,000 doctors."[20] Moreover, these same South Asian migrants to the USA, who have come in increasing numbers since 1965, are, like their Iranian counterparts, attracted to major urban areas, such as New York, Chicago, Washington, Houston, and, of course, Los Angeles. While one might expect a similar interest in maintaining cultural authenticity through TV programming in the language of the home country, it is modest, at least on the major overseas programmed TV station in L.A., KSCI-TV. Naficy's breakdown shows only one hour per day of Hindi/English programming, compared with three hours of Arabic and fifteen and a half hours of Persian.[21] Again, I would suggest that it is not religious affiliations or cultural moves to hybridity or creolization that is at stake here; rather, the notion of being Asian and being American is channeled through bourgeois forms of cultural capital that are produced and consumed, then reproduced and often exported from L.A. to the rest of the United States, then from the United States to the rest of the world.

The Urban Context

While Los Angeles television programming is a valuable window into the dynamics of transnational civil society, I would like to conclude this selective view of transnational immigrant (ir)religion by repeating my major argument: All studies that highlight religious affiliation as their key variable in looking at the sociocultural identity of immigrants are two-edged. As crucial as religious practice may be, in public and in private, in building structures and networking communities, other indices compete with religious affiliation or the lack thereof. Especially when one looks at the context of religious practice it is impossible to escape attention to the familiar trio of race, gender, and class along with another, pivotal index: location. For in every instance, whether it is recent immigrants or those dating back to the pre-1965 period, relocation in North America is, above all, charted as relocation in its cities. Those who choose to, or are forced to, come to North America do not go to Arkansas or North Dakota, at least not in large numbers. Instead, they go to New York, Chicago, and Los Angeles, along with other major metropolitan centers. As the religious historian Tom Tweed observed in his study of diasporic religious practices among Cuban immigrants, his Cuban Catholic subjects overwhelmingly preferred urban America. "Most Cuban exiles," notes Tweed, "like other recent American migrants, have lived in cities."[22]

In part, this magnet quality of cities is a result of the changing nature of labor in North American mega-cities. Many have shifted from heavy industry to soft information, with cities such as Los Angeles now marketing themselves and their services to an unprecedented degree.[23] Yet which is the real L.A.? Of the alternative downtowns that define present-day L.A., does one prefer the downtown of Bank City or its opposite, Shopping City? Bank City is "landscaped with fountains and trees, offering stores and restaurants to workers who travel from one office complex to another by shuttle bus and drive home to their (tweaky) neighborhoods by nightfall." Its consumers are upscale Anglos and immigrants, including Iranians.

Shopping City, on the other hand, is populist, mainly Mexican and Latino. In its open markets and sidewalk displays one finds "the immigrant shop-keepers, the empty department stores and old movie palaces, the schlock and sleaze, the mingled scents of tacos and danger."[24]

Future studies of immigrant religion will have to chart the reciprocal impact of particular cities, and even of boroughs or discrete neighbor-hoods, on specified groups in order to make sense of the range of diasporic religious practice that is taking place at the outset of a new millennium. Will it also mark a new moment in American religious history? The portents are not clear, but following Naficy's assessment of Iranians in L.A., we may find that liminality, rather than hybridity, best describes the several layers of negotiation within and between subcommunities. The mixtures are not of solids but of fluids, and the range of options for discrete groups, such as Iranian Americans in L.A., reflects multiple notions of belonging and competing, even within a single generation. What Tom Tweed wrote about Cuban Americans also applies to other immigrant groups: the best way to understand multiple, often conflicting images of homeland within a single immigrant community is to expect difference rather than sameness, conflict rather than conformity. "Diasporic images of nationhood," argues Tweed, "are multiple and contested, even within the same immigrant community,"[25] with the result that religion is always fungible, its invocation as much dependent on its location as on its history. Especially when urban and urban-dependent regions are the most significant sites, they, like their religious immigrant citizen subjects, exhibit a fractious, irreducible difference that may be finally more quintessentially American than the Anglo-American monoculture that animates the white overclass and conjures nostalgic longing for a past that never existed while also denying immigrants a future kaleidoculture that they have helped to create.

We can make some tentative conclusions. At least about Los Angeles, and Irangelinos, we have seen that no one can take numbers for granted. One must revisit every effort to say "so many" Muslims live in America or in L.A. The process is complicated by the U.S. Census ambiguity, but it is complicated equally by the members of local communities, including the L.A. Iranian community, who want to claim higher numbers for themselves.[26]

At the same time, one must note the near impossibility of pursuing Ashis Nandy's idealized strategy, namely, to have Asian Americans decouple their links with the mother country in order to enter the political realm of their new and adopted country. South Asian immigrants, Nandy suggests, "must see this as an opportunity to create a new life, just like other settlers did in Australia, North and South America. Their demands on India should be cut. They should not expect India to redeem their self-esteem. Nor should they seek a proxy presence in the public realm of South Asian societies. The diaspora must work towards dismantling links with the mother country and entering the political realm of their new country."[27] Yet neither Iranian Americans nor South Asian Americans have the will to sever their emotive as well as personal links to their places of origin; their politics, like their personas, remain transnational, and the strategy of stressing accommodation misses the deeper reflex to remain between two cultures, two countries, two worldviews. Far from enhancing emotional anxiety or social instability, the ambivalent outlook of Iranian Americans mirrors that deeper reflex of polyvalence that is crucial to the kaleidoculture of twenty-first-century America.

For Iranian Americans, as for other Asian Americans, the long-term struggle to be both American and non-Anglo is made more, not less, difficult by the power of the media. In the final chapter we will examine the several roles of the media, whether print or visual or virtual. The euphoria of cyberspace may translate seamlessly into the lives of overclass Anglo-Americans, but it translates less evenly into the professional and personal future of immigrant Americans. Especially those who fall at the lower end of the socioeconomic scale of late capitalist global economy may never achieve the cyberfantasy that one geek has labeled "techgnosis."[28] It is to that ambivalent influence of the media on all social expectations, but especially those framed as immigrant cultural and religious options, that I will now turn.

CHAPTER 5

Reimagining Religious Pluralism

Americans need images that help us picture religious, racial, and cultural diversity not merely as tolerable but as irreducible and delightful. . . . By analyzing and criticizing public [which is to say, media] images, religious studies can serve religious institutions that seek to propose images representing values alternative to those of a culture based on entertainment and consumption. Like Plato, we still "strain after images" that help us to imagine our lives fruitfully, enjoy our differences, and relate lovingly to one another and the natural world.

— Margaret Miles, "Image"[1]

The media, through their powerful presentation of the Other and their recasting of culture, have made everyone feel increasingly that they live in the presence of the Other, and no longer the demonized other.

— Rabbi Irving Greenberg, "Jewish Denominationalism"[2]

Framing Narrative 1: *Time* Finds God.com

The year was 1996, and as it approached its end, the editors of *Time* decided to highlight God in the December issue. December 1996 was not so long ago, yet in terms of chronic/cyber time, it was a momentous year. It was the year when the impact of the Net/Internet and cyberspace communication was just beginning to be felt in its broad, seemingly global impact. Onto a picture that mirrored a new dawn breaking was the simple but elegant

A very different version of this chapter, with some overlapping references and themes and images, appears as "God on Line: Locating the Pagan/Asian Soul of America in Cyberspace," in Susan Mizruchi, ed., *Religion and Cultural Studies*, 236–54 (Princeton: Princeton University Press, 2001).

BURMA'S ANGRY STUDENTS

TIME

God.com

Finding Religion
On the Internet

"God.com," with an cursor pointing at the G, which was highlighted in Gothic floral relief, its yellow and purple hues offsetting the stark black of the letter G. Beneath the announcement of God.com was the subheading "Finding Religion on the Internet." The cover story features a monk scrolling through his computer, and with numerous references to the first and second Information Ages, it makes the point that just as the first Information Age was sparked by a religious document, the Gutenberg Bible of

1456, so the second Information Age will be marked by a religious transformation no less dramatic and interactive.[3] As the collective authors, five in all, from Rome, Paris, New York, and New Orleans, conclude:

> As much as the Net is changing our ideas of God, it may be changing us even more. For many, signing on to the Internet is a transformative act. In their eyes the Web is more than just a global tapestry of personal computers and fiber-optic cable. It is a vast cathedral of the mind, a place where ideas about God and religion can resonate, where faith can be shaped and defined by a collective spirit. Such a faith relies not on great external forces to change the world, but on what ordinary people, working as one, can create on this World Wide Web that binds all of us, Christian and Jew, Muslim and Buddhist, together. Interconnected, we may begin to find God in places we never imagined.

Framing Narrative 2: *The Economist* Finds God in Cyberspace

A year later *The Economist* followed the lead of *Time*. The November 15, 1997, issue included a sidebar on the theme of religion and the Net. The essay, of course, was marked by the typical *Economist* penchant for understatement and irony. Yes, we are told, thousands of religious denominations have taken their message to the World Wide Web in the past four or five years. Yes, some of them also use it not for information but for proselytization, and, most surprisingly, one of the most evangelical is Judaism. Consider the high quality and wide dispersion of the site on Project Genesis at *www.torah.org*. Not only observant Jews but also multicultural Catholics, Parsis and Bahais, Muslims and Hindus, even the staid Church of England/Anglicans use the Net for their own advocacy. But, as *The Economist* article rightly concludes:

> These are still pioneering days for the electronic media. While it is already apparent that the Web can perform some useful functions for religions: it can educate, make accessible the workings of large organizations, answer the questions of the curious and coordinate

community activities, [it also has limits]. What it cannot do, not yet anyway, is convert cyberspace into a place of virtual worship. The times of religious services can be posted on the Web but congregations still need to gather.[4]

Framing Narrative 3: The Baby Buddha for Baby Boomers

Midway through 1998 the fascination with religious pluralism and the possibilities of the World Wide Web found vivid expression in the alternative press. It was again in a cover issue, the cover of the July-August 1998 issue of the *Utne Reader*.[5] The cover outdoes all others in capturing what Homi Bhabha would call religious hybridity, or the rest of us might call syncretistic or creole expressions of American questing. It is the baby Buddha, probably Tibetan, springing off an invisible trampoline, or tossed into midair by invisible but gleeful parents. With designer pink silk pants and a brown mock monk's shirt, he sports three necklaces—a cross, a crescent and star (Muslim), a yin-yang (Taoist)—and a toothy, leafy bracelet that could be Sikh. A Hindu *tikka* marks his forehead, a Jewish *kippa* and sidelocks adorn his smiling face—impish or beatific or both? Writ large across his piebald body is the phrase "Designer God," and beneath the question mark: "In a mix-and-match world, why not create your own religion?"

The article that the cherubic pluriform baby god on the cover touts is titled "God with a Million Faces (Thank You, Joe Campbell)," and the subtitled message/thesis is "Critics call it 'cafeteria religion,' but the new mix-and-match approach to faith may be the truest spiritual quest of all." The body of the article addresses privatized faith in a way all too familiar to academics who have read, and tried to make sense of, Robert Bellah's *Habits of the Heart*. In both instances the focus is on individualism as the American religion, with attention to the spiritual imagination and energy of women. Sheila in one case, Anne-marie in another, represents all women who seek to form their own religion of various beliefs and practices, pursuing the pastiche spirituality first made famous in California but now extant in many upscale communities of the United States.

For all its populist features, the *Utne Reader* article stresses two familiar points over and over. The first shift is temporal: we have entered a new era

How to Think Like a Genius

UTNE ᵁᴿ READER

THE BEST OF THE ALTERNATIVE MEDIA

JULY-AUGUST 98

Designer God

In a mix-and-match world, why not create your own religion?

Sex Food
Isabel Allende

Science and Soul
Ken Wilber

The Velvet Planet
Václav Havel

Mothers of Invention
Maya Angelou, Julia Cameron, Frank Zappa

in American religious practice, an era that began with the Immigration and Naturalization Act of 1965, for it was that act that eliminated a long-standing bias against Asians and other people that had been enforced through quotas based on national origin. Among the new immigrants from Asia were many spiritual teachers whose influence would eventually extend beyond their immediate followers into the popular culture.

The second shift is technical. The information explosion has led to the rise of do-it-yourself spirituality:

> Esoteric texts once known to a privileged few now fill the bookstores, their myriad truths laid open to be read and recombined at will. And virtually every work of sacred art, from the caves of Altamira onward, circulates endlessly now, free for the appropriating. This robust spiritual marketplace perfectly suits the consumer mentality that has turned Americans into a nation of comparison shoppers. In an age when we trust ourselves to assemble our own investment portfolios and cancer therapies, why not our religious beliefs?

Beyond the historical accent on the 1965 immigration act and the invocation of Net-based resources for spiritual adventurism, the *Utne Reader* article also underscores the changed climate for so-called traditional religions, and in so doing it introduces a dimension absent from most popular writing about New Age spirituality. "We're living in what observers call an age of extreme 'religious pluralism,'" observes the author, "[yet] the same cultural forces that have driven many to leave their inherited faiths have also affected others who have stayed. Almost all the major denominations now contain internal movements that are trying to transform them."[6] These forces, of course, are opposed by traditionalists and fundamentalists, but they persist within the familiar sites of Christian, Jewish, and Muslim institutional expression.

Framing Narrative 4: *Life* Sees GOD

And nowhere is the force of institutional religion more keenly registered than in the December 1998 issue of *Life*. Like *Time* two years earlier, *Life* featured Religion on a special year-end cover. "GOD" on the cover of *Life* is hardly

surprising. After all, the huge Christmas market shapes all strategies for journal formatting and topic selection at the end of a calendar year. Especially
inviting is the opportunity for increased sales in a calendar year that is one
shy of marking the end of the second millennium in the Christian calendar
and the beginning of its third millennium. How many of us can say we don't
think of that strange occurrence in our lifetime, whether with amusement,
disdain, or awe? And so GOD is in the news as well as on our minds.

Nor is it surprising that the December 1998 cover of *Life* asks a single

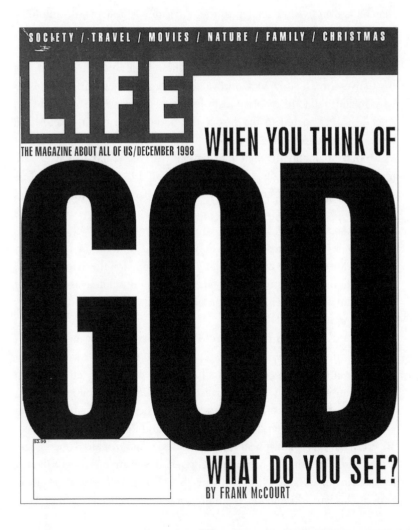

SOCIETY / TRAVEL / MOVIES / NATURE / FAMILY / CHRISTMAS

LIFE

THE MAGAZINE ABOUT ALL OF US / DECEMBER 1998

$3.99

WHEN YOU THINK OF

GOD

WHAT DO YOU SEE?
BY FRANK McCOURT

question in two parts: "When you think of GOD what do you see?" A high-brow audience would not make this connection. Thought is a reflective, and also a literary-based activity, while image belongs to the lower world, the world of hoi polloi or undereducated folk. There persists, as Castells noted, "a social hierarchy between literate culture and audiovisual expression."[7] And the *Life* feature story acknowledges this same hierarchy even while trying to subvert it. Look at who answers the question: "When you think of GOD what do you see?" It is not a theologian, nor is it a film director. It comes instead from a man of letters. The person who answers the question is no less an authority on religion than Frank McCourt. McCourt may be known to some readers as the renegade Catholic whose autobiography of his Irish abusers, *Angela's Ashes*, rebuts not only Trinitarian belief but also hidebound institutional practices. McCourt pokes fun at all the pomp and circumstance that cloak the patriarchical, hieratic structures of his native church. It is McCourt's deep-seated iconoclasm that explains why, in addition to its redolent lustfulness and knack for the quick phrase, *Angela's Ashes* soared to the top of the best-seller list in the USA and remained there for well over a year.[8]

To make palpable my own engagement with the visual display of contemporary religious artifacts, I have highlighted the aspects of the *Life* story that catch the casual reader. First is the cover: A stark black and white with red borders, and in the center, beckoning the eye to linger, is "GOD." Above "GOD" is written "when you think of" and below "GOD" is written "what do you see?" The double effect could not be more alluring to a lower-middle-class would-be purchaser, nor the name "Frank McCourt" more intriguing to a middle- or upper-middle-class reader of fiction who is familiar either first- or secondhand with McCourt's raunchy autobiography.

A second signifier is the layout of the opening spread of the article. It pictures four audiences, each in spiritual rapture, each wearing institutionally mandated dress, each sexually segregated. The top left is a group of Mormon women, all eyes downcast. Below them is a group of Muslim men, all at prayer, in nearly symmetrical rows. They resemble the Mormon women, except that their backs are in the air and their bottoms up. There are no faces here; Islam appears to be a faceless religion of blind obedience, we are told. Opposite the Mormon women and Muslim men are Orthodox Jews, all in black and white, with heads covered, gathered at Madison Square Garden, while below them are Protestant evangelicals from Minnesota, part of an eight-thousand-member choir, decked out in green sport shirts to grace a Billy Graham crusade in the Twin Cities and eyeballing the photographer.

The third and most problematic signifier for the *Life* article is the cumulative etching of other religious groups in distinctive settings. Each is marked with an explanatory insert, though not all groups are identified with membership statistics. It is mainly the groups that came to the United States in significant numbers after 1965 who are marked, whether by their global numbers and their new representation in the USA or just by the latter. In other words, the insert boxes try to capture and also to epitomize what is new and also irreversible about the altered American religious landscape: Hindus, 800 million in India, 30 million outside India, 1 million in the USA; Russian Orthodox, 2 million in the USA; Sikhs, 20 million worldwide, 2 million in North America; Roman Catholics, 60 million in the USA; Christian Fellowship (no stats); Jains, 10 million in India, 100,000 in the USA; Christ Clubs (no stats); Pentecostals, 130 million global, 12 million in the USA; African Orthodox (no stats); Greek Orthodox, 15 million global, 2 million in the USA; Holy Rollers (no stats); Buddhists, 780,000 in the USA; storefront Baptist girls at prayer (no stats). Though Roman Catholics, Russian Orthodox, Pentecostals, and Greek Orthodox all predate 1965 in large numbers, it is only Jews, Muslims, and Mormons from the initial four-group picture who are given totals: 6 million Muslims (in North America), 6.8 million Mormons worldwide, and 6 million Jews also worldwide. No membership statistic is given for Evangelicals, nor for the majority of smaller Christian groups: African Orthodox, Christian Fellowship(s), Christ Clubs, Holy Rollers, Baptists. In other words, they count but are not to be counted; their numbers do not register beside those who really count—Jews, Muslims, and Mormons.

Some might like to pause and revisit those figures or that absence of figures. They are jarring, since they reflect how tenuous are *all* efforts to particularize religious or denominational membership. In earlier chapters, we have already seen how controversial are the numbers attributed to Muslims; the same could be said for Mormons, Pentecostals, and Buddhists. Consider the extent to which this picture of religious catchments or labels contrasts with the one provided by Diana Eck under the rubric "World Religions." For Eck, as for most who do introductions to world religions, no religion can get more than one button, so Christianity encompasses Roman Catholics, Protestants, Greek Orthodox, and also Mormons. All

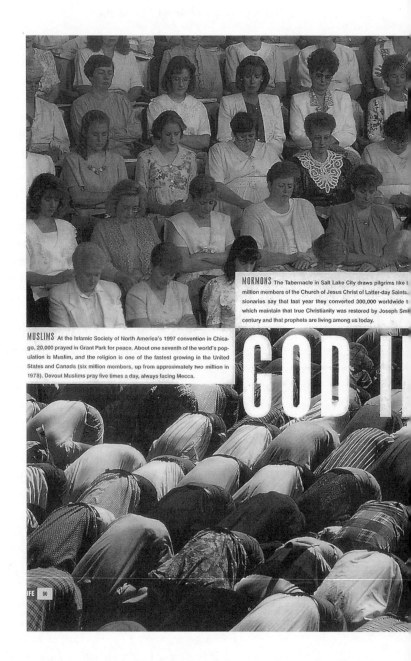

MORMONS The Tabernacle in Salt Lake City draws pilgrims like t
million members of the Church of Jesus Christ of Latter-day Saints.
sionaries say that last year they converted 300,000 worldwide t
which maintain that true Christianity was restored by Joseph Sm
century and that prophets are living among us today.

MUSLIMS At the Islamic Society of North America's 1997 convention in Chicago, 20,000 prayed in Grant Park for peace. About one seventh of the world's population is Muslim, and the religion is one of the fastest growing in the United
States and Canada (six million members, up from approximately two million in
1978). Devout Muslims pray five times a day, always facing Mecca.

GOD I

ent Hebrews founded their religion on reverence of a transcendent
vealed Himself to Abraham, Moses and other prophets. Today there
on Jews in the U.S., up 100,000 since 1996. Some 26,000 Orthodox
ding these celebrants, gathered at Madison Square Garden in Sep-
to mark the end of a seven-and-a-half-year reading of the Talmud.

ERICA

EVANGELICALS Rev. Billy Graham's most recent U.S. crusade drew 283,00
Christians in Tampa. (The men seen here are part of an 8,000-member choir pe
forming at an earlier appearance in Minneapolis.) When Graham first wer
abroad, in 1954, he preached his traditionalist view of the Bible to two million i
London; in 1995 he reached one billion via satellite from San Juan, Puerto Rico.

Christian groups become subsets of something larger called Christianity. Yet *Life's* editors have no hesitation about splicing up the world's most schismatic religion, Christianity. It consists of Mormons, Evangelicals, Russian Orthodox, Roman Catholics, Christian Fellowships, Christ Clubs, Pentecostals, African Orthodox, Holy Rollers, and Baptists, ten subgroups in all. Yet every other major religion gets but one picture: Muslims, Jews, Hindus, Sikhs, Jains, and Buddhists, six in all. It is as if to say that there is no internal diversity among Muslims or Jews, or Hindus or Buddhists! Yet no intelligent person would accept such an assertion: even Jains and Sikhs, though smaller groups than Hindus and Buddhists, are significant Asian religious communities that also exhibit their own internal diversity.

It is difficult to avoid the conclusion that the visual smorgasbord offered by *Life* is for mainly Christian—that is to say, mainly Anglo-Protestant Christian at that—consumers. In other words, racialized class prejudice has become so internalized that it does not need to be defended, only per-petuated. Instead of genuine polyvalence, there is but one dominant reli-gion—Christianity—and instead of a cultural kaleidoscope or kaleidocul-ture, *Life* offers but a fig leaf for the continued dominance of Progressive Protestant Patriotism.

And its message is made more appealing through a double virtuosity: the photo virtuosity of *Life*, which is unmatched in popular media, and also the verbal virtuosity of McCourt, whose words are almost as graphic as the pictures accompanying them: America on the cusp of a new millennium offers nothing less than "a spiritual smorgasbord." "I don't confine myself to the faith of my fathers anymore," intones McCourt. "All the religions are spread before me, a great spiritual smorgasbord, and I'll help myself, thank you."

Reimagining Religion in an Age Awash with Images

Life's marketing of global, Polyanna, smorgasbord religion, the shopping mall approach to American-style spirituality, is not *Life's* alone. It is more than just a few journals, whether *Time*, *Life*, the *Utne Reader*, or even the staid *Economist*, that seem to see religion as now a topic of vital interest. If we are to believe communications experts, the readers of these journals reflect the tastes and values of the baby boomer producers/consumers whose wealth still accounts for much of American commerce, and so their views on Religion resonate with a broad segment of the knowledge class and the affluent class, which tend to elide.[9]

What characterizes the media approach to religious pluralism American style is a common commercial strategy, from *Time* to *The Economist* to the *Utne Reader* to *Life*. The most effective way of talking about religion is through images combined with text, or text that conjures images. It was Hans-Georg Gadamer, the German cultural critic, who has argued that the deepest structure of religion is not cognitive but visual. "The transition from the stage of representation to that of the concept," says Gadamer, "cannot be made without art."[10] Why could not the deepest structure of religion be tactile or aural, tasty or even odoriferous? It could be, of course, except that the register common to Euro-American or, better, Anglo-Protestant norms is visual.[11] Images drive the media, from newspapers to journals to television and now the Internet. Not images of private devotion but those of public advertising, and mass marketing, create expectations about spirituality, expectations that are as consumer-driven as the food we eat or the cars we drive or the clothes we buy.

And so there are two major forces about religious images in the twenty-first century that coexist uneasily with one another. The first is the culture-specific attachment to images that links back to Hellenistic philosophy mediated but not reversed by Enlightenment philosophy, Marxist, and Freudian interventions, and then the capitalist market.[12] Our attachment to images is not universal, yet it appears so prevalent as to seem at once universal, natural, taken-for-granted. The second point is that the new media do not merely add more pictures to the everyday repertoire of expectations, fueling desires and reinforcing needs that Americans share; the new media, including print and cyber journalism, extol images as symbols of the deepest spiritual reality, which becomes more authentic as it becomes more visually arresting. Though it is a collective appeal to individual taste, it is always packaged as a choice or, better, the illusion of choice, which prevails even when the predisposition to pick certain images, to make particular pitches, is driven by expectations of consumer interest, desire, readiness, and ability to buy. I call this reciprocal process that depends on a deep level of ideological consumerism *hyper-visualization*.

In the interest of instantaneous appeal, buyer "need," and higher sales, the media gloss difference primarily through pictures, and then elide pictures with subordinate, though often superfluous, text. And spirituality is a high-consumer product, at least for baby boomers—meaning, Anglo, middle-aged, Protestant-minded, well-heeled patriots. Progressive Protestant Patriots are more prone to buy magazines, or watch movies, or explore tapes and books that have to do with spiritualized difference. Whether it is the Baby Buddha or the Dalai Lama or the Immigrant Guru, all these images, and persons, suggest a difference that has already been domesticated, regularized, and assimilated to an American idiom of faith. That idiom presupposes faith as private belief, public ritual, and political non-advocacy. It is the paradigm of cultural fundamentalists as well as their neoliberal opponents. Except for wars in the Supreme Court and over government support for faith-based initiatives under the Bush 43 administration, both sides want to reduce, rather than expand, government interference with the exercise of religious freedom.

But beyond the surface appeal of the Baby Buddha phenomenon lies a deeper force: the long arm of racialized class prejudice . While it affects *all* minority group experience in the USA, and not just Asian immigrants, it imposes parameters on Asian immigrants in social as well as professional domains, in religious and cultural pursuits as much as in educational or residential options.

Racialized class prejudice inserts itself into the new media, just as it did into the old media. To understand its role in the new media one must first revisit and highlight its genesis in the old. The old media include radio, television, and phonographs, but they are epitomized by Hollywood, and in Hollywood films of ethnic/racial minorities the gaze of the Anglo-Protestant majority pervades, in ways that are consistently negative. Even when movies celebrate ethnic-cultural polyphony, it rarely leads to the kind of polyvalence that is the major goal of the current study. First of all, the kind of heteroglossia that movies such as *The Pawnbroker* (1965) and *Brother from Another Planet* (1984) celebrate is drawn from urban sites, usually New York or Los Angeles, where one can see different classes, races, and generations in such intimate exchange that there is a dazzling polyphonic potential.

Yet it remains a staged, manipulated potential; it always stops short of questioning power structures that would reveal the unequal relations of the principal characters. Rather than subvert existing power relations between diverse communities, the films tend to orchestrate superficially defined ethnic interaction. Some acclaimed films such as Spike Lee's *Do the Right Thing* (1989) do celebrate a North American polyphonic culture, foregrounding music, dance, and food as sites of meeting, matching and mixing the texture of minorities' lives. Whether the minorities are the oldest, forced immigrants, who are African Americans, or newer, "voluntary" immigrants, such as Europeans, Hispanics, and also Asians, cultural fusion does not erase structural inequity, and the other message of Spike Lee's movie, for instance, is that Italians (along with other immigrants) "have used blacks as a kind of 'welcome mat,' as a way of affirming, through antiblack hostility, their own insecure sense of American identity."[13]

And Native Americans in their filmic representation stand beside, or perhaps below, African Americans as the undesirable other, the unwelcome mat. Even an acclaimed countercultural film such as *Little Big Man* (1970), with Dustin Hoffman, emphasizes Native Americans' downtrodden existence. Because it does show many different personalities and cultures among American Indians, it may seem to evoke a plea for greater understanding to a largely Anglo audience. Yet given the history of the First Nation during the past three hundred years, it may also confirm for this same audience that *all* Indians are beyond help. "In that sense, falsifying, simplifying and romanticizing the image of the Indian may unwittingly succeed in making the overall message more appealing and more palatable to white audiences."[14] The most recent Hollywood adaptation of James Fenimore Cooper's *The Last of the Mohicans* (1992) goes still further. Not only does it stress the apartness and otherness of Native Americans but it also moralizes the doomed nature of love between white and Indian. The not-so-subtle message is that Indian represents Black represents the "alien" other. One may dabble in music or art or dance or food, one may feel pity and attempt public acts of good faith, one may even pray. Progressive Protestant Patriots refuse to cross, or allow others to cross, the white line.

Even countercultural films cannot avoid projecting, rather than simply protesting, racialized class prejudice. Third World Newsreel produced a socially critical, politically engaged documentary of one of the poorest rural communities in the United States, the Mississippi Delta. Titled *Mississippi Triangle*, it was shot in 1985. It has three groups as its subjects: the Chinese/black Chinese community, the black community, and the white community. It projects a broad lens that puts new immigrants alongside fourth- and fifth-generation Delta Mississipians. It includes Protestant and Catholic, Asian, Anglo, and African American participants.

At first blush, this film seems to have little do with Asian religion. There are no Buddhists or Hindus among its subjects; even the Protestant/Catholic distinction is minimal. The film focuses on the many social institutions in the Delta area: the cotton industry and the small retail economy frame the school system, local politics, the family and also the church. In each instance the views of all three groups are intercalated so that no one predominates as the "truth," but the truth that does emerge from the film's collective engagement with multiple subjects is that racialized class preju-dice is all too alive in rural Mississippi, despite—or perhaps because of—the influx of immigrants. The prejudice revolves most clearly around dat-ing and marriage. Each subgroup has internal norms that govern the behavior of the next generation. One young Chinese interviewee explains that he dated mostly Chinese girls, even though they were "more conser-vative and sexually uptight than the other kind—the off-brand." At one point he qualifies the off-brand: they are never African American, since "by dating black women he [a Chinese American] would risk ostracism from both the white and the Chinese communities."[15]

But the psychological and social separation of Chinese in the Delta from their black neighbors is not a dilemma of race relations unique to rural Mississippi. Rather, the cautionary tale of *Mississippi Triangle* forces us to revisit and revise our notion of how Asian Americans fit into the ethno-racial pentagon. The engagement with racialized thinking in twenty-first-century America affects the new media as much as the old. It is impossible to read the *Utne Reader* or any other New Age magazine and not come up against a startling contradiction. Why are Asian Americans so desirable as spiritual lodestones if not because, in part, they are an accept-able racialized difference? Against the invisible, but invincible, line that militates against miscegenation with Amerindians or with African Ameri-cans, Asian Americans become a liminal racial other. Questions about intermarriage may still arise, but not with the same class/race disparity firmly in place against African and Native Americans.

To put the case still more strongly, Asian Americans both spiritually and socially are the unintended beneficiaries of the long history of racialized social policy and media representation in the USA. Without awareness of that history, and attention to its pervasive effect, one cannot understand either the reception of Asian Americans in general or their spiritual options. The latter are twofold. They are spiritual options for themselves, what they can do, where they can live, what temples or mosques they can build, but they are also the options that others, others from the white overclass, have for eliding with them. Whether they elide as fellow worshipers or as marital partners, they modify the ethno-racial pentagon without displacing its firmest barrier, the barrier against African and Native American others. What emerges are other strands of polyvalence within twenty-first-century American kaleidoculture, yet the foundations of class/race difference that first led to the pentagon's construction are attenuated rather than obliterated.

The Latest Phase of Hypervisualization

Despite its limits, the 1965 Immigration and Naturalization Act did change the U.S. religious landscape forever. While it did not and cannot eliminate racialized class prejudice, it has ensured that, despite conservative opposition, the United States will never again be merely a three-religion nation-state of Protestants, Catholics and Jews.[16]

But how do most Americans register this difference? I have argued from the outset that we cannot answer this question by quibbling about academic distinctions between religion and culture. Instead, we must see the two as elided, and above all, we must account for the power of popular culture to determine how "others" are represented, their presence Americanized if not domesticated.

Here I want to argue that the most powerful stimulus for normalizing Asian, and also non-Asian, others comes from media images—not just images but packaged images that depend on a process of production and consumption that I call *hypervisualization*. The CD-ROM, *On Common Ground*, as we have noted above, depends on this process without ever raising questions about the multiple assumptions that it requires. *On Common Ground* condenses, then projects fifteen religious traditions in eighteen sites as the "new" religious landscape of turn-of-the-millennium America. In doing so through a medium that relies on visual appeal, its iconic effect as much as its indexical content determines how viewers respond to it.

Hypervisualization is not limited to religion; it is an aspect of global culture that pervades, even as it now has begun to transform, religious sensibilities. What do I mean by *hypervisualization*? I mean the extent to which popular culture has become synonymous with images and the imaginary, driven by very recent advances in media technology. The most obvious consumers are sports fans and moviegoers or video watchers, even though some studies have shown how limited is the number of movies that "average" Americans can bear to watch.[17] Yet images, and image-based learning, also have a huge audience in all levels of education, from grade school through the university, not only in technical fields but also in liberal arts and social sciences. Religion remains anchored in the humanities, and so its study reflects a text-oriented approach, yet ours is no longer a text-based culture: whether we look at Generation X, Y, or E, most of today's students rely on images or image-based learning much more than did their predecessors a mere decade ago, and they use image-based learning to supplement, if not to replace, both the literary representation of scripture and the textbooks that trace religions through written artifacts.

What drives most college-level students, above all, is engagement with the Internet as the lodestone of image-based learning. The Internet, or the Net, is a very recent advance in media technology. It was not until January 1993 that the first graphical, mouse-based hypertext system was conceived, but by late 1993 Mosaic, the first graphical Windows-based browser, had appeared, and now, less than a decade later, both the WWW (the World Wide Web) and Mosaic have become inextricable, though the Web dominates, even as it has been paralleled and upgraded by Netscape, yet another Windows-based graphical browser. Yet the domain of the Net, cyberspace, offers random, detailed, labyrinthine templates of almost any subject or set of subjects. It offers at once too much information and too little structure or criteria for its usage. The Info Age or the High-Tech Revolution is still in its earliest stage.

When one lives through a revolution, it is difficult to theorize the tidal wave of change. Consider the brilliant and comprehensive writings of Manuel Castells. Noting that before the twentieth century, among educated elites there was "a social hierarchy between literate culture and audiovisual expression," Castells charts the revenge of the audiovisual in the twentieth century. It began with film and radio, then television, and then the multimedia system of the 1990s. For Castells the current revolution is equivalent to the creation of the alphabet in 700 B.C.E. Greece. What we are witnessing, in his words, is "a technological transformation of similar historic dimensions," since "the formation of a Super-Text and a Meta-Language integrates into the same system the written, oral, and audiovisual modalities of human communication for the first time in history."[18] According to Castells we are witnessing nothing less than the Second Information Revolution; the computer will be to future generations what the Gutenberg Bible was to sixteenth-century North Europeans and their descendants.

What does that mean for the academy? It means that groups within the academy also form digital communities, each with its own citizenry or, what some veterans of cyberspace call, netizenry. Netizens find information about almost everything, they make contacts unimagined or impossible a few years ago, and they discuss all sorts of topics. They may rely on E-mail but they also surf the Net, and they do so far more systematically than anybody predicted.

There is a danger; it is the danger of numbing referentiality to cyber-data, without acknowledgment of other experiences and other sources of engagement. I call this danger cyberpsychosis, and it afflicts "average" teenagers, not just techies. Yet despite the danger of cyberpsychosis, the Net is here to stay, and I would like to project a notion of culture/religion that acknowledges the potential of the Net rather than bemoans its intrusiveness. Hypervisualization can be a tool, rather than an impediment, to rethinking religious studies in general. It may yet assist the project invoked by Margaret Miles in the first epigraph, "to propose images representing values alternative to those of a culture based on entertainment and consumption," but the path must lead through a maze of popular culture representations of religion, including representations of the new faiths of Asian immigrants to the United States since 1965.

In fact, countercultural images and the values they convey must reflect an engagement with mainstream culture, and if we are entering the Second Information Age, as Castells has argued, it is time to offer an alternative theory of religion/culture. It is a theory that begins with the new Asian immigrants and their faith loyalties. It has five points. They constitute the circuit of religion, mirroring the circuit of culture announced by the Open University course team, headed by Paul du Gay and Stuart Hall.[19] The outline of this theory of culture[20] offers an interlocking grid:

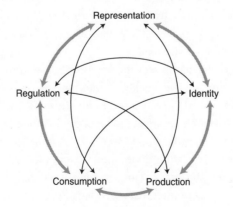

We can adapt this same model to religion, but with some significant adjustments. First, we must complicate Representation by adding the element of Contestation, i.e., Representation always inscribes a choice and often a conflictual choice of what gets represented and for whom. Identity also requires its complementary other, Community, at the same time that Production must be paired with Reproduction since there is never a production *de novo*, and the pattern of continuity is crucial for capitalist markets, even though Consumption, which is the goal and the goad of Production/ Reproduction, must itself be linked to technologies of the self expressing both need and desire.

Finally, in applying the du Gay/Hall model to immigrant religious groups, one has less concern with Regulation than Location. Location itself is not inherently stable as a category, and to reflect its malleability one must link it to its prefix correlates: dis-location, re-location, bi-location, all of which are crucial for studying diasporic groups.

And how does Identity emerge from this interactive process? First, identity is never given, it is always constructed, and constructed by social relationships that themselves reflect power differentials. The major arena for identity construction is always civil society. For Castells, there are three stages of identity formation: legitimizing identity, which is distinct from resistance identity, and then project identity, which is an amalgam of the two.[21] Castells, following Gramsci, projects legitimizing identity as the work of civil society: Within approved civic associations and voluntary groups, individuals find their social identity, while resistance identity emerges on the margins of civil society and often threatens to disrupt its routinizing functions. Project identity therefore is the effort to incorporate elements of resistance into legitimizing identity, to make the uncivil civil, and for Castells this prefigures the transformative labor that takes place through the network society rather than a new version of civil society, whether national or transnational.

Hall, on the other hand, sees the key issue for identity to be the link between social and psychic reality.[22] Suturing is the metaphor for the knowing subject who at once recognizes identities as "mere" representations yet searches the repertoire of modes of production embedded in special social contexts in order to discover "why certain individuals occupy some subject positions rather than others" (a question Foucault failed to answer).[23] Relating the unconscious to ideology is the work of psychoanalysis; it was the one frontier that remained closed to Foucault. Yet, once we have related not only production but self-production to specific choices and specific modes of conduct, suggests Hall, we may be able to forge what Foucault himself dimly glimpsed but never fully articulated: a genealogy of the technologies of the self.[24]

Whether we reassess identity through the civil society prism or through its opposite, the psychoanalytic prism, we still need to analyze immigrant religion with fresh insight. We might pursue a five-fold sequence, or a five-node circuit of religion that helps us to see new faiths in twenty-first-century America as contingent both historically and contemporaneously. We could investigate how they are media-ted in several directions, including most recently, cyberspace and the new marvels—at once magical and mischievous—of the World Wide Web.

Our new diagram would look like this:

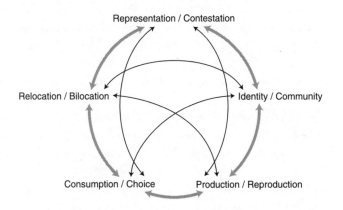

Let us signal points on the circuit marking the New Faiths as cultural artifacts by noting questions that they address. Let us characterize them as: two whats, two whens, and one where. The two whats: What is religion? What are Asian religions? The two whens: When did Asian religious actors begin to relocate outside Asia? And when did they become critically significant in their relocation to the New World? Finally, where within the New World are the newest Asian religious actors most prominent?

Even while raising these questions, I must stress that neither the questions nor the terms are stable, isolated points; rather, they are interrelated, changing nodes, open to negotiation as well as reversal. They remain contingent.

1. *Religion*. What is it in the third millennium? Whether we follow a functionalist like Steve Bruce or a poststructuralist like Talal Asad, we must always affirm, following the dictum of Dipesh Chakrabarty, that we cannot simply speak *about* religion; we must also speak *from* a particular religion and, even more, from a particular place. Even if our register is a blank—that is, a secular disavowal of any religious commitment or orientation, practice or ritual—we must still say from which norms we are demurring when we say, "I have no religion; I live in Antarctica, etc." At the 1998 gathering of the American Academy of Religion I attended a session on comparative theology. It featured the work of the Oxford theologian Keith Ward, and one of the respondents to Ward's corpus was Paul Griffiths of the University of Chicago Divinity School. Griffiths attacked Ward for his feeble attempt to distinguish between attenuated, revised confessionalism, deemed broad in its approach to other religions, and strong but narrow confessionalism, unengaged by the other, especially the creedally other. Griffiths demolished the distinction but did so while hoisting up his own dyadic clutch, namely, the home religion and "alien" religions. It was a peculiarly inter-Christian type of disputation, with almost no relationship to other groups that are autonomous from, and irreducible to, Christian categories.

I was especially struck by the punctuated tone of Griffiths' reference to "alien" religions. Why are they deemed "alien"? Why did no one in the audience take up the cause of the "aliens"? Because, I suggest, most theologians are wedded to Religion One—wholesale encatchments called Christianity, Hinduism, Buddhism, and so on. On the other hand, I take religion to be much closer to the specific and always local contexts out of which "religious" actors arise and the circumstances to which they relate, the memories that they claim, and the realities that they contest and then re-vision. If it must be called something, call this approach to Religion Two "anthropological," since without the anthropological appreciation of local context and agency, with the nuance and hope that both unfold, there would be no immigrant Asian religion worth studying.

2. *Asian religions*. What then are Asian religions and where do they exist? They were not constituted as religions till the nineteenth century, as Jonathan Z. Smith has made pointedly clear, and one can never be too attentive to their historical specificities.[25] One may doubt whether Asian religions, or religions of Asia, exist as an analytical category except within Euro-American academic circles—and there as a subset of

"world religions." While not wishing to descend into nominalism, claiming that both "Asia" and "religions of Asia" exist only as mental constructs, I would argue that we must be very clear how limited is their discursive value beyond an audience of middle- to highbrow Euro-American elites.

3. *Asian religions in diaspora.* When does the greater dislocation/relocation of Asian laborers begin to take place? Not till the nineteenth century, and then in response to global capitalism and colonialism with, e.g., Muslims and Hindus relocating in South Africa, Hindus in Malaysia and Singapore, still others in Europe and the New World, America. The second wave of colonialism saw large numbers of Asians leaving their initial countries of relocation to seek still better opportunities within other parts of the expanding European empires. It is this mobility of labor that has to be more keenly nuanced in our understanding of the latest, third wave of colonialism that continues into the twenty-first century, for it is only because of this third wave of colonialism that we have witnessed the large-scale immigration marking post-1965 America. To avoid the illusion of equality or equivalence between various groups and also often competing religions, it would be more accurate to approach the latest diaspora, which brought many Asians to North America post-1965, with the following grid:

JUDAISM–CHRISTIANITY–ISLAM
(still the dominant traditions in numbers and influence)
and
Hinduism–Buddhism, along with Jainism and Sikhism
(lumped together in much popular understanding as
the minor "Asian" alternatives)

And if we choose to match lesser to greater, we might look beyond numbers and try to gauge perceived influence in the public square of media representation. Despite its wholesale distortion (as we saw especially in the case of the *Life* 1998 cover essay), media projection of religious groups does both reflect and reinforce the way many Americans, especially the white American overclass, think of religion. The *Life* image recognizes internal divisions within Christianity, but mostly sees them as Protestant/Catholic, according to the following grid:

Judaism — Islam

//

PROTESTANTISM — ROMAN CATHOLICISM

****

Hinduism — Buddhism

In other words, while Judaism and Islam are not identical, they parallel each other, as do Protestantism and Catholicism, and all four circulate within an Abrahamic arc that is defined by Protestant-Catholic norms and values. By the same criterion, Hinduism and Buddhism, despite the hype about their popular appeal and media notoriety, continue to represent external and minor "others."

Exoticizing the Oriental other is also an acceptable move within the continuing paradigm of racialized class prejudice that dominates all American culture, including religious practice. It is not the same as demonizing the Other, and Rabbi Greenberg is right to stress that a major benefit of modern media is to make the Other familiar and acceptable, but acceptable only within limits, and those are the limits of racialized class prejudice. Often it goes unnoticed. Consider again the Baby Buddha. The Baby Buddha is not a dark black but a light brown Buddha, and bell hooks (among others) has suggested that the humility as well as the otherness of being black makes African American Buddhists difficult to acknowledge, a black Buddha beyond the pale, for Anglo converts to Buddhist practice.[26] Indeed, one would be hard-pressed to think of any figure in the collective imaginary of the white overclass that extols black as divine. Saint John Coltrane, for instance, is a spiritual giant in the African Orthodox Church, a church that also boasts a vivid, compelling Web site, yet to most Americans John Coltrane is just another jazz great who died before his time, not a saint, and certainly not a divinized figure for *all* Americans.

The logic of these two grids accords with hypervisual projections of religious practice in twenty-first-century America. While neither grid reflects the "reality" of the *Life* inserts, together they problematize the seamless equality of traditions that is implied in the set of fifteen buttons used to depict "World Religions in America" in the *On Common Ground* CD-ROM. It is not just that the technology limits the possibility of having more buttons, or bigger and smaller, or brighter and dimmer, buttons. It is rather that we must continually question the assumptions of hypervisualization and test its limits. Religious pluralism can be hypervisualized, but the resulting images should not be overvalued. They cannot, and do not, substitute for a more accurate ground-level engagement with the internal complexity of immigrant religious communities in urban America. Religion Two finally is more necessary for analytic precision than Religion One!

4. *Asian religions in the USA.* When did they become critically significant? In preceding chapters I have argued repeatedly that they became significant only after 1965. We still need to confront the difficulty of theorizing such a recent occurrence. The most crucial set of issues is to go beyond "mere" religious identity, and to see how identity is constructed and reconstructed through contested representation, through production/reproduction of images that are imposed as much as chosen. In the arena of resistance, one must look to the force of cultural citizenship, a category first raised in Latino circles but now increasingly prominent in Asian immigrant circles.[27]

5. *And where—namely, in which cities—do the Asian immigrants relocate?* For all the prominence given to the new immigrant religious communities as North American, or just plain American, they are in reality urban-based Americans. The choice of residence for most immigrants is driven by the reality of labor opportunities but also previous small-scale immigrations to large metropolitan catchments. Today's immigrants cannot be disconnected from their precursors, and not surprisingly, most of those coming after 1965 appropriately choose "familiar" metropoles as the most hospitable to their own long-term interests as American residents and future citizens.

The importance of the dominant urban location for Asian religious practices is not yet fully marked in extant literature. Karen Leonard, for instance, the cultural anthropologist who has done one of the most systematic studies of South Asian American immigrants, notes that Asian Indians are more concentrated in metropolitan areas than the general U.S. population, with 70 percent being in seven industrial-urban states: New York, California, New Jersey, Texas, Michigan, Illinois, and Ohio, but actually more than half are located in just three urban areas—New York, Chicago, and Los Angeles.[28] Leonard's work, while valuable, needs to be expanded to other, non–South Asian communities, and it also needs to intersect some of the latest research on world cities.[29]

The Next Step

How do we probe, and continue to probe, the deeper reflex of journalistic and academic highlighting of diversity? That move requires us to acknowledge the power of theology but also the greater power of ideology in charting the social significance of religion. Religious ideology alone, according to historian of religions Bruce Lincoln, underscores the "linkage of different levels [personal, social and cosmic] which gives religions their tremendous persuasive power."[30] The cyber age, far from diminishing the tremendous persuasive power of religions, has extended those powers in forums that were not previously imagined. Globalization, instead of producing cultural homogenization, has produced its localization. In Stuart Hall's apt dictum, "the return to the local is often a response to globalization [not its antithesis]."[31] One might even say that the global imaginary introduced by the cyber age not only extends the mass media field but also produces a new discursive field, one in which all of the salaried classes have become migrants, uprooted from the presuppositions that lingered in a text-driven age.

Yet those Asian migrants who relocate in America have become doubly mobile. They are doubly mobile in a way that Arjun Appadurai highlights when he writes, "More people than ever before seem to imagine routinely the possibility that they or their children will live and work in places other than where they were born: this is the wellspring of the increased rates of migration at every level of social, national, and global life."[32] Appadurai's optimistic note needs to be qualified by the reminder that those who migrate out of choice tend to go to advanced industrial/high-tech societies, so that while, according to United Nations reports, "in 1993 there were 100 million people living outside their place of birth; a majority of them (67%) were economic migrants who left their native lands in search of work or better wages."[33]

Nonetheless, Appadurai's basic insight is correct. Whether we are looking at diasporas of hope, diasporas of terror, or diasporas of despair,[34]

> in every case, these diasporas bring the force of the imagination, as both memory and desire, into the lives of many ordinary people . . . and not just as a counterpoint to the certainties of daily life. They move the glacial force of the habitus into the quickened beat of improvisation for large groups of people. [Today, unlike in the past,]

those who wish to move, those who have moved, those who wish to return, and those who choose to stay rarely formulate their plans outside the sphere of radio and television, cassettes and videos, newsprint and telephone (and also the Internet). For migrants, both the politics of adaptation to new environments and the stimulus to move or return are deeply affected by a mass-mediated imaginary that frequently transcends national space.

What is crucial to note here is the degree to which a break from the past does not occur as a once-and-for-all moment; rather, technology mediates the forces of production and consumption, as also representation and identity, with reference to location. One must be somewhere in the redefined global imaginary but never pinned to that place without resort to others: while the national space may be transcended by the immigrant, it is not forgotten, and it is this double movement of leaving yet lingering, of relocating but remembering, that defines the religious imaginary of migrants and ensures that religion will continue to be a crucial element of culture for the next generations as it has been for the survivors of the 1960s.

It is by no means clear, however, that the cosmopolitan dream is shared by all, or even the majority of, immigrants. In purely religious terms there is the large segment of Asian immigrants who are defined not by the Baby Buddha but by the Baby Jesus. They are Filipino Catholics or Korean Presbyterians, and they have little interest in the collage experiments with the spiritual East that inspire so many of the consumers of all mainstream publications and even alternative media such as the *Utne Reader*. It is for this reason that beyond critical cosmopolitanism, or self-critical multiculturalism, at least one modern observer has suggested that the current debate is characterized by corporate multiculturalism. Corporate multiculturalism combines Religion One and Culture One. Specifically, it does not yield multiculturalism as a shifting kaleidoscope of equal polyvalent parts; rather it projects "corporate-sponsored, liberal-pluralist versions of multiculturalism that abstract the study of religion and culture from struggles over power and reduce the ethical project of religious studies to learning how to appreciate different ways of being spiritual."[35] In the accusatory language of Michael Lind, multiculturalism is but a fraud perpetrated by the white overclass in the USA since 1965.[36]

Whether it is real and beneficial or false and harmful, the religious edge is as crucial to multiculturalism as is the cultural dimension to religion. To reconstruct the recent history of religious pluralism, or at least its North American chapter, one must go back to the link between religion and culture, and to the double-edged quality of cyberspace. For those Asian immigrants or students of Asian religions who acknowledge spiritual issues and pursue religious trajectories will likely do so increasingly on the Internet. They will engage a polyvalent notion of culture online, and they will both absorb and perpetuate kaleidoculture through their own participation in chat groups. Certainly, none will read *Life* magazine's next picture spread issue on cyber religion. Due to appear in the year 2020, it has been canceled, since *Life* ceased to exist, at least as a monthly journal, in March 2000. But even had the magazine continued to be published regularly, the World Wide Web can, and will, provide a fuller exposition of the varieties of religious experience, and expression, for immigrants and for others, than *Life* or any print journal could portray. Polyvalent kaleidoculture will be as much cyber culture as print or television culture, and its social impact will grow with Generations X, Y, and E.

Conclusion

Grateful Here

After a sit-in at the Pentagon,
the arresting marshal misspelt my name.
Actually, though, I know I should feel grateful here.
In fact, just last week on the radio, I heard
that the Red Guards had broken the wrists
of a most promising young pianist. Among other things,
he had journeyed to the West to play Beethoven and Brahms.

—Wing Tek Lum[1]

On Being Asian American—For My Children

Of course, not everyone
Can be an Asian American.
Distinctions are earned,
and deserve dedication.
. . . .
You are at the head
of succeeding generations,
as the rest of the world
comes forward to greet you.

—Lawson Fusao Inada[2]

The first epigraph speaks to public life in the 1970s. It was then that there were protests, not just by Asian Americans but by Asian Americans along with other Americans, against the war in Vietnam. The protest presents a double assault. Not just arrested but having one's name misspelled! Yet at

Conclusion

the same time the Asian American dissident recalls another rhythm of public protest in 1970s mainland China, where the offense was seemingly less confrontational yet the punishment more severe. The poet evokes the tension: to protest against U.S. militarism while still recognizing and protesting Communist Chinese authoritarian practices. To choose to exercise one's conscience is a cultural act, yet within Confucian norms and values it is also a religious act; it is as religious as going to temple or taking part in a prescribed ritual. And so the protest poem counts as authentic Asian American experience, at heart a moral evocation with both religious and cultural value.

More than a quarter of a century later, the same issue of protesting both countries—one's homeland and one's new location—is still alive for Asian and African Americans. Following the September 11 attacks, the FBI in tandem with the Immigration and Naturalization Service arrested more than 1,200 immigrants to the USA, many of them Muslims from Mauritania (in West Africa) to Malaysia (in Southeast Asia). The poem of Wing Tek Lum could have been recited by one of the Mauritanians from Kentucky who was among those arrested. Though it was later confirmed that Mr. Ould Belal of Louisville had nothing to do with the World Trade Center bombings, or with the terrorist network that planned and carried them out, the experience of being interrogated, then imprisoned for forty days on an immigration violation, left him unnerved. Some Mauritanians protested his treatment, yet others noted that in his homeland he would have been treated far more harshly, as would all "foreigners" who looked like the terrorists. "If an attack like this happened in other countries," observed a leader of the Mauritanian community in Louisville, "they [the government security forces] would be out there killing people to find out what happened."[3] Arrest with a misspelled name versus incarceration with broken wrists, arrest with forty days' imprisonment versus murder as revenge—the scales of response seem disproportionate, the actions of the U.S. government better, even when heavy-handed, compared to some other political regimes of Africa and Asia.

And, if one is speaking to the next generation, as Lawson Inada does in the second epigraph, then the pride of American identity would seem to triumph over the pain of social exclusion or intermittent injustice. Asian Americans, in Inada's view, will coalesce as a symbolic group in the future, projecting a force that will be felt not just in the USA but by "the rest of the world." Is this a matter of pride or fear or both? Pride that the rest of the world will take note may be the hope, but it is a hope laced with fear, fear that the distinction "Asian American" may not be evident unless it is earned; indeed, it will only deserve recognition, both at home and abroad, if it is earned.

We are then left with two contrasting messages for the future. On the one hand, there is the ambivalence about identifying too closely with any political agenda, especially one that advocates war abroad against one's co-religionists or former countrymen, and on the other hand, there is the utopian call for Asian American global superiority, a superiority marked by distinctiveness earned at home and recognition generated from abroad as "the rest of the world comes forward to greet you."

How do we hold in tandem these very different scenarios for the future of Asian Americans? Will Asian Americans stand with or apart from other non-Asian immigrants? Do they stand together as Asian Americans, or will each be linked to the part of Asia from which they have become American? At the very least, the lyrical quandary conjures questions that go beyond the notion of a dialogue among equals. There is neither a common ground nor a single table. There is instead a kaleidoscope of cultures, or kaleidocul-ture, and each culturally empowered group brings its own valence to the checkered future that it will help shape in twenty-first-century America.

The questions also underscore how unresolvable yet productive is the constant tug-of-war between religion and culture broached throughout this book. The core issue may be summarized in a double aphorism: Religion is about more than religion, Asian Americans are about more than Asia. Initially, religion must be linked to culture, for the very structures and practices as well as the beliefs and rituals of any religious community are affected by the cultural markings of its members. African American Muslims do not share the same outlook as Arab or Iranian American Muslims. At the same time, Asian Americans are not the first immigrants or the only minorities in the United States. Asian Americans were preceded by African Americans, who, though involuntary immigrants, have become the minority in contemporary America that defines race, both racial perceptions, which are subjective, and racialized prejudice, which is institutional. American Indians are the most aggrieved minority, having been the First Citizens of the USA five hundred years ago and now reduced to the tiniest of minorities, made even tinier by the strategies of the Bureau of the Census. Conjoined with both Amerindian and African Americans as yet another ethno-racial minority are Latinos. Large, growing, internally dis-

Conclusion

parate, Latinos are neither homogeneous nor reducible to a single reflex, yet in the Anglo-dominant view of America, for Progressive Protestant Patriots and their allies, Latinos remain defined as "yet another" racial minority.

Both the culture of religion and the plurality of minorities make Asian immigration a topic of explanatory value beyond the dyadic discourse about in-group integrity (cultural citizenship) versus top-down assimilation (national cohesion). An analytic lever to the larger problems posed by Asian immigration comes through capital. Economic capital has shaped the turn-of-the-twentieth-century European immigration and now the turn-of-the-twenty-first-century Asian/Latino immigration. Then rich countries like the United States most needed unskilled workers in industry and agriculture; now the top needs have been for skilled workers in the high-tech, medical, or commercial sectors of the workforce. As we saw in chapter 3, the temptation is to turn away or to reduce the poorest would-be immigrants, which is hard to justify in humanitarian terms, though seemingly necessary to justify in pragmatic terms.

Yet the mechanisms of global capital explain only the surface of change. While the regime of transnational corporativism produces a flow of "voluntary" immigrants that shows no signs of abating, bringing more and more Asians and other skilled immigrants, along with their less skilled countrymen, to the USA, that aspect of capital does not account for some of the most significant dimensions of Asian immigration. These come not through economic but through social or symbolic capital. Symbolic capital mirrors but also refracts the logic of economic capital. It involves the perception and reception of persons who are defined as other by the prevalent norm. In the United States that norm, despite disclaimers to the contrary, remains the Anglo-Saxon Protestant norm. It now includes Catholics and Jews, but it does not yet include Muslims or Buddhists or Hindus, though anecdotal evidence may be mustered to highlight exceptions.

Jews, especially, provide one of the most interesting test cases for how difference and sameness are commingled in the self-perception of a notable minority, American Jewry. Many are the mechanisms by which American Jewish groups have bridged the social and religious side of their American identity.[4] But theoretically what the case of American Jews demonstrates is the fungible, productive value of civil society as an analytical rubric. On the one hand, one could make the argument that civil society is but a flattening force, at once hegemonic and homogenizing, extending the power of Anglo-Protestant elites in cultural guise; yet one could also make the contrary argument, that civil society is a genuine third track, mediating between the state and the market in ways that are less predictable than either the market or the state would suggest. Civil society can pose a challenge both to the dominant paradigm and to its own former profile: it offers not a blueprint but a blurry map to the future of America as a polyvalent kaleidoculture.

And everywhere civil society depends on the self-perception and agency of individuals. Self-perception may translate as accommodation, but its goal is prestige—to find not just acceptance but validation and success in the host culture. The other side of symbolic capital is equally important, though less pleasant. It is the side that reflects isolation or resistance from the immigrant group, but also from elements in the host society. This translates as prejudice, and as I have argued above, it means that in terms of the Asian immigrants to the United States, there is a double side to prejudice: it is, in the first instance, the prejudice of extant norms and those who both enforce and perpetuate those norms, but it is also the internalization of those same norms by immigrants seeking success in the host country even while retaining residual loyalty to their country of origin. It is this double effect of prejudice that works so persistently against African Americans in general and African American Muslims in particular. Though they are a major, not a minor, component of whatever is defined as American Islam, they do not enjoy equivalent social status with other, non-African American Muslims or with other non-Muslim Americans.

A major analytical strategy that emerges from our study is to underscore and expand the doubling. Double location, double consciousness, double speaking position. The key is not to stop at the doubling, but to realize that the multiplying effect of doubling continues at levels beyond the familiar frames. The doubling extends to gender, to location, to jobs, and to religion. Religion is not less significant for being part of the doubling process that pervades immigrant experience, yet its true significance can not be gauged apart from this doubling. It is in fact the multiplying of doubling strategies that produces what I deem to be a particular advantage of the immigrant experience, polyvalence. Polyvalence is not mere diversity increased or difference deepened. Polyvalence is engagement with other, and otherness, as the constructive component of one's own changing but hopeful outlook. Polyvalence is the metastrategy for survival in a culture where one norm lurks beneath many structures, from the census to the courts to the schools to the media, and where the opportunity for difference needs to include imaginative, then planned, then actual engagement with others.

It is possible to see as an outcome of each of the chapters of this book the seeding of polyvalence for Asian immigrants. Examples abound in the journal produced by the Association for Asian American Studies. Though it remains tilted toward Asian Pacific perspectives and interests, with only one South Asian scholar on its thirteen-person editorial board, it nonetheless produced a thorough and evocative review of Asian American pedagogy in its first issue of the new millennium,[5] and it has also included reviews of new monographs on immigrants and the law,[6] essays on post-1965 legislative and bureaucratic shifts on the "race" question,[7] and attention to the popular media and their impact on perceptions of Asian immigrants.[8]

What I have not answered is the philosophical quandary: can cultural difference survive societal change, in this case, the change from multiple Asian settings to the setting of twenty-first-century North America and the challenges of cultural citizenship in the USA? This philosophical issue has been argued in the abstract. It has fueled a debate between Thomas McCarthy and Charles Taylor. Taylor has set forth in bold form the argument that while the normative view of modernity is said to be acultural, it, in fact, conceals a hegemonic, flattening cultural agenda—conformity to dominant norms that are the more insidious for being marked not as culturally specific but as universally evident and inevitable. A key example for Taylor is the slippage between "progressive" and "religious" as attributes: to progress or modernize is to become more rational is to become more secular is to become less religious. Yet Taylor challenges this set of equivalencies, showing how other cultural contexts can be both modern and religious without being laced with dimorphism, or its psychoanalytic extension, schizophrenia. Yet McCarthy disagrees. He believes that there has been not just a regional but a global pattern of rapid change during the last two centuries. Initiated by the West and labeled modernity, it promotes cultural convergence, or what others call assimilation. Instead of signaling loss, McCarthy argues that such cultural convergence can fulfill the project of Immanuel Kant—namely, to reconcile nationalism with cosmopolitanism, for as more multicultural nation-states move toward greater agreement on principles (e.g., human rights, democratic structures, open markets), the entire world will move toward mutual understanding and peace.[9]

Conclusion

While this battle may seem like an abstract battle between utopian idealists, it should be clear that the evidence and argument of this book is weighted toward Taylor rather than McCarthy. Progressive Protestant Patriots try to have both religion and modernity in a single container: the Anglo-dominant brand of cultural fundamentalism that produces not just slogans like "In God We Trust" and "One Nation Under God" but also census forms, media stereotypes, and policy manuals that reinforce the inner and outer alien as the African/Asian/Latino other. Polyvalent kaleidoculture, on the other hand, argues that citizenship can be cultural as well as political, that it can express many forms of location and loyalty that expand rather than inhibit an impulse to Americanness. Michael Lind may have been right that "the white overclass in the United States since the 1960s has specialized in ruling by fraud," but he is not correct when he says that the two biggest frauds are racial preference and multiculturalism.[10] While the multiculturalist project has been skewered by both neoconservatives and neoliberals, there remains a trajectory of hope within cultural citizenship. Cultural citizenship can be polyvalent, and it can function at many levels for the same individual and for different sets of individuals. It is not culture refracted but culture multiplied in piebald forms, some religious, some nonreligious; together they indicate a culture in the making, a polyvalent kaleidoculture.

This approach will annoy many folk. It does not put religion center stage as an isolate from other features of American history or global exchange. Nor does it privilege Asia as a site for immigration different from, and ranked above, that of other countries/regions economically disadvantaged in the current global system with workers seeking opportunities abroad. Nor does it make of race a card that can be played on behalf of one group against others. Rather it makes race a historic process, or series of intersecting processes, endemic to the USA. While racialized class prejudice is so laced into American economic and political, social, and religious life that it can never be fully eliminated, it can be recognized, combated, and reduced through individual and collective strategies that extend beyond Asian Americans to other minority groups.

Sustained attention to these issues will hardly affect the lives of Ali Rizwani or Ramesh Gupta, but they will become a part of the expanded repertoire for being Asian American that Lawson Inada wants for his children. When the rest of the world looks to Asian Americans, it may not be able to see them, except as Americans, not because they are part of a single homogeneous culture but because America itself will have been redefined as a kaleidoscope, a polyvalent kaleidoculture, where each part makes the whole more vivid, more colorful, more capacious without exhausting the limits for contest and for experiment, for challenge and for change. It is not a stable future. Nor is it predictable. But it is viable, and it may also be inevitable.

Yet it will not be a "common" future. Despite its other flaws, Hollinger's analysis underscores why "common" is itself a problematic qualifier. "Americans have become too afraid of each other," he observes, "and too unwilling to take up the task of building a common future. Part of the problem is with the notion 'common,' which when coupled with 'ground' is often taken rather preciously to imply a uniform opinion on whatever questions are at issue."[11] Stated more directly, the difficulty with a common ground is that for many it appears not as a level ground but as the leveled ground, the leveled ground where all are made to seem like the dominant or Anglo-Protestant group, which still would define the norm for some, even when to others it no longer does or should!

As we have suggested throughout, kaleidoscope in flux is the better metaphor for multiethnic and multireligious America than a common ground. And the kaleidoscope can work only if it is also seen as combining traits without collapsing them into a single profile, even a democratic profile that promises the greatest good for the greatest number. To build such a kaleidoscope, one must prescind both the Enlightenment bias against religion and the religious exclusion of culture. While religion and culture hardly elide, they can be related through expanding the connotation of both, and only then can one make the link of religious studies to cultural studies. Scarcely charted, it is fiercely resisted both by divisions of academic labor and by public queasiness, yet its convergence is overdue, with analytical and practical benefits that accrue to Anglos and Asians, indigenes and immigrants.

Time and again I have tried to show how New Faiths do more than elicit Old Fears. I have tried to articulate how an image of Religion One matches too often with Culture One, in giving the impression of a chess match. Each side has a limited number of players. Each move is fraught with peril. Each side must work out its own strategy and remain wary of its opponent. It is an endgame, where finally one group will checkmate the other. There can be only one winner.

Yet the reality of twenty-first-century America is far more complex. We can only begin to understand that complexity in religious terms if we acknowledge the underlying persistence of race-class prejudice that mocks alike the ennobling beliefs/rituals of religion and the hopeful ideals of equality and justice in democratic politics. Religion and culture elide through civil society. Not an autonomous space but the necessary realm between the fictively separate public and private spheres, civil society is a negotiated space where various groups, including religiously based and scripturally motivated groups, compete with each other but also comple- ment the potentials of family, state, and market to define the common good as well as the ultimate value of human existence. To come to terms with civil society one must first understand Religion Two and Culture Two: one must prize the plurality and polyvalence of viewpoints within each reli- gious tradition, and also their counterparts within the sociocultural spec- trum of each democratic polity, not least the USA. Everyone has to have the chance to be a winner.

And who are the winners in mixed marriages? Without denigrating those who are themselves partners in, or products of, racially mixed mar- riages, one must ask whether such marriages produce a genuine kaleido- scope or just another telescope. Can it really still be the case that equality is pegged exclusively to intermarriage? I bristle to think that Robert Park's dictum, voiced in the binary, overtly racist period of 1920s America, still projects the worldview of most Americans. "A social equal, as ordinarily defined in America," he says, "is one that you will be willing to have your daughter marry." And in a similar vein Schlesinger intones: "sex—and love—between people of different creeds and colors can probably be counted on to arrest the disuniting of America."[12] But is the only goal unity or uniformity? Must the route to liberation be obliteration of difference? If the marginal man (and woman) is to be liberated, must the strategy be the obliteration of racial differences through intermarriage?

The answer to all three questions—which in fact are one question— comes not from Park's hero, Booker T. Washington, but from the other major black intellectual in early twentieth-century America, W. E. B. Du Bois. Just as Du Bois understood the importance of educated blacks and the black public intellectual to African American solidarity, so he resisted not only Negro assimilation into Anglo culture but also racial admixture through interracial marriage, or what he called "amalgamation." A chief benefit of the polyvalent kaleidoculture is to dispense with amalgamative solutions to social inequity and racialized class prejudice. In Du Bois's view, not everyone needs to intermarry to produce a viable twenty-first-century America; instead, one needs to grasp how unliberating are social "liberals" from Park to Schlesinger when they advocate "amalgamation" as the ultimate solution to the endemic American problems of racialized thinking and socioeconomic inequities.

How then does one look positively at America's kaleidoculture and prize polyvalence as a gain and the equivalence of all groups—racially, economically, and religiously—as a near-term ideal? At the very least, one must go beyond either the Polyanna of multiculturalism or the dystopia of its opponents, and in the third millennium one place where one must go is cyberspace. Arjun Appadurai, as we have seen, argues that electronic media and immigration are interconnected diacritical markers of modern subjectivity. Together they create diasporic public spheres that transcend the boundaries of nation and narrowly defined ethnicity. Yet in both the USA and the Republic of India there is a contest between religious or communitarian status and the rights of citizenship. The boundaries of Hindu national identity, as seen by BJP, are not transcended through diasporic public spheres, and they may be reinforced, as they are in the case of North American Sikhs supporting Khalistan. Nor is it clear that the resistant groups who use the World Wide Web have had greater result than the corporativist neoconservatives, some of whom are also religious groups, also using the World Wide Web.

And so one ends not with answers but with more questions:

- How does Internet-generated, or -accelerated, globalism affect the formation of immigrant subjectivity?
- Have recollection and reconnection become so instantaneous that immigrant subjectivity is now no longer a physical reflex but rather a mental one, just a matter of inhabiting a particular node in the global network?
- Have loss, rootlessness, and nostalgia simply been replaced by a new brand of consumerism, a circuit of commodities that interpellate and reinscribe immigrant desire into the discrete transactions of an affective economy?

For cultural theorists, these remain the central questions, but they need to be expanded. The list should include questions about the internal variation that persists in the USA and elsewhere:

- What happens to huge disparities within the economic/social status of immigrant communities, for instance, between Bangalore/Silicon Valley immigrants, who are high-tech mavens and Afghani refugees driving taxicabs in New York City?
- How does one account for intergenerational differences, for instance, between those older Asians who built Hindu and Buddhist temples in California and New Jersey, and those younger Asians who create communities via the Internet?
- And how does one connect with pro-immigrant interest groups in cyberspace while also opposing those who oppose not only immigrant desire but also the immigrant presence in the USA?

Whatever the answer to these questions, two senses of religion/market will persist. One is the limited, uppercase Religion One. Religions—defined institutionally and marked by creedal, ritual accents—will continue to be seen as both producers and vendors of the God product, whether they are Hare Krishna airport hawkers, Salvation Army volunteers, or Web site managers. But the other, deeper sense of Religion Two, religion as fractious, fungible, and polyphonous, will also persist. It will be shaped but not contained by global capital forces. It will reflect racialized class prejudice, yet its practitioners will make choices that reflect other norms, other values, and other visions. The choices will not be the same for those who fill the skilled, elite labor market demands at the top end, as they are for those who are unskilled mass laborers, at the lower end of the U.S. economy. Yet both will be part of immigrant culture/religion in the twenty-first century, and the benefit for Asian studies will be to grapple with the contradictions and the irreducible differences, not just of Asians from Anglos, new elites from old elites, but of illegal from legal immigrants, lower-class from middle-class workers, heterodox from orthodox believers. The turmoil will not abate, and it may make global civil society less civil, and certainly less tidy, yet it will finally be the third way that cannot, and should not, be denied.

And it will be the way that proves increasingly necessary for more Americans to pursue in the aftermath of September 11, all the more so since profiling, far from being questioned, has now become a legal policy aligned with the international war on terrorism declared by President Bush. It is a war to be fought on domestic as well as foreign soil, and at home it means that security officers, from the FBI to National Guard to airport screeners, look more closely at those who look like the nineteen men who committed the crimes of September 11. Those nineteen men were Arab nationals from Muslim countries. Arab-Muslim-male cluster as a set of traits that places one minority group of Americans apart from others, and no matter how persistent is the claim, especially from the Japanese-born Transportation Secretary Norman Maneta, that no one can be targeted for how they look, the olive-complexioned, dark-haired Other, especially if his name is Muhammad or Ali, becomes a subject for a long, furtive gaze in public space, and nowhere more so than on public transportation and at airports.

Can one prevent a slur on Arab Americans? Can one limit the implicit attack on Islam? Can one take steps to separate all Asians—not just Arabs but Arab look-alikes, Asians from Pakistan and India as well as Bangladesh and Afghanistan—and not just Muslims but also Sikhs and Hindus—from the terror of unwarranted scrutiny that follows the war on terrorism and perpetuates its harm on innocent Others?

That is the challenge for American courts and schools and government agencies, but it is equally the challenge for ordinary American citizens. The answer is to affirm polyvalence, to admit that difference is not just possible but healthy, and at the same time to work for a kaleidoculture, to have every building block in the future of American society given its worth and its place in the land of the free that is also the home of the brave. Who are the free? Who will dare to be brave? Every American, not just those with the privilege and power and history to claim America as their, not others' homeland, but also Asians and Latinos who share, with African Americans and Amerindians, a dream that America's future is greater than its past. Progressive Protestant Patriots will have to move over and share the dream with other Americans who are not less patriotic or progressive because they happen not to be Protestant or Anglo. Polyvalence will succeed because it must.

NOTES

PREFACE

1. Lamont B. Steptoe, "Election Time," in Maria M. Gillan and Jennifer Gillan, eds., *Unsettling America: An Anthology of Contemporary Multicultural Poetry*, 250 (New York: Penguin, 1994).

2. Chogyam Trungpa Rinpoche, "Command," in Jeffery P. Chan et al., eds., *The Big Aiiieeeee!: An Anthology of Chinese American and Japanese American Literature*, 601 (New York: Meridian, 1991).

3. There are, of course, numerous other Asian religions: Confucianism and Taoism from East Asia, Jainism and Zoroastrianism or Parseeism from South Asia, as well as Bahaism from West Asia. All these would warrant mention, and detailed analysis, in a comprehensive study of Asian religions in contemporary America, but the purpose of the current work is to probe and expose, then interpret and explain the contours of racialized class prejudice as it affects all Asian immigrants, but especially Muslims and Hindus. There are, of course, also Asian Christians, notably Protestants from South Korea and Roman Catholics from the Philippines. They will be considered, though not emphasized, since a study of them would stress the East Asian dimension of Asian religious immigrants, whereas the current study highlights the understudied and often neglected South Asian immigrant communities.

4. A noted authority on American religion, Martin Marty, has observed that "while Christianity [in the United States] is growing by only 0.8 percent annually and Judaism not at all, Buddhism and Hinduism enjoy annual growth rates of 2.75 percent and 3.38 percent, respectively, and Islam outpaces them all [yet starts from a much smaller base]." At the same time, Marty does not see the preeminence of either Christianity or Judaism under threat in the near term ("New Faces of God: The Third Millennium," in *Religion and Ethics Newsweekly* [1999], 2–3). The figures for Marty's projections come from David B. Barrett and Todd M. Johnson, *Annual Statistical Table on Global Mission*, 1999, and while these figures may exaggerate some numbers, especially those for Christians, given as 2 billion in 2000, and understate others, including those for Jews, given as 14 million, they still provide benchmark approximations that help explain why, in addition to Judaism and Christianity, the major religious communities to consider in twenty-first-century America are Islam, Hinduism, and Buddhism, with Sikhism a lesser but still

notable fourth Asian religion. Neither Shintoism nor Confucianism is included in these tallies, and their exclusion would seem justified in terms of both global populations and their representation in the United States.

5. The gap remains, despite some valiant interventions by South Asianists to engage the question of Asian American location from an integrated perspective that is inclusive of South as well as East Asian Americans. Among the advocacy publications by South Asian scholars, see especially the anthology edited by Lavina D. Shankar and Rajini Srikanth, *A Part, Yet Apart: South Asians in Asian America* (Philadelphia: Temple University Press, 1998). The introductory essay, "Closing the Gap? South Asians Challenge Asian American Studies," 1–22, summarizes several issues, elsewhere addressed by both South Asian and occasionally non–South Asian scholars. For a full list of references as of February 2000, see Shilpa Dave et al., "De-Privileging Positions: Indian Americans, South Asian Americans, and the Politics of Asian American Studies," *Journal of Asian American Studies* 3, no. 1 (February 2001): 67–100. Many East Asian scholars either omit reference to South Asian immigrants or give them limited space, as does Ronald Takaki in *Strangers from a Different Shore* (New York: Penguin, 1989), in which Asian Indians are the major subject of but one short chapter (chapter 8) and hardly visible elsewhere. David Palumbo-Liu also excludes South Asians and South Asian evidence from his wide-ranging analysis of Asian immigrants, *Asian/American: Historical Crossings of a Racial Frontier* (Stanford: Stanford University Press, 1999), and he is explicit in his reasons for excluding them. He is concerned with "how the discourse on the modernizing of America has been deeply linked to East Asia and how the development of the global economy has focused on the specific expansion of East Asia and Southeast Asian regions" (8). He defers until the conclusion of his book "the deconstruction of this Asia Pacific paradigm," which he deems to be "a crucial task for Asian American studies, one that might be facilitated by an analysis of alternative modernities in South Asia" (8), yet the actual conclusion gives little hint about what might be the actual shape of an inclusive pan-Asian paradigm (392).

6. See Jack Forbes, "Undercounting Native Americans: The 1980 Census and the Manipulation of Racial Identity in the United States," *Wicazo Sa Review* 6, no. 1 (1990): 2–26. Forbes highlights how the actual number of First Nation tribes and tribal members was systematically discounted by the 1980 census takers.

7. Despite the limitations of a participant perspective, either because the immigrant is transformed into a theorist or because the immigrant voice is undertheorized as a voice from somewhere, the participant view is often acutely dissident and opposed to taken-for-granted American norms and values. At the head of each chapter, as also in subsequent analysis, it is participant voices that will be highlighted.

8. One could expand this lament from poetry to prose, indicating that in the spectrum of groups occupying American space in the early third millennium no

group comes close to the dispossession—physical and territorial, political and economic, cultural and religious—that characterizes Native Americans. In July 2001 a Seneca spokesperson reacted to an *Economist* article lauding Tiger Woods's achievement as a biracial, Asian-African American. "Your article on Tiger Woods [16 June] displays a singularly ignorant and revisionist view of the plight of Native Americans. No fair-minded person would deny that blacks have suffered a tragic and awful history, but it is reasonably safe and sane to regard the enslavement and subsequent segregation of blacks as less harrowing than the state-sponsored genocide inflicted upon our native peoples" (*The Economist*, July 6, 2001, 14). While it is a comparison deemed to please no one, it is framed by the reality that indigenous Americans were reduced from perhaps 10 million in 1600 to fewer than 300,000 by 1900, so that from an Amerindian perspective, one could say, as the author does, "African Americans have been 'allowed' to journey much further from their subjugated roots and are well [?] represented in all aspects of the mainstream American government, culture and economy."

9. Derrick Bell, *Faces at the Bottom of the Well: The Permanence of Racism* (New York: Basic Books, 1992): 197–98, as quoted in William Ayers, "To the Bone: Reflections in Black and White," itself a response to Tahar Ben Jelloun, *Racism Explained to My Daughter* (New York: New Press, 2000), 170–71, provided as an epilogue to his book.

10. I am, of course, not claiming that all Latinos, or African Americans, or Native Americans act with one motive or claim one strategy or speak with one voice. On the contrary, what several studies have shown, perhaps none more compellingly than Michael Omi and Howard Winant, in *Racial Formation in the United States: From the 1960s to the 1980s* (New York: Routledge, 1986) and *Racial Formation in the United States: From the 1960s to the 1990s* (2d ed., New York: Routledge, 1994), is that shifts in both the structural and the subjective dimensions of race formation in the United States, especially since 1965, have eliminated the possibility of intragroup consensus: Neoconservatives, but also neoliberals, have co-opted minority perspectives, splintering the discourse of minorities and assuring the continuity of structural inequities. See Omi and Winant, *Racial Formation in the United States*, especially 128–54. With respect to African and Native Americans, however, there remains a refreshing clarity to bell hooks's argument that pre-Columbian Africans and Native Americans shared a hospitality code that persists despite "white supremacist constructions of history [that] have effectively erased from public collective cultural memory the recognition of solidarity and communion among Native Americans, Africans and African Americans" (bell hooks, *Black Looks: Race and Representation* [Boston: South End Press, 1992], 181–82).

11. I will elaborate on this point in chapter 3, where I deal with the issue of immigrants and the law. I am especially indebted to the lucid essay of Renato Rosaldo, "Cultural Citizenship, Inequality, and Multiculturalism" (in William V. Flores and

Notes

Rita Benmayor, eds., *Latino Cultural Citizenship: Claiming Identity, Space, and Rights*, 31 [Boston: Beacon, 1997]), not just for the citation from an anonymous Chicana poet but also for framing the issue of *respeto*, or respect, as crucial to the cultural citizenship that Latinos seek in twenty-first-century America.

12. While the United States does not account for all of North America, I consistently use the term *America* as synonymous with the United States of America. In a fuller study of the issues raised here, one would like to expand the geographical coverage to include Canada, especially the urban areas of Vancouver and Toronto, two of the largest magnets for South Asian as well as East Asian immigrants during the last half of the twentieth century. Lack of experience and time has imposed on me the more circumscribed reference to the United States as (North) America.

INTRODUCTION

1. W. E. B. Du Bois, *The Souls of Black Folk* (1903; reprint, New York: Norton, 1999), 162–63, partially cited in Lawrence H. Fuchs, *The American Kaleidoscope: Race, Ethnicity, and the Civic Culture* (Hanover, N.H.: University Press of New England, 1990), 106, and here elaborated to provide the accent of Du Bois on African American labor in the New World as gifts, involuntarily given but still gifts without which America could not have become America. One of the finest commentaries on this line from Du Bois's classic is provided by Robert Gooding-Williams, who argues that "the Negro has played so important a role in creating America," according to Du Bois, "that America's identity as a distinct political [and cultural] community is not conceivable absent the centuries-long presence of blacks in America." See Robert Gooding-Williams, ed., *Reading Rodney King/Reading Urban Uprising* (New York: Routledge, 1993), 163.

2. This lament comes from an actor playing the role of an Asian immigrant in the movie *Mississippi Masala*; it is here cited from Binita Mehta, "Emigrants Twice Displaced: Race, Color, and Identity in Mira Nair's *Mississippi Masala*," in Deepika Bahri and Mary Vasudeva, eds., *Between the Lines: South Asians and Postcoloniality*, 192–93 (Philadelphia: Temple University Press, 1996).

3. On the unintended consequences of the 1965 immigration act, see David Palumbo-Liu, *Asian/American: Historical Crossings of a Racial Frontier* (Stanford: Stanford University Press, 1999), 444. Others, notably Alejandro Portes and Ruben G. Rumbaut (*Immigrant America: A Portrait* [Berkeley: University of California Press, 1996]), have argued that the 1965 act was not itself the explanation for the major increase of immigrants during the last third of the twentieth century. Privileging the motives of the underprivileged—namely, the illegal, mostly migrant laborers who immigrate to the United States for multiple motives, they still have to account for middle-class professional immigrants, almost all of whom, acknowl-

Notes

edge Portes and Rumbaut, do immigrate because of "the gap between life aspirations and expectations and the means to fulfill them in the sending countries" (12). And later, they support the lifestyle elevation motive as primary when they note that European immigration did *not* increase dramatically after 1965 precisely because the same professional classes among newly prospering West European nations did not find the change in American law after 1965 to be "a cause for much excitement" (65).

4. Howard Winant, "Racial Dualism at Century's End," in Wahneema Lubiano, ed., *The House That Race Built*, 108 (New York: Random House, 1998).

5. Howard Winant, *Racial Conditions: Politics, Theory, Comparisons* (Minneapolis: University of Minnesota Press, 1994), 131.

6. Ibid., 165. While Winant lauds the multipolar system that has evolved since 1965, he is quick to note that it has not changed the underlying racialized structure of American society and that "white identities," in particular, "remain largely unitary and unreflexive."

7. While there are problems with Martha Nussbaum's presumptive individualism, and her triumphant brand of cosmopolitanism, her essay "Religion and Woman's Rights" does nonetheless combine South Asian data with North American issues in a way that is as exemplary as it is rare. See "Religion and Woman's Rights: The Case of India," in Nancy L. Rosenblum, ed., *Obligations of Citizenship and Demands of Faith: Religious Accommodation in Pluralist Democracies*, 335–402 (Princeton: Princeton University Press, 2000).

8. These are the terms preferred by David Hollinger (see *Postethnic America: Beyond Multiculturalism* [New York: Basic Books, 1995], especially 84–86), though his own position is now seen as one that falls within the universalist camp of cosmopolitans, especially given his assessment of current immigrants as uniformly and unqualifiedly attached to the United States as their homeland of choice (153).

9. While the differences between these camps are interesting, they constitute a digression from the major issues occupying me in the current monograph. For their fullest staging in an archcritical reading of the contentious debate among cosmopolitan theorists, see Srinivas Aravamudan, "Guru English," *Social Text* 19, no. 1 (2001): 19. For Aravamudan, the biggest cleavage is between those who "insist on the careful reconstruction of cosmopolitanism as an efficacious (but always provisional) lingua franca," such as James Clifford, Homi Bhabha, Bruce Robbins, and others who "are apologists for the grand normative scaffolding of Western liberalism and universalism," such as Martha Nussbaum, Tzvetan Todorov, and Julia Kristeva.

Neither David Hollinger nor Michael Walzer is cited in this overview, but one may safely consign them to the latter or liberal/universalist camp.

10. Hollinger, *Postethnic America*, 151–56.

11. Shahnaz Khan, *Muslim Women: Crafting a North American Identity*

Notes

(Gainesville: University Press of Florida, 2000). In this series of interviews, framed by an introduction and conclusion from the interviewing author, sixteen Muslim women immigrants to Canada are all identified by class and by sectarian loyalty— Shi'i, Ahmadi, Sunni—but their own ethnic differences are never addressed. While the dominant Anglo culture is commendably theorized, especially with reference to the work of Ali Rattansi, it is never grounded in the actual racialization of those who immigrate to Canada from regions of Asia, Africa, and Europe. Hence the rearticulated politics of difference, which the author advocates fervently (125), remains mired in unexamined notions of race and class.

12. Karin Aguilar-San Juan, *The State of Asian America: Activism and Resistance in the 1990s* (Boston: South End Press, 1994), especially 11–12, for South Asian voices.

13. George J. Borjas, *Heaven's Door: Immigration Policy and the American Economy* (Princeton: Princeton University Press, 1999), 40–41. I have abbreviated the data in some parts to streamline the argument.

14. Ibid., 41. Emphasis is Borjas's.

15. Arthur M. Schlesinger Jr. *The Disuniting of America: Reflections on a Multicultural Society* (New York: Norton, 1992), 17–18.

16. I have summarized and shortened the narrative here, and also, for reasons that will be made clear in chapter 2, all figures about religious adherence and institutional affiliations must remain provisional.

17. Thomas A. Tweed and Stephen Prothero, *Asian Religions in America: A Documentary History* (New York: Oxford University Press, 1999), 8–9.

18. A notable exception, which also includes extensive bibliographic notes, is Edward J. W. Park and John S. W. Park, "A New American Dilemma? Asian Americans and Latinos in Race Theorizing," *Journal of Asian American Studies* 2, no. 3 (October 1999): 289–309. The major point that the authors make again and again is that American race theory remains locked into binary categorization: black vs. white dominates most thinking and writing about race, so that Asians and Latinos are still assessed on this biracial criterion. It is as if whiteness is the norm and assimilation the only process by which Asians and Latinos become fully American. The two authors mount a broad-gauged critique of this simplistic and reductive treatment of the 15 million latest immigrants from below the border and across the sea, yet they never mention religion or religious identity.

19. Many examples will come up in following chapters, but among those that include close attention to local detail are William V. Flores and Rita Benmayor, eds., *Latino Cultural Citizenship: Claiming Identity, Space, and Rights* (Boston: Beacon, 1997) on Latinos in Los Angeles; Hamid Naficy, *The Making of Exile Cultures: Iranian Television in Los Angeles* (Minneapolis: University of Minnesota Press, 1993) on Iranian television in Los Angeles, and Helen R. Ebaugh and J. S. Chafetz, eds., *Religion and the New Immigrants: Continuities and Adaptations in Immigrant*

Notes

Congregations (New York: Altamira, 2000), on Houston's new communities. Attention to individual experience is foregrounded in Khan, *Muslim Women*, on immigrant Muslim Women in Canada, and also several authors in *Amerasia Journal* and again in literary collections such as Nurjehan Aziz, ed., *Her Mother's Ashes and Other Stories by South Asian Women in Canada and the United States* (Toronto: Tsar, 1994), or Maria M. Gillan and Jennifer Gillan, eds., *Unsettling America: An Anthology of Contemporary Multicultural Poetry* (New York: Penguin, 1994).

20. See, for instance, Peter McLaren, *Revolutionary Multiculturalism: Pedagogies of Dissent for the New Millennium* (Boulder: Westview, 1997).

21. Fuchs, *American Kaleidoscope*, has used the kaleidoscope metaphor creatively, asserting that American shared identity can no longer be viewed exclusively as Judaeo-Christian but must also accommodate an expanded Asian community that is often non-Abrahamic in outlook and practice. I expand Fuchs's helpful insight and terminological usage by making class the crucial marker to racial/religious elasticity; class must inform both racial discourse and religious identity in any inclusive assessment of the polyvalent population of twenty-first-century America.

22. Another metaphor that recurs in some studies of American ethnicity is palimpsest or celluloid palimpsests, so that for literary scholars Werner Sollors and William Boelhower, "all the components of American culture become palimpsests, tablets upon which are written and rewritten numerous codes and traditions." See Lester D. Friedman, "Celluloid Palimpsests: An Overview of Ethnicity and the American Film," in Lester D. Friedman, ed., *Unspeakable Images: Ethnicity and the American Cinema*, 19 (Urbana: University of Illinois Press, 1991). Yet the palimpsest achieved less success than the melting pot as a metaphor for American-style assimilation, and its overly literary connotation also underscores a static, authorial voice for the makers of culture rather than a changing active agency for those whose cultural destiny is being writ.

23. Jonathan Z. Smith, "Close Encounters of Diverse Kinds" in Susan L. Mizruchi, ed., *Religion and Cultural Studies*, 14 (Princeton: Princeton University Press, 2001).

24. Sunaina Maira, "Henna and Hip Hop: The Politics of Cultural Production and the Work of Cultural Studies," *Journal of Asian American Studies* 3, no. 3 (October 2000): 329–69, especially 348–62, where Maira stresses that hip-hop, like henna, is not just hybridized but polycultural, i.e., "it is a cultural practice that is always already complicated by its affiliations with multiple communities, rather than a product of two or more discrete, 'pure' cultural strands. The South Asian Americans who wear mehndi, a form of henna, are disrupting 'the binaries of pure/inauthentic national cultures and memories'" (353).

25. A notable exception is Ronald Takaki, *A Different Mirror: A History of Multicultural America* (Boston: Little, Brown, 1993). While it paints a much broader canvas than his earlier book, *Strangers from a Different Shore: A History of Asian*

Americans (New York: Penguin, 1989), it suffers from a huge topical omission since the Asians included in *A Different Mirror* are only Chinese and Japanese. It also repeats the same accent on selective detail and personal testimonies rather than structural or comparative analysis.

26. Haeyoung Yoon, "Reciprocity: Human Identity Through Interdependence," *Amerasia Journal* (1996): 168.

27. The worst-case example of academic blindness to this process must be Richard D. Alba, *Ethnic Identity: The Transformation of White America* (New Haven: Yale University Press, 1990). Focusing on the tenacity of ethnic pride and adherence to ethnic identities among European immigrants to the United States, Alba almost systematically excludes even mention of all other "minorities": Hispanics, American Indians, and African Americans (listed under "Blacks") become a mere backdrop for his paean to symbolic identity, which has now produced, according to him, a European-American identity that coexists alongside, and often in tension with, an older, unhyphenated American identity (315). Had this book been written in 1955, it would have seemed quaint, but in 1990 it flies in the face of both indigenous and immigrant experience of cultural citizenship as multivalent. Polyvalent kaleidoculture?! That is a future drama unimagined, and unimaginable, in this myopic study of American ethnicity.

28. Lisa Cacho, review of Chang and Louie, *Journal of Asian American Studies* 3, no. 3 (October 2000): 378.

29. Mehta, "Emigrants Twice Displaced," 192–93. Mehta's essay provides both an analysis of the movie and also a response to the movie's critics, notably bell hooks and Anuradha Dinghwaney. It also draws on cultural theories about the power of representation in popular media, for example, Ella Shohat and Robert Stam, eds., *Unthinking Eurocentrism: Multiculturalism and the Media* (London: Routledge, 1994).

30. It is most fully developed in Hollinger, *Postethnic America*.

31. Throughout this study I have used the term *Latino* because I am referring solely to the Latino component of the Hispanic population, yet in a broader survey of race-religion-culture among post-1965 immigrants, the distinction between Latino and Chicano would merit further study.

32. In highlighting Haley's choice—the choice of Alex Haley to be African American rather than Irish American, though in fact he is both—Hollinger makes the point that it is social prejudice, and public policy derived from but also reinforcing that prejudice, that determines the African American bloc as separate from, and unequal to, the others. The source of this prejudice? Empowered whites, the Anglo-Protestant majority. "Nothing illustrates the selective suppression of diversity and the socially constructed character of these ethno-racial blocs more tellingly than the historic denial, by generations of empowered whites, that they share with black Americans a substantial pool of genes" (*Postethnic America*, 27).

Notes

33. David Hollinger, "Multiculturalism and the Jews," *Tikkun* 13, no. 6 (1998): 68–69.

34. Of course, it does happen, often in semipublic forums, that some "white" groups continue to experience public discrimination, whether because of their Italian accent or their Polish ancestry or their variant lifestyles.

35. For the most thorough longitudinal study on the mechanics of classificatory strategies within the U.S. Bureau of Census, see Sharon M. Lee, "Racial Classifications in the US Census: 1890–1990," *Ethnic and Racial Studies* 16, no. 1 (January 1993): 75–94. Her best hope is not to remove the census classifications by race but rather to allow each respondent to the census to exercise the "ethnic options," identifying himself or herself historically rather than by color coding (91). Currently that choice is open only to whites, but even were it expanded, it would disguise rather than eliminate the underlying problem of racialized class prejudice. Blacks, identified as African Americans, would still be at one end of the spectrum, while whites, or European Americans, would be at the other end, and participants would still weigh their choices in terms of that built-in biracialized value system.

36. My own view engages, but does not replicate, two extreme views of prejudice. On the one hand, there is Robert Park's apology for prejudice as normal and necessary: "A man without prejudices is a man without conviction, and ultimately without character." On the other hand, there is the neoliberal protest against Anglo-conformity as "the price of linguistic extinction and cultural loss" that the early twentieth-century European immigrants paid for the privilege of white racial status in the United States. What Park overlooks is the bigotry against African Americans, as well as Amerindians and now Hispanics and Asians, that was reinforced by the biracialism of American public policy during most of this century. The neoliberal protest, by contrast, claims that West European immigrants in general, and Jewish immigrants in particular, paid too high a price for federal program assistance that in effect led to the postwar whitening of Jews, along with other eastern and southern European immigrants. Yet notable Jewish intellectuals, among them Rabbi Irving Greenberg cited below, disagree. For references in this debate, see Robert Park, "The Basis of Race Prejudice," in *Race and Culture*, 230–43 (Glencoe: Free Press, 1950); Portes and Rumbaut, *Immigrant America* (1996), 182–84; and Karen B. Sacks, "How Did Jews Become White Folks?" in Stephen Gregory and Roger Sanjek, eds., *Race*, 78–102 (New Brunswick, N.J.: Rutgers University Press, 1994).

37. I am not speaking of The Fundamentalism Project, and its staggering five-volume set of collected essays, which continue to define the topic for many inquirers, even while the public at large remains lost in the miasma of Christian fundamentalist discourse framed by Hal Lindsay in *The Late Great Planet Earth* (New York: Bantam, 1981). Lindsay's book set the tone for a whole spate of apocalyptic books that heralded the end time, "subtly" coinciding with the end of a Christian

Notes

millennium and also marking a moment when Jerusalem, the major sacred space shared by Jews and Christians (as also Muslims), was facing heated contestation.

38. Henry R. May, *Ideas, Faiths, and Feelings: Essays on American Intellectual and Religious History, 1952–1982* (New York: Oxford University Press, 1983), 171–72.

39. The Republic of India, which has seen the rise of both Hindu and Muslim (as well as Sikh) fundamentalisms since independence (1948) but more especially since the 1980s, is the most evident counterpart to the United States. Links between American and Indian constitutionalism, above all through the U.S.-educated untouchable who became one of India's foremost advocates of secular justice, B. R. Ambedkar, make the comparison even closer, as is evident in Martha Nussbaum's extended essay "Religion and Woman's Rights,"

40. Harold Bloom, *The American Religion: The Emergence of the Post-Christian Nation* (New York: Simon and Schuster, 1992), 37.

41. Ibid., 39.

42. Todd Gitlin, in *The Twilight of Common Dreams: Why America Is Wracked by Cultural Wars* (New York: Metropolitan Books, 1995), has detailed how ambiguous and open to reassessment is the slogan "the American dream." "A dream may be evocative, illuminating, fascinating, or frightful but one thing it is not is a fait accompli. It is incapable of verification. It invites revision. Intrinsically ambiguous, it invites interpretation and reinterpretation" (47).

43. See Kamala Visweswaran, "Diaspora by Design: Flexible Citizenship and South Asians in U.S. Racial Formations" *Diaspora* 6, no. 1 (1997): 5, where he quotes D'Souza's remark that "in the United States I am no stranger to xenophobia, prejudice and discrimination. I also feel a particular debt to the civil rights movement. Yet I am not an uncritical cheerleader for every parade that carries the minority banner" (*The End of Racism* [New York: Free Press, 1995], vii). In effect, D'Souza is positioning himself against the radical perspectivists for whom there can never be a defining center. "From the logic of their point of view," notes Todd Gitlin, "it is never possible to be polycentric enough" (*Twilight of Common Dreams*, 197). Yet this dystopic view of centrifugal anarchy is less an imminent social reality than a deft rhetorical ploy by neoconservatives to argue for fewer centers, or actually for just one center, the beleaguered but still vibrant Anglo-Protestant hegemonic center.

44. David Hollinger asserts that "Anglo-Protestant chauvinism" had become diminished by the 1950s and 1960s, at least among the knowledge class (*Postethnic America*, 97), while Todd Gitlin argues that the neoconservative backlash that mimicked black, Chicano, and Indian consciousness movements while claiming privilege for PIGS (Polish, Italian, Greek, and Slavic workers who immigrated to America in the early twentieth century), was launched by Michael Novak's book *The Rise of the Unmeltable Ethnics*, published in 1972 (*Twilight of Common Dreams*, 139).

45. I omit Mexico only because it falls outside the analytic gaze of almost all studies of North American culture to date, but in future inquiries it will come from

the margins to the center, as Hispanic persons, along with Hispanic language and customs, culture and religious expression, become increasingly visible elements in a broadened North American ethos.

46. Aminah Beverly McCloud, *African American Islam* (New York: Routledge, 1995), 169–70.

47. Amritjit Singh, "African Americans and the New Immigrants," in Bahri and Vasudeva, *Between the Lines*, 99.

48. Even though not implemented till 1968, the 1965 immigration act forever changed the pattern of Asian and Latino presence within the United States, and the major scholarly challenge has been to assess just how great will be its impact on all American cultural options.

49. Fuchs, *American Kaleidoscope*, 476.

50. Ibid., 477. While Fuchs may have overstated the general impact of the civil rights movement in all sectors of U.S. society, he has certainly epitomized the view of the knowledge class, those most attuned to social changes and most in favor of aligning democratic principles with current practices. The cultural fundamentalists, whom we examine in detail below, were not persuaded, and they mounted their own challenge to this change in both the composition and the contours of American society.

51. Christopher Jencks, "Who Should Get In? Part II," *New York Review of Books* 48, no. 20 (December 20, 2001): 96. While Jencks maintains that immigration can be healthy for the United States in the long term, he, like Borjas (who is both his colleague and his friend at Harvard), argues that the number of immigrants must be curtailed at the same time as their social/economic location must be fixed at the upper end of class indices—that is, they must look and act and profess like their Progressive Patriot Protestant contemporaries; they must be "model minorities" who conform to majoritarian standards. The economistic argument allows for no cultural ambiguity, precluding both kaleidoculture and polyvalence as categories in twenty-first-century America.

52. Garbi Schmidt, *American Medina* (Lund, Sweden: University of Lund, 1998), 151.

53. Hoda Bakr, "Al-Noor Mosque," in Ebaugh and Chafetz, *Religion and the New Immigrants*, 213.

54. Hollinger, "Multiculturalism and the Jews," 69.

1. AMERICAN RELIGION AS COMMODITY CULTURE

1. Cornel West, foreword to Marjorie Garber and Rebecca L. Walkowitz, eds., *One Nation Under God? Religion and American Culture* (New York: Routledge, 1999), viii.

Notes

2. David Yoo, "Racial Spirits: Religion and Race in Asian American Communities," special issue of *Amerasia Journal* 22, no. 1 (1996): xiv. I have summarized some of the other contributions in order to highlight their contrast with the one contribution still lacking, in the domain of religious studies.

3. I am acutely aware of the multiple levels at which this study could be expanded to address gender perspectives, including the gendered hybridities announced by Cornel West in the first epigraph. Though I do refer to American Asian women in some of the examples introduced in later chapters, I defer till another time, and another book, the range of gender-related issues that combine with, even as they further complicate, racialized class prejudice. See, for example, Leslie Bow, *Betrayal and Other Acts of Subversion (Feminism, Sexual Politics, Asian American Women's Literature* [Princeton: Princeton University Press, 2001]).

4. Cited from the project description in a pamphlet distributed at the first national gathering of the conference "Education as Transformation," at Wellesley College, September 27–28, 1998.

5. Immanuel Wallerstein, "Culture as the Ideological Battleground of the Modern World-System," in *Theory, Culture, and Society* 7 (1990): 33. The examples are mine, and the thrust of the cultural wars is far more closely linked to religious data, actors, and issues in my view than in Wallerstein's.

6. See Hollinger (*Postethnic America: Beyond Multiculturalism* [New York: Basic Books, 1995], 98), though the criticism that he voices against Herberg seems to overlook the particular terrain of public discord that marred 1950s America, when everything to do with foreign "culture" was suspect as "socialist," or worse, tainted as "communist." For Herberg to make his argument publicly acceptable he had to couch it in terms of religious rather than cultural pluralism. Forty years later, with the end of the Cold War, the revival of African American legacy claims, the clamor for Hispanic cultural citizenship, and the maturity of Asian American intellectuals, it seems beneficial to again make the link between cultural and religious forms of polyvalence instead of bracketing one from the other.

7. See Eliott R. Barkan, "Race, Religion, and Nationality in American Society: A Model of Ethnicity—from Contact to Assimilation," *Journal of American Ethnicity* 14, no. 2 (1995): 10.

8. James Hunter, *Culture Wars: The Struggle to Define America*, and now Alan Wolfe, *One Nation Under God*, as well as Martin Marty's *America Indivisible*, all depend on a taken-for-granted notion of Euro-American continuities. Tom Tweed alone of current American religious historians challenges this view in his several writings, including the edited *Retelling U.S. Religious History* (Berkeley: University of California Press, 1997). What is crucial about Tweed's approach but missing in others is the stress of historical location rather than philosophical debate. Those, such as Stephen Carter and Bill Bennett, who want to define America as beset with cultural decline or political retardation do so by raising contemporary America as a

mirror reflecting the age-old philosophical question, Is truth eternal and unchanging or is it relative? The evasive disingenuity of this approach is, to paraphrase the mirror image, its neglect of the stand. No mirror rests in space; it rests in some place, on some support. And in the case of the turn-of-the-millennium United States, the location is late global capitalism still dominated by a Protestant Christian moralism, one that political conservatives such as Pat Buchanan or Bill Bennett will support in cultural if not in creedal terms.

9. As Eck herself notes in the *Guide for Teachers and Students Using "On Common Ground: World Religions in America"* (New York: Columbia University Press, 1997), "this visual image of separate boundaried circles—graphically convenient as it is—is highly misleading, for every religious tradition has grown through the ages in dialogue and historical interaction with others" (17). She then goes on to explain both the internal complexity and the dynamic character of specific traditions, using the metaphor of rivers. "Religions are far more like rivers than like boundaried circles or even complex structures." And again, "Today all these rivers of faith are flowing through the landscape of America." The problem with the metaphor, as with her approach generally, is its failure to acknowledge the cultural patterns that are not banks of a river but part of the liquid elements that give shape, force, and meaning to *all* religious traditions; it is these cultural elements that I examine as "religious ideology" or "religious ideologies" in chapter 5.

10. Peter A. Kivisto, "Religion and the New Immigrants," in J. William Swatos, ed., *A Future for Religion? New Paradigms for Social Analysis*, 95 (Newbury Park, Calif.: Sage, 1992). Kivisto also makes the point that in addition to uneven attention to specific groups, the religion of new immigrants itself has been an understudied topic, anticipating the Yoo (1996) epigraph to this chapter.

11. Diana L. Eck, "The Multireligious Public Square," in Garber and Walkowitz, *One Nation Under God?*, 11.

12. Sunaina Maira, "Henna and Hip Hop: The Politics of Cultural Production and the Work of Cultural Studies," *Journal of Asian American Studies* 3, no. 3 (October 2000): 358.

13. Paraphrased from conversations with Professor Charles H. Long both during and after the delivery of an earlier version of this lecture at the University of Michigan on February 10, 1999. Adding substance to Long's rebuke is Eck's casual, almost diffident reference to Arthur Schlesinger Jr.'s invidious book *The Disuniting of America: Relections on a Multicultural Society* (New York: Norton, 1992). Arguing that Schlesinger sees too much *pluribum* and not enough *unum*, she maintains, along with others, that "the *pluribus*, the diversity, is the very stuff out of which the *unum* is created, a oneness marked not by uniformity but by the engagement of our deepest differences in the common covenants of citizenship" (Eck, "The Multireligious Public Square," 5). What mars her disclaimer is her inattention to how weighted "common covenants of citizenship" are against African Americans, as the

recent immigrant experience makes even more clear than did the pre-1965, which was also the pre–civil rights, period of American history. Schlesinger's attack on Afrocentrism as itself an invented tradition (while Anglo dominance remains unspoken and above the fray) is assailed by Leith Mullings,ed., in *On Our Own Terms: Race, Class, and Gender in the Lives of African American Women* (New York: Routledge, 1997), cited by Michael Eric Dyson, "What's Derrida Got to Do with Jesus? Rhetoric, Black Religion, and Theory" in ibid., 92 n. 4.

14. There has been extended coverage of both Falwell's and Graham's infelicitous comments. For a sample of the attention to Graham's, see *Raleigh News and Observer*, December 8, 2001, A-9.

15. The critique of Eck's project from the Religious Right only serves to underscore how necessary it is to include Latino Christian and Asian Christian pluralism as part of her project. While rejecting outright the pernicious insinuation that Eck's lesbian identity and her pluralism are equally compromising of her value as a public intellectual, I agree with Neuhaus's contention that she needs to have more Christians in the profile of American pluralism if it is to have even a semblance of inclusiveness. See the anonymous attack "Pluralism's Proponent," *IRD: The Institute on Religion and Democracy*, February 15, 2001, also available online at http://www/ird-renew.org/About/About.cfm?ID=76.

16. See especially his essay "The Clash of Definitions," forthcoming in Michael Sells and Emran Qureishi, eds., *The New Crusades: Demonizing the Muslim Enemy* (New York: Columbia University Press).

17. V. S. Naipaul has written a number of books on the subject of Islam, all of which convey a single message: Lodged within every Muslim is a fundamentalist instinct, the curse of Islam is the rise of the West, the hope of every Muslim "fundamentalist" is to bring down the West, or at least to damage enough Westerners to avenge the insult to his civilizational hubris that modern secularized civilization has wrought. It would be a laughable message, except that Naipaul is a skilled practitioner of the English language, whose venom appeals to an Anglo overclass that sees him as a brown ally.

18. Samuel P. Huntington, "The Erosion of American National Interests," *Foreign Affairs* 76, no. 5 (September–October 1997): 28–50.

19. I elaborate this perspective in an earlier lecture, "Towards a History of Global Religion(s) in the Twentieth Century: Parachristian Sightings from an Interdisciplinary Asianist" (Sixteenth Annual University Lecture in Religion, published by Department of Religious Studies, Arizona State University, Fall 1995).

20. See Helen R. Ebaugh and J. S. Chafetz, eds., *Religion and the New Immigrants: Continuities and Adaptations in Immigrant Congregations* (New York: Altamira, 2000). While I have relied on the Hoda Badr chapter concerning the Muslim community of Houston, the entire range of case studies (fifteen in all), coupled with evocative thematic studies (totaling seven), makes this work a ground-

Notes

breaking venture in the study of post-1965 immigrant Americans and their religious practices.

21. Since sociologists are not concerned with fine historical detail of the sort that delights, and bedevils, documentarians, it is unfair to fault Herberg for underpluralizing America, as does Wentz when he declares, "The ink was hardly dry in this very important book [*Protestants, Catholics, Jews*] before it became evident that America's diversity was much more radical than Herberg's trinitarian formula made it out to be" (Richard E. Wentz, *The Culture of Religious Pluralism* [Boulder: Westview, 1998], 13). The pattern of Americanization, whether applied to three or thirteen or three hundred ethnic/religious groups, was the sustaining premise of Herberg's bold and unprecedented analysis.

22. Henry F. May, *Ideas, Faiths, and Feelings: Essays on American Intellectual and Religious History, 1952–1982* (New York: Oxford University Press, 1983), 171–72.

23. Lawrence Levine, *The Opening of the American Mind: Canons, Culture, and History* (Boston: Beacon, 1996), 119, criticizes our limited view of the American past as a Henry Ford–style Anglo-conformist melting pot.

24. Paraphrased, and expanded, from Walter D. Mignolo, "The Larger Picture," in Jorge J. E. Gracia and Pablo De Greiff, eds., *Hispanics/Latinos in the United States: Ethnicity, Race, and Rights*, 104 (New York: Routledge, 2000).

25. Some of these same methodological points have been raised, and pursued, though with more specifically ethnographic language, in Akhil Gupta and James Ferguson, "Culture, Power, Place: Ethnography at the End of an Era," in Akhil Gupta and James Ferguson, eds., *Culture, Power, Place: Explorations in Critical Anthropology*, 49–50 (Durham: Duke University Press, 1997).

26. Hollinger, *Postethnic America*. For a thorough critique of Hollinger's failure to locate his own privileged gaze, see Mignolo, "The Larger Picture," 116–19.

27. Ronald Takaki, *A Different Mirror: A History of Multicultural America* (Boston: Little, Brown, 1993).

28. I am following the terminology of Michael Teitelbaum and Jay Winter in *A Question of Numbers: High Migration, Low Fertility, and the Politics of National Identity* (New York: Hill and Wang, 1998), 247, though without the deterministic linking of all issues of migration to internal labor demands of the host country/ries that require migration as a "fix," albeit one with uncertain outcomes.

29. William V. Flores and Rina Benmayor, eds., *Latino Cultural Citizenship: Claiming Identity, Space, and Rights* (Boston: Beacon, 1997), 87–89, unfortunately makes no or very little mention of religious affiliations as part of the basis for conflict; here the very absence of religion as a marker on internal rivalry/conflict is a telling point against the Huntington thesis, as is the very different citation of religion in Jean Bacon, *Life Lines: Community, Family, and Assimilation Among Asian Indian Immigrants* (New York: Oxford University Press, 1996), 63.

30. Lawrence Levine, *The Opening of the American Mind: Canons, Culture, and History* (Boston: Beacon, 1996), 118.

31. See not only Hamid Naficy on world cities, with L.A. as his model, but also Sharon Zukin, *The Cultures of Cities* (Oxford: Blackwell, 1995).

32. Ibid., 119–20, 131.

33. Cited from Barbara Christian, "The Crime of Innocence," in David Batstone and Eduardo Mendieta, eds., *The Good Citizen*, 58 (New York: Routledge, 1999).

34. Eduardo Mendieta, "The Making of New Peoples," in Batstone and Mendieta, *The Good Citizen*, 49.

35. W. E. B. Du Bois (*The Souls of Black Folk* [1903; New York: Norton, 1999], 11) was the first African American intellectual to use the term *double consciousness* as a badge distinguishing "the Negro people." His invocation of the term at the beginning of his classic study has subjected it to intense scrutiny and even outright rejection. Cornel West, in *Race Matters*, 138–139 (New York: Random House, 1994), quotes the critical passage and then comments that Malcolm X rejected its implication, namely, that because of double consciousness, in Du Bois's view, the Negro could "only see himself through the revelation of the other world," suggesting instead, that "this tragic syndrome can be broken through psychic conversion" (139). But in fact, as Dickson D. Bruce Jr. makes clear in his essay on Du Bois's use of *double consciousness*, the term evoked at least three levels of meaning: (1) the real power of white stereotypes in black life and thought, (2) the double consciousness created by the practical racism that excluded every black American from the mainstream of American society, and (3) the double consciousness of being both an American and not an American—that is, the internal conflict in the African American individual between what was "African" and what was "American" (*The Souls of Black Folk*, 238). While the first two senses would reinforce a sense of powerlessness that Malcolm X, along with others from the 1960s, defiantly opposed, the latter sense, which seems to be the core of Du Bois's usage, offers a hope to recover what is African and not American while remaining American. It is this element of hope despite the structural limits of normative constructions of race and racism that leads West himself to postulate at the end of *Race Matters* (144–45) a vision beyond Malcolm X's rage, a vision of cultural hybridity generated from the resources of black religion but not limited to them. Indeed, the cultural hybridity of which West speaks has parallels in themes etched later in this book, a cultural hybridity in which the complex nature of African, European, Amerindian (but also Latino and Asian) elements can constitute something that is new and polyvalent in the modern world.

36. Huntington, "The Erosion of American National Interests," 28.

37. Michael W. McConnell, "Believers as Equal Citizens" in Nancy L. Rosenblum, ed., *Obligations of Citizenship and Demands of Faith: Religious Accommo-*

dation in Pluralist Democracies, 105–6 (Princeton: Princeton University Press, 2000).

38. Among the best documented has been the December 10, 2001, *Newsweek* cover story, "Secret Trials. Justice vs. Terror: How Far Should We Go?" 38–47. It details the lives of some of the 1,200 Arab Muslim men swept up in the post–September 11 dragnet; it also highlights the irony of their willingness to show more respect for the attorney general than he ever showed them. Even after being held without cause for three weeks, one detainee, on being released, still professed "my love for America," before adding, "but with all due respect to Mr. Ashcroft, if somebody wants to accuse you of something, they should tell you what it is." In one part of the United States, Portland, Oregon, the police chief refused to obey Justice Department orders to "interview" twenty-three Arab resident aliens because the state law of Oregon bars police from collecting information about the political and religious views of anyone who isn't specifically charged with a crime. In the same vein, some older Japanese Americans from San Francisco, still mindful of their own incarceration during World War II, have raised questions and spoken out publicly on behalf of American Muslims, whom they see as but the newest victims of a government-directed policy of racial/religious discrimination that makes enemies of all residents who seem to resemble the external enemy (*Raleigh News and Observer*, December 8, 2001, A-9).

2. CIVIL SOCIETY AND IMMIGRANTS

1. Adam Seligman, *The Idea of Civil Society* (Princeton: Princeton University Press, 1992), 168–69.

2. J. P. S. Uberoi, *Religion, Civil Society, and the State* (New Delhi: Oxford University Press, 1999), ix–x; I have slightly modified and abbreviated the text here to fit the tone of an epigraph.

3. The entire episode, including the final quotation, is taken from Garbi Schmidt, *American Medina* (Lund, Sweden: University of Lund, 1998), 85. While the episode is vivid in its characterization of differences within the Muslim community of Greater Chicago, one is tempted to discount the final statement about family structure and religious morals, as being attributable to the author's projection of class differences. Yet the internalization of a notion of the "model minority" is as real a part of the outlook of some immigrant Muslims as of other Asian immigrants, and lacking specific attribution, we must presume that she captured the tone, if not the language, of her interviewee's reasons for avoiding the announced festival from IMAN.

4. Not surprisingly, two of the III&E pamphlets try to place these last two movements outside the pale of Islam: "Islam and Farrakhanism Compared" and

"Qadiyanism: A Brief Survey." I have also benefited from Schmidt's detailed survey of Chicago Muslim organizations in constructing the brief portrait of Amir Ali and III&E; see *American Medina*, 172–80.

5. The citation, together with the thumbnail capsulation of the VHP, comes from Arvind Rajagopal's comprehensive essay "Hindu Nationalism in the U.S.: Changing Configurations of Political Practice," *Ethnic and Racial Studies* 23, no. 3 (May 2000): 473–76. The essay demonstrates how transnational circuits of communication and exchange between North America and South Asia perpetuate Hinduism as an implicitly conservative, optimally insular community, marked by its enemies, especially Muslims, but also by centrist Hindus as well as Sikhs, Jains, and untouchables.

6. This argument is best framed in Jose Casanova, *Public Religions in the Modern World* (Chicago: University of Chicago Press, 1994), especially 216–19, which I have reiterated here in summary form, excluding references internal to social science debates and terminology favored in those debates.

7. I am summarizing the argument of Dominique Colas, *Civil Society and Fanaticism* (Stanford: Stanford University Press, 1997).

8. Seligman, *Idea of Civil Society*, 202. Elsewhere, Seligman accents the preeminence of America as the showcase of modernity and also, for that very reason, the place where the public sphere, on which civil society depends, becomes infused with issues of individual choice that reflect more the equality of citizens than their concern for collective consensus (138–39).

9. Max Weber, *The City*, 233, cited in Bryan Turner, "Outline of a Theory of Citizenship," *Sociology* 24, no. 2 (May 1990): 203.

10. Laurie Brand, " 'In the Beginning was the State . . ': The Quest for Civil Society in Jordan," in A. R. Norton, ed., *Civil Society in the Middle East*, 151–52 (Leiden: Brill, 1995).

11. Martin Malia, *Russia Under Western Eyes: From the Bronze Horseman to the Lenin Mausoleum* (Cambridge: Harvard University Press, 1999). The excerpts here are quoted from the Sunday *New York Times Book Review*, April 11, 1999.

12. This view of civil society as the node and catalyst for a global utopia is not limited to Seligman or to Malia; it is shared by most global theorists who approach civil society through the post-1989 perspective. See also Jean L. Cohen and Andrew Arato, *Civil Society and Political Theory* (Cambridge: MIT Press, 1992); John S. Hall, ed., *Civil Society* (Cambridge: Polity, 1998); John Keane, *Old Images, New Visions* (Cambridge: Polity, 1998); and Stephen Baron et al., *Social Capital: Social Theory and the Third Way* (New York: Oxford University Press, 2000).

13. The argument here is paraphrased from McNeill's "Project Report: Fundamentalism and the World of the 1990s," *Bulletin of the American Academy of Arts and Sciences* 47, no. 3 (December 1993): 29–30. It is cited in Susanne Rudolph and James Piscatori, eds., *Transnational Religion and Fading Nation-States* (Boulder:

Notes

Westview, 1997), 221–22. Elsewhere ("Epilogue" in Martin E. Marty and R. Scott Appleby, eds., *Fundamentalisms and Society: Reclaiming the Sciences, the Family, and Education*, vol. 2 of The Fundamentalism Project, 572 [Chicago: University of Chicago Press, 1993]), McNeill went still further, offering a future prescription from historical analysis:

> Because cities are places where strangers meet and trade with one another, complete ethnic and religious uniformity is inconceivable. The high level of ethnic uniformity that modern European nations took for granted was very unusual. . . . When cities recruit from afar and across cultural lines, as is now coming to be the case in all the richest countries in the world (except Japan), assimilation to a common norm becomes impractical. In such urban milieux, therefore, religiously defined communities seem very likely to become increasingly important, just as they were in olden times throughout Asia and Europe.

14. Indeed, much of recent critical reflection on key terms indicates that not only *civil society* but also *civilization* are terms reshaped through the prism of global European expansion and colonial rule, which provided not only the antecedents to the current world order but also the basis for its rethinking from the formerly marginal perspectives of postcolonial subjects. See especially Walter Mignolo, *Local Histories/Global Designs* (Princeton, N.J.: Princeton University Press, 2000), especially 305–8, which unpacks the dyadic logic, and the unexamined aporia, of Huntington's categories.

15. Sheila Carapico, *Civil Society in Yemen: The Political Economy of Activism in Modern Arabia* (Cambridge: Harvard University Press, 1998), 2. Though focused on one marginal member of the Arab nation-state club, this monograph illumines the ambiguous arc of scholarship that has shaped current usage of the term *civil society*.

16. Ali Kazancigil, quoted in Kevin Robins, "Interrupting Identities: Turkey/Europe," in Stuart Hall and Paul du Gay, eds., *Questions of Cultural Identity*, 70 (London: Sage, 1996).

17. Robbins, "Interrupting Identities," 76.

18. Michael Walzer, "The Idea of Civil Society," *Dissent* 39, no. 3 (Spring 1991): 293–304.

19. Emile Durkheim, *Professional Ethics and Civic Morals* (1958), as quoted in Seligman, *Idea of Civil Society*, 122.

20. Robert W. Hefner, *Civil Islam: Muslims and Democratization in Indonesia* (Princeton: Princeton University Press, 2000), 219–20.

21. For a thorough analysis of Islam in Senegal, including the Sufi leaders or marabouts as agents of civil society, one should consult the pioneering study of Leonardo A. Villalon, *Islamic Society and State Power in Senegal: Disciples and Citizens in Fatick* (New York: Cambridge University Press, 1995). While Villalon's

own study was limited to the commercial crossroads of Fatick, he brings other parts of Senegal into sharp focus, at the same time demurring from the anti-religious bias of most civil society theorists. An example of confrontational activity by the marabouts, in tandem with other Islamic groups, was the protest against the revised Family Code in the early 1970s. Their opposition led to its effective non-implementation in many areas, including Touba, the capital of the Mouridiya brotherhood (227–30). An example of dissociative activity is the refusal of the marabouts to be drawn into the heated national elections in 1988 and again in 1993 (262–65).

22. The cases of Sufi, Buddhist, and Christian activists in a third space are provided in Rudolph and Piscatori, *Transnational Religion and Fading Nation-States.*

23. Some, of course, feel that civil society can never be independent of the values of the dominant, or bourgeois, group in society. A noted Latino scholar, for instance, argues that it is not just the state but also civil society that becomes an arena for contest, since "the notion of a civil society with all its diverse institutions . . . constitutes the cultural domain in which hegemony is enforced." In other words, civil society is an adjunct of the oppressive state rather than a counterfoil to it. (See William V. Flores, "Citizens Versus Citizenry," in William V. Flores and Rita Benmayor, eds., *Latino Cultural Citizenship: Claiming Identity, Space, and Rights,* 275–76 (Boston: Beacon, 1997). His answer is Marx's answer extended by Gramsci to include the tacit forces of control that make hegemony at once so pervasive and so elusive. Yet Hegel's answer is different: To the extent that civil society helps to maintain the state—i.e., is a genuine partner rather than a co-opted appendage of centrist control—it can contribute to a nonoppressive state. This is the view of Uberoi, as we will see below.

24. The most extensive treatment of Chinese American Christians is provided in F. Yang, *Chinese Christians in America: Conversion, Assimilation, and Adhesive Identities* (University Park: Penn State University Press, 1999). On Filipino immigrants, with a more dispersed attention to issues of religious identity, see Jonathan Y. Okamura, *Imagining the Filipino American Diaspora: Transnational Relations, Identities, and Communities* (New York: Garland, 1998).

25. Marshall G. S. Hodgson, "The Great Western Transmutation," originally published in *Chicago Today* (1967), then included in *The Venture of Islam,* vol. 3 (Chicago: University of Chicago Press, 1974): 176–200, then reprinted as a chapter in Edmund Burke III, ed., *Rethinking World History: Essays on Europe, Islam, and World History* (New York: Cambridge University Press, 1993), 44–71, here cited from p. 63.

26. Manuel Castells, *The Information Age: Economy, Society, and Culture,* 3 vols. (Oxford: Blackwell, 1996–1998). Like Hodgson's earlier trilogy, Castells's opus is at once spatially comprehensive, boldly predictive, and enormously controversial.

27. On heteronomic networks, see Ronnie D. Lipschutz, *After Authority: War, Peace, and Global Politics in the Twenty-first Century.* (Albany: State University of New York Press, 2000), chapter 11.

28. For an analysis of these downside aspects of cybernetic globalism, I have relied on both Saskia Sassen, *Globalization and Its Discontents: Essays on the New Mobility of People and Money* (New York: New Press, 1998), and Zillah Eisenstein, *Global Obscenities: Patriarchy, Capitalism, and the Lure of Cyberfantasy* (New York: New York University Press, 1998).

29. James Holston and Arjun Appadurai, "Cities and Citizenship," *Public Culture* 8 (Winter 1996): 202.

30. Sassen, *Globalization and Its Discontents,* 182.

31. The contrast is with the lucid and provocative analysis of shifting notions of cultural citizenship, especially for South Asians, set forth in Kamala Visweswaran, "Diaspora by Design: Flexible Citizenship and South Asians in U.S. Racial Formations," *Diaspora* 6, no. 1 (1997): 5–29.

32. Peter Mandaville, "Digital Islam: Changing the Boundaries of Religious Knowledge," *ISIM Newsletter* 2, no. 1.

33. David Palumbo-Liu, *Asian/American: Historical Crossings of a Racial Frontier* (Stanford: Stanford University Press, 1999), 263.

34. There are many theoretical studies that elaborate the ambiguities laced into the core concept of a digital culture, but none relates them so frontally to the contradictions of commodity logic in a late capitalist global economy better than D. N. Rodowick, *Reading the Figural, or, Philosophy After the New Media* (Durham: Duke University Press, 2001). See especially "Three Questions Concerning Digital Culture" and its sequel (210–34), where Rodowick relates the nature of representation and communication to the changing forms of commodity. As market forces redirect networks of social exchange, access becomes the key concept of digital culture, marking the fine line between perpetuating inequities and challenging them. For new immigrants and Asian religious practices in twenty-first-century America, there is a crucial difference between an ethical principle of reciprocity (information potlatch), which allows countercultural advocates to participate freely in cyberspace, and the logic of top-down commodity exchange, which restricts "complex sites of social struggle and myriad choices whose historical outcomes have political (and also economic) consequences" (229).

3. NEW IMMIGRANTS AS PARIAHS

1. Robert Park, *Race and Culture* (Glencoe: Free Press, 1950), 354. Also cited in Alejandro Portes and R. G. Rumbaut, *Immigrant America: A Portrait* (2d ed., Berkeley: University of California Press, 1996), 146.

Notes

2. Akhil Gupta and James Ferguson, eds., *Culture, Power, Place: Explorations in Critical Anthropology* (Durham: Duke University Press, 1997), 47.

3. From Lalita Gandhbir, "Free and Equal," in Nurjehan Aziz, ed., *Her Mother's Ashes and Other Stories by South Asian Women in Canada and the United States*, 68–74 (Toronto: Tsar, 1994). I have abbreviated and also adapted the story in order to make the double point that free and equal is not a status *anywhere*, either in India or in the United States, for this young South Asian couple.

4. Her daughter, my first cousin, has now produced a copy of this and other recipes from my aunt Lil. Called "Lil's Kitchen," it contains the best of Lillian Beck's culinary delights, even for those whose ancestries do not connect their palates to Hungarian cuisine.

5. Lisa Lowe, *Immigrant Acts: On Asian American Cultural Politics* (Durham: Duke University Press, 1996), 4.

6. Jean Bacon, *Life Lines: Community, Family, and Assimilation Among Asian Indian Immigrants* (New York: Oxford University Press, 1996), 264.

7. The critique of Lowe here, and also of Palumbo-Liu in other passages, must be framed within the recognition of (a) their broad, stunning and theoretical advances in thinking about immigrant America through East Asian eyes as well as (b) their attention to precisely the flip side of Asian immigration to America, namely, American imperialist occupation of the Philippines and an interventionist agenda that also had imperialist goals in both Korea and Vietnam. Both books have been deftly reviewed by Ketu Katrak, though without accounting for their slight of South Asia, in *Journal of Asian American Studies* 3, no. 3 (October 2000): 371–74.

8. Native American anthropologist Jack Forbes has unraveled the implications of this bureaucratic formulation for Native Americans in compelling detail. See his "Undercounting Native Americans: The 1980 Census and the Manipulation of Racial Identity in the United States," *Wicazo Sa Review* 6, no. 1 (1990): 2–26.

9. My analysis, including the above reference to Jack Forbes, is indebted to Roger Sanjek, "Intermarriage and the Future of Races in the United States," in Stephen Gregory and Roger Sanjek, eds., *Race*, 108–9 (New Brunswick, N.J.: Rutgers University Press, 1994). It is also featured in Michael Omi and Howard Winant, *Racial Formation in the United States: From the 1960s to the 1980s* (New York: Routledge, 1986), 53–54. The most comprehensive treatment of the Louisiana woman is provided in Virginia Dominguez, *White by Definition* (New Brunswick, N.J.: Rutgers University Press, 1992). Since the 2000 Census, the inherent contradiction between subjective recognition and institutional rights applies to multiracial Americans with even more ironic, and painful, twists, as Rebecca Chiyoko King makes clear in her deft essay "Racialization, Recognition, and Rights: Lumping and Splitting Multiracial Asian Americans in the 2000 Census," *Journal of Asian American Studies* 3, no. 2 (June 2000): 191–217.

10. Benedict Anderson offers some confusing figures in a footnote to his widely

Notes

cited article, "Exodus: Long Distance Nationalism," first published in *Critical Inquiry* 20, no. 2 (1994): 326–27 n. 23, then republished in his collected volume, *The Spectre of Comparisons* (London: Verso, 1998), 73 n. 29. While the commentary by Myron Wiener is interesting, the sources for his numerical conjectures are not provided, and since the 2000 Census results have yet to be made fully available as this book goes to press, I must defer any further speculation on the actual number of South Asian Americans in 2002.

11. Beyond the conjectures of Anderson and Wiener above, see Bacon, *Life Lines*, 8, on the combined statistics for East, Southeast, and South Asian immigrants, and for the Hispanic figures, consult Richard del Castillo and Arnoldo De Leon, *North to Aztlan: A History of Mexican Americans in the United States* (New York: Twayne, 1996), 149.

12. Peter Brimelow, *Alien Nation: Common Sense About America's Immigration Disaster* (New York: Random House, 1995): 1, 58–59, 217–19.

13. Richard J. Herrnstein and Charles Murray, *The Bell Curve: Intelligence and Class Structure in American Life* (New York: Free Press, 1994), 479–526.

14. Michael S. Teitelbaum, "The Population Threat," *Foreign Affairs* 71, no. 5 (Winter 1992): 8.

15. See Jagdish Bhagwati, *A Stream of Windows: Reflections on Trade,Immigration, and Democracy* (Cambridge: MIT Press, 1998); *Boston Review*, October/November 1998, 22; and also Bhagwati and Francisco Rivera-Batiz, *In the Eye of the Storm: Targeting Illegal Aliens*, forthcoming.

16. Bhikhu Parekh, "Some Reflections on the Hindu Diaspora," *new community* 20, no. 4 (July 1994): 603–20, provides a broad overview without the theoretical reflection on this Indian diaspora that included Muslims and Sikhs as well as Hindus. For a staging of the capitalist process that produced this and other migrations as well as class formations for the overseas Indian communities of the past century, including the latest subset in the United States, see Kamala Visweswaran, "Diaspora by Design: Flexible Citizenship and South Asians in U.S. Racial Formations," *Diaspora* 6, no. 1 (1997): 5–29.

17. Nussbaum's essay was later published, with several responses, some of them sharply critical, in Joshua Cohen, ed., *For Love of Country* (Boston; Beacon, 1996). For a further critique of Nussbaum, see Linda Bosniak, "The Citizenship of Aliens," *Social Text*, 56, vol. 16, no. 4 (fall 1998): 32, 35.

18. Myron Wiener, "Messy Realities," *Boston Review* 23, no. 5 (October/November 1998): 20.

19. Owen Fiss, "The Immigrant as Pariah," *Boston Review* 23, no. 5 (Fall 1998): 6. The entire *Boston Review* issue was later published as a book: Owen Fiss, *A Community of Equals: The Constitutional Protection of New Americans* (Boston: Beacon, 1999).

20. Yen Le Espiritu, *Asian American Panethnicity: Bridging Institutions and*

Notes

Identities (Philadelphia: Temple University Press, 1992). A more complex assessment of this issue is set forth in Maria Root, *The Multiracial Experience: Racial Border as the New Frontier* (Thousand Oaks, Calif.: Sage, 1996), and also Roger Sanjek, "Intermarriage and the Future of Races in the United States," where the author argues that "in the end, the critical racial issue will continue to be the place that persons of African descent occupy within the U.S. social order" (122). In other words, one cannot make too much of inter-Asian marital strategies or successes within the total structure of an American society that remains hostage to racialized class prejudice in the twenty-first century as it was in the twentieth.

21. One of the most cogent studies of why the model minority argument fails comes from Martin Carnoy, *Faded Dreams: The Politics and Economics of Race in America* (New York: Cambridge University Press, 1994). Carnoy shows in graphic detail how both African and Hispanic Americans, given the same educational and job opportunities as Asian Americans, will likely succeed. "The blame that the model-minority argument casts on blacks for their disadvantaged earnings and employment situations would have much greater validity were not the history of blacks in the United States so different from that of Asian-Americans. Blacks have always been at a greater disadvantage in the labor market because they did not bring commercial skills with them from the 'old country.' They were always more dependent on white employment and white government policies for their economic well being . . . and when punitive policies did change, the black community made gains that might have been as rapid as those of Asian-Americans had the policies been supported over a long enough period of time" (85).

22. Jeffery P. Chan et al., eds., *The Big Aiiieeeee!: An Anthology of Chinese American and Japanese American Literature* (New York: Meridian, 1991), 145–65.

23. R. Stephen Warner and J. G. Wittner, eds., *Gatherings in Diaspora: Religious Communities and the New Immigration* (Philadelphia: Temple University Press, 1998), 28.

24. Karen Leonard, *The South Asian Americans* (Westport, Conn.: Greenwood, 1997), 76.

25. Ibid., 82.

26. Technically speaking, Latino is an ethnic grouping rather than a racial category. The semantic difference conceals a bureaucratic sleight of hand, as Lawrence Wright, among others, has demonstrated; see his "One Drop of Blood," *New Yorker*, July 25, 1994, 46–55.

27. David A. Hollinger, *Postethnic America: Beyond Multiculturalism* (New York: Basic Books, 1995), 8–9.

28. Robert N. Bellah, "Is There a Common American Culture?" *Journal of the American Academy of Religion* 661, no. 3 (Fall 1998): 624.

29. Anderson, "Exodus," 311.

30. Leonard, *The South Asian Americans*. See also Karen Leonard, "State, Cul-

Notes

ture, and Religion: Political Action and Representation Among South Asians in North America," *Diaspora* 9 no. 1 (2000): 21–39.

31. Some of these same issues have also been pursued in Susan Koshy, "Category Crisis: South Asian Americans and the Questions of Race and Ethnicity," *Diaspora* 7, no. 4 (1998): 285–320.

32. Yvonne Haddad and John Esposito, eds., *Muslims on the Americanization Path?* (New York: Oxford University Press, 1998).

33. Yvonne Haddad and Adair T. Lummis, *Islamic Values in the United States: A Comparative Study* (New York: Oxford University Press, 1987).

34. Ali Mazrui, "An Interview on Muslims in America," *Middle Eastern Affairs Journal* 3, nos. 1–2 (Winter/Spring 1997): 177, which echoes the same intra-Muslim racial tensions noted by Aminah Beverly McCloud, *African American Islam* (New York: Routledge, 1995), 4–5.

35. Two notable further examples are Kambiz GhaneaBassiri, *Competing Visions of Islam in the United States: A Study of Los Angeles* (Westport, Conn.: Greenwood, 1997), and also Diana Eck, discussed in chapter 1. In the CD-ROM *On Common Ground*, the section "Islam: Identifying Issues in America" shows Muslims facing external issues, not internal problems, and certainly not those of community self-identity, racial preference, or class prejudice. Jane Smith, in her recent broad survey, *Islam in America* (New York: Columbia University Press, 1999), provides frequent insights on major issues but nonetheless glosses these same problems.

36. It matters not whether these ties are prompted by patriotic nostalgia or by a penchant for cultural/religious authoritarianism, both of which Anderson explores in "Exodus."

37. Park, *Race and Culture*, 250.

38. Ibid., 366.

39. Rick Fields, "Confessions of a White Buddhist," *Tricycle: The Buddhist Review* 4 (1994): 54–56.

40. Jan Nattier, "Visible and Invisible: Jan Nattier on the Politics of Representation in Buddhist America," *Tricycle: The Buddhist Review* 5 (1995): 42–49, where Nattier also describes a third, or evangelical, track of American Buddhists, but this track, echoing a Protestant model, detracts from the value of her race/class critique that forms the core of her argument about the internal fragmentation of Buddhist America. Neither Diana Eck's recent book nor Richard H. Seager's *Buddhism in America* (New York: Columbia University Press, 1999) takes up the challenge posed by Nattier's seminal article.

41. Irene Lin, "Journey to the Far West: Chinese Buddhism in America," *Amerasia Journal* 22, no. 1 (1996): 121–22.

42. Lucie Cheng and Philip Q. Yang, "Asians: The 'Model Minority' Deconstructed," in Roger D. Waldinger and Mehdi Bozorgmehr, eds., *Ethnic Los Ange-*

Notes

les, 329 (New York: Russell Sage Foundation, 1996). Numerous other attacks on the model minority hypothesis also exist. Gary Y. Okihiro demonstrates how it allies with consumerist strategies that seem to assimilate Asian minorities to the Anglo majority, while in reality raising the fear that Asian Americans can be "too success-ful" and hence remain "the yellow peril" (*Margins and Mainstreams: Asians in American History and Culture* [Seattle: University of Washington Press, 1994], 141), while David Palumbo-Liu goes still further, arguing that "the myth of Asian Amer-ican success took hold only because it suppressed specific differences in the mate-rial histories and contemporary realities of many Asian groups in America and fore-grounded the rise of certain Asians (primarily among second and third generation Chinese and Japanese Americans) while ignoring the continuing struggle of oth-ers" (*Asian/American: Historical Crossings of a Racial Frontier* [Stanford: Stanford University Press, 1994], 396).

4. RELIGIOUS OPTIONS FOR URBAN IMMIGRANTS

1. Ali Zarrin, "Made You Mine, America," in Persis M. Karim and Mohammad M. Khorrami, eds., *A World Between: Poems, Short Stories and Essays by Iranian Americans*, 52–57 (New York: George Braziller, 1999). The entire poem weaves a tapestry of memories and hopes, experiences and images that echo the poet's tran-sition from Iran to the United States, to which he emigrated in 1970. I have high-lighted certain sections that relate to the theme of this book, but I commend the entire poem, since it emblematizes not only a cross-cultural but also a cross-gener-ational passage to "another" America.

2. Barry Kosmin and Seymour Lachman, *One Nation Under God: Religion in Contemporary American Society* (New York: Harmony Books, 1993), 4.

3. These numbers are, of course, contested. Two of the most nimble discussions are set forth in Ron Kelley and Jon Friedlander, eds., *Irangeles: Iranians in Los Angeles* (Los Angeles: University of California Press, 1993), especially Mehdi Bozorgmehr et al., "Beyond Nationality: Religio-ethnic Diversity," 59–81, and Mehdi Bozorgmehr, "Diaspora in Microcosm: Middle Easterners in Los Angeles," in Alison Feldman ad Mehdi Bozorgmehr, eds., *Middle Eastern Diaspora Com-munities in America*, 17–33 (New York: Hagop Kevorkian Center for Near Eastern Studies at New York University, 1996).

4. Susanne Rudolph and James Piscatori, eds., *Transnational Religion and Fad-ing Nation-States* (Boulder: Westview, 1997).

5. While Anderson's view of long distance nationalism is largely negative, Rudolph and Piscatori are less confident, noting the confusion among social scien-tists about the multiple roles of religion in "postnational" contexts; see especially the introductory and concluding essays by Rudolph. An alternative reading is pro-

Notes

vided from Yasmin Soysal in *The Limits of Citizenship: Migrants and Postnational Membership in Europe* (Chicago: University of Chicago Press, 1994). Examining six West European countries (Great Britain, France, Germany, Netherlands, Sweden, and Switzerland), she argues that distance between citizen and foreigner has declined; foreigners have acquired many of the rights previously reserved for citizens, e.g., access to social security and health care systems. In her optimistic view, a postnational model of membership, or collective identity, has emerged, with universal personhood instead of nationhood as the implicit ideal and the increasing reality.

6. A detailed review of this and all the manifold economic problems facing the Islamic Republic of Iran is set forth by Hooshang Amirahmadi in *Revolution and Economic Transition: The Iranian Experience* (Albany: State University of New York Press, 1990), 70–82. Amirahmadi's class analysis of the debate on development planning is unprecedented. Its value in interpreting modern Iranian politics is discussed more fully below.

7. Karen Leonard, *The South Asian Americans* (Westport, Conn.: Greenwood, 1997), 76.

8. Kosmin and Lachman, *One Nation Under God*, 82–86. While the category is valuable, it is doubtful that it can be projected with quite the determinism suggested by these authors. Both take the frontier phenomenon to be emblematic of the switch to a broadly secular outlook, based on their own survey, the National Survey of Religious Identification (NSRI); conducted in 1990, it generated significant popular media attention and is still widely cited as authoritative. Yet it leads to wholesale generalizations, such as "religious diversity and high levels of irreligion go hand in hand"(84) or "Eastern religions have established a beachhead in American culture, not just through immigration but through the conversion of many white Americans, especially in California"(152), that cannot be proved or disproved but that project a murky relativism as the core of American-style pluralism. Our conclusion leads us in a different direction, making racialized class prejudice a much more significant marker of actual religious experience, both individual and collective, than Kosmin and Lachman suggest.

9. See Harjot Oberoi, *The Construction of Religious Boundaries: Culture, Identity, and Diversity* (Oxford: Oxford University Press, 1993), 260.

10. Hamid Naficy, *The Making of Exile Cultures: Iranian Television in Los Angeles* (Minneapolis: University of Minnesota Press, 1993), 26.

11. George Sabah and Mehdi Bozorgmehr, cited in Naficy, *The Making of Exile Cultures*, 26.

12. The example of a secularized Iranian woman emigrant with a dilemma similar to Ali's is provided at the outset of Ron Kelley, "Ethnic and Religious Communities from Iran in Los Angeles," in Kelley and Friedlander, *Irangeles*, 81.

13. David Yoo, "Racial Spirits: Religion and Race in Asian American Communities," special issue of *Amerasia Journal* 22, no. 1 (1996).

Notes

14. R. Stephen Warner and J. G. Wittner, eds., *Gatherings in Diaspora: Religious Communities and the New Immigration* (Philadelphia: Temple University Press, 1998).

15. The observation is made by Shahnaz Khan at the end of *Muslim Women: Crafting a North American Identity* (Gainesville: University Press of Florida, 2000). Two visions exist: (1) to incorporate religion into a strategy of women's empowerment, or (2) to work outside religious frameworks to seek empowerment as "post-religious" women (128).

16. Naficy, *The Making of Exile Cultures*, xv.

17. See Raymond Rocco in William V. Flores and Rita Benmayor, eds., *Latino Cultural Citizenship: Claiming Identity, Space, and Rights*, 102 (Boston: Beacon, 1997).

18. I am indebted to the excellent study on this issue by Raymond Rocco, "Citizenship, Culture, and Community: Restructuring in Southeast Los Angeles," 97–123, in Flores and Benmayor, *Latino Cultural Citizenship*.

19. Leonard, *The South Asian Americans*, 77.

20. Bhikhu Parekh, "Some Reflections on the Hindu Diaspora," *new community* 20, no. 4 (July 1994): 606.

21. The figures for some of the other East Asian immigrant communities are equally fascinating: there are also 14.5 hours of Japanese, 9.5 hours of Mandarin, and a whopping 22.5 hours of Korean! (Naficy, *The Making of Exile Cultures*, 233).

22. Thomas A. Tweed, *Our Lady of the Exile: Diasporic Religion at a Cuban Catholic Shrine in Miami* (New York: Oxford University Press, 1997), 88. See also now Robert A, Orsi, *Gods of the City: Religion and the American Urban Landscape* (Bloomington: Indiana University Press, 1999).

23. See Mattei Dogan and John D. Kasarda, eds., *The Metropolis Era: Mega-Cities* (Newbury Park, Calif.: Sage, 1988), but more readable and making a point about the cultural ambiance of modern urban sites is Sharon Zukin, *The Cultures of Cities* (Oxford: Blackwell, 1995).

24. Zukin, *The Cultures of Cities*, 274–75.

25. Tweed, *Our Lady of the Exile*, 86.

26. Kelley and Friedlander, *Irangeles*, 70, offer an apt characterization of the problem of ingroup hyperinflation of population figures.

27. Nikos Papastergiadis, "The Limits of the Diaspora: A Conversation with Ashis Nandy," in *Dialogues in the Diasporas: Essays and Conversations on Cultural Identity*, 111 (London: Rivers Oram Press, 1994).

28. Erik Davis, *Techgnosis: Myth, Magic, and Mysticism in the Age of Information* (New York: Harmony Books, 1998). Davis's appreciation of New Age religion, including its Asian component, is reflective, often insightful, yet it remains oblivious of both class and racial markers for the youthful consumers, who are often also the producers, of techgnosis.

Notes

5. REIMAGINING RELIGIOUS PLURALISM

1. Margaret R. Miles, "Image," in Mark C. Taylor, ed., *Critical Terms in Religious Studies*, 170–71 (Chicago: University of Chicago Press, 1998).

2. Rabbi Irving Greenberg, "Jewish Denominationalism Meets the Open Society," in Marjorie Garber and Rebecca L. Walkowitz, eds., *One Nation Under God? Religion and American Culture*, 35 (New York: Routledge, 1999).

3. No acknowledgment is made of the early 1960s Canadian theorist Marshall McLuhan, but one sees his fingerprints throughout this comparison. For a fuller assessment of McLuhan, both his insight and its limits, see Manuel Castells, *The Information Age: Economy, Society, and Culture*, 3 vols. (Oxford: Blackwell, 1996–1998), 1:340–41. In the new media system, the medium is no longer the message (McLuhan); rather "the message is the medium"(340). So much so that instead of living in a global village (McLuhan), we are now living "in customized cottages globally produced and locally distributed"(341).

4. Since November 1997, of course, there have been efforts to establish cyberworship. For one such site, which provides links to others, see http://www.execpc.com/chender/.

5. The *Utne Reader* remains the best repository of the alternative media, and it is common fare, in both public and private spaces, for middle-class, or overclass, Anglo-Americans. Eric Utne, the founder and editor of the *Utne Reader*, is adroit at providing mainstream journals with highly literate and also entertaining quotes about major issues from computer technology to environmental legislation to new religions.

6. Jeremiah Creedon, "God with a Million Faces," *Utne Reader*, July–August 1998, 42–48.

7. Castells, *The Information Age*, 1:328.

8. One of the most exquisite parts of McCourt's story is its sense of delayed triumph. A retired high school teacher, he had tried for thirty years to write his life story. Finally he resolved to dedicate a whole year to nothing but this deferred wish. The results must have exceeded even the wildest Irish oracle of commercial and literary success in America, yet all the more reason that one has to gasp at his instantaneous status not just as a late-blooming autobiographer but also as a religious authority!

9. Among others who have analyzed this phenomenon generationally is Wade Clark Roof, *Spiritual Marketplace: Baby Boomers and the Remaking of American Religion* (Princeton: Princeton University Press, 1999).

10. Hans Georg Gadamer, in Jacques Derrida and Gianni Vattimo, eds., *Religion* (Stanford: Stanford University Press, 1998), 209.

11. David Howes, in his essay "Sensorial Anthropology," shows that the anthro-

pology of the senses has scanned the role of the senses in different non-Euro-American cultures. The Wolof culture of West Africa, for instance, privileges touch over speech-taste-sight, while in some cultures sight and smell are both deemed to be antisocial or animal-like functions. See David Howes, ed., *The Varieties of Sensory Experience* (Toronto: University of Toronto Press, 1991), 177–85.

12. The discusssion of Cornel West in chapter 1 anticipates the issues raised here.

13. Robert Stam, "Bakhtin, Polyphony, and Ethnic/Racial Representation," in Lester D. Friedman, ed., *Unspeakable Images: Ethnicity and the American Cinema*, 264–68 (Urbana: University of Illinois Press, 1991). In addition to the direct quotes from Stam in the above paragraph, I have also benefited from his subtle reading of ethnic/racial characters in mainstream Hollywood movies.

14. Paul S. Cowen, "A Social-Cognitive Approach to Ethnicity in Films," in Friedman, *Unspeakable Images*, 371.

15. Gina Marchetti, "Ethnicity, the Cinema, and Cultural Studies," in Friedman, *Unspeakable Images*, 300–303, for both the quotations and the vivid analysis that informs them.

16. Or arguably, the United States never was merely a three-religion nation-state, since one must count nonreligion as a religious option with distinctively American qualifiers; see chapter 4 on recent Iranian immigrants and their status as "a model minority."

17. The limits to the ideology of the leisure society have been charted by Castells in *The Information Age*, 1:364–72. Discussing multimedia as symbolic environment, Castells refers to the study made in Colorado in 1993–1994 that indicated that most households, despite increased options, watched about 2.5 movies per month (1:368).

18. Ibid., 1:328.

19. Totaling six volumes, *Culture, Media, and Identities* was published simultaneously from London, Thousand Oaks, and New Delhi in 1997. Its coeditors included Linda Janes, Hugh Mackay, and Keith Negus.

20. A thumbnail but dense recapitulation of this scheme is provided by John Kraniauskas, "Globalization Is Ordinary: The Transnationalization of Cultural Studies," *Radical Philosophy* 90 (July–August 1998): 13.

21. Manuel Castells, "The Power of Identity," in *The Information Age*, 2:8f.

22. Stuart Hall, "Who Needs 'Identity'?" in Stuart Hall and Paul Du Gay, eds., *Questions of Cultural Identity*, 5 (London: Sage, 1996).

23. Ibid., 10.

24. Ibid., 14.

25. Jonathan Z. Smith, "A Matter of Class: Taxonomies of Religion," *Harvard Theological Review* 89, no. 4 (1996): 387–403, but especially 399–401, where "universal" and "living," along with "world" are shown to be qualifiers of "religion" that

Notes

simultaneously denigrate hybridization and privilege the purity of originary belief, which is characteristic not of all religion but of one above all others: Protestant Christianity.

26. bell hooks, "Waking Up to Racism," *Tricycle* (Fall 1994): 42–45, reprinted in Thomas A. Tweed and Stephen Prothero, *Asian Religions in America: A Documentary History* (New York: Oxford University Press, 1999), 277–81.

27. See William V. Flores and Rita Benmayor, eds., *Latino Cultural Citizenship: Claiming Identity, Space, and Rights* (Boston: Beacon, 1997), and also Aihwa Ong, "Cultural Citizenship as Subject-Making: Immigrants Negotiate Racial and Cultural Boundaries in the United States," *Current Anthropology* 37, no. 5 (December 1996): 737–62.

28. Karen Leonard, *The South Asian Americans* (Westport, Conn.: Greenwood, 1997): 70. Also notable is her more recent essay, "State, Culture, and Religion: Political Action and Representation Among South Asians in North America," *Diaspora* 9, no. 1 (2000): 21–38.

29. The leading essay remains Janet Abu-Lughod, "Comparing Chicago, New York, and Los Angeles: Testing Some World Cities Hypotheses," in Paul L. Knox and Peter J. Taylor, eds., *World Cities in a World System*, 171–91 (Cambridge: Cambridge University Press, 1995), though it must now be supplemented with her new major study, *New York, Chicago, Los Angeles: America's Global Cities* (Minneapolis: University of Minnesota Press, 1999). While hers is a splendid landmark in urban sociology, it accounts for race chiefly through Latino-black competition at the lower end of the labor market in Los Angeles (396–98), scarcely mentioning the Hart-Celler Act of 1965 and not touching on the religious outlook or practice for any immigrant group.

30. Bruce Lincoln, "Rethinking Ideology and Religion," in *Method and Theory in the Study of Religion* 10, no. 3 (1998): 323.

31. Stuart Hall, "The Local and the Global," in Anne McClintock, Aamir Mufti, and Ella Shoat, eds., *Dangerous Liaisons: Gender, Nation, and Postcolonial Perspectives* (Minneapolis: University of Minnesota Press, 1997), 183.

32. Arjun Appadurai, *Modernity at Large: Cultural Dimensions of Globalization* (Minneapolis: University of Minnesota Press, 1996), 6.

33. Rosaura Sanchez, "On the Racialization of Culture and Class: Transnational Latino Spaces," working draft of paper given at Latino Subaltern Conference, Duke University, Fall 1998, 11.

34. Appadurai, *Modernity at Large*, 6.

35. Mark D. Wood, "Religious Studies as Critical Organic Intellectual Practice," *Journal of the American Academy of Religion* 69, no. 1 (March 2001): 130. The entire article "encourages scholars to link the academy to society and the study of religion to economics, politics, and other social forces" (148). In terms of this book, the largest of those social forces that the academy needs to confront is racialized

Notes

class prejudice; it affects Asian Americans but also other minority groups both internally and externally, both in the immediate inequities of U.S. society and in the long-term prognosis for collective health.

36. Michael Lind, *The Next American Nation: The New Nationalism and the Fourth American Revolution* (New York: Free Press, 1995), 139.

CONCLUSION

1. Wing Tek Lum, last stanza of a five-stanza poem "Grateful Here," in Jeffery P. Chan et al., eds., *The Big Aiiieeeee! An Anthology of Chinese American and Japanese American Literature*, 596 (New York: Meridian, 1991).

2. Lawson Fusao Inada, "On Being Asian American—For Our Children" in Chan et al., *The Big Aiiieeeee!*, 619. The above quotation also comes from a poem by Inada in the same collection.

3. The incident concerning Mauritanian immigrants in Kentucky is reported in the *New York Times*, December 5, 2001. See David Firestone, "Federal Sweep Shifts Attitude of Immigrants About the U.S.," B-1. The civil problem is much greater than Mauritanians or Muslims, whether from Africa or Asia. It evokes the insidious danger of profiling, that any group, simply because of the way its members look, can be identified with similar-looking enemies, or terrorists. The line from Japanese Americans imprisoned during World War II to Asian Americans arrested after September 11 is too clear to be ignored, and it remains one of the public ironies of the post—September 11 world that the Bush administration's transportation secretary, Norman Maneta, is a Japanese American who was incarcerated during the 1940s.

4. See Rabbi Irving Greenberg, "Jewish Denominationalism Meets the Open Society," in Marjorie Garber and Rebecca L. Walkowitz, eds., *One Nation Under God? Religion and American Culture*, 32–59 (New York: Routledge, 1999).

5. Five essays, including a bibliographic review essay on the experiences of Asian Pacific Americans in higher education, are provided in *Journal of Asian American Studies* 3, no. 1 (February 2000): 1–109.

6. See especially Angelo N. Ancheta, *Race, Rights, and the Asian American Experience* (New Brunswick, N.J.: Rutgers University Press, 1998), which offers a careful synthesis on the relation between Asian Americans and specific areas of civil rights and immigration law. The line between others' perception and self-perception remains slippery, as A. S. Chen makes evident in his comprehensive review of the book in *Journal of Asian American Studies* 1, no. 3 (October 1998): 293–97.

7. A notable example is Rebecca Chiyoko King, "Racialization, Recognition, and Rights: Lumping and Splitting Multiracial Asian Americans in the 2000 Census," *Journal of Asian American Studies* 3, no. 2 (June 2000): 191–217.

8. Many examples could be provided, but certainly the showcase is the third in

Notes

a trilogy of dedicated issues that marked the *Journal of Asian American Studies* at the outset of a new millennium. The February 2000 issue was dedicated to pedagogy, and the June 2000 issue to race, while the third and final issue offered essays on cultural performance from Asian American perspectives. Again, the tilt to East Asia is evident, as three of the four articles focused on Asian Pacific Americans, and only one, a fascinating exploration of Indo-chic and its elision with Afro-Am chic, highlighted South Asian Americans. See Sunaina Maira, "Henna and Hip Hop: The Politics of Cultural Production and the Work of Cultural Studies," *Journal of Asian American Studies* 3, no. 3 (October 2000): 329–69.

9. Charles Taylor, "Two Theories of Modernity," and Thomas McCarthy, "On Reconciling Cosmopolitan Unity and National Diversity," in Dilip Parameshwar Gaonkar, ed., *Alternative Modernities*, 172–96 and 197–236, respectively (Durham: Duke University Press, 2001).

10. Michael Lind, *The Next American Nation: The New Nationalism and the Fourth American Revolution* (New York: Free Press, 1995), 139.

11. David A. Hollinger, *Postethnic America: Beyond Multiculturalism* (New York: Basic Books, 1995), 157.

12. Arthur Schlesinger Jr., "Has Democracy a Future?" *Foreign Affairs* 76, no. 5 (1997), cited in David Palumbo-Liu, *Asian/American: Historical Crossings of a Racial Frontier*, 384–85 (Stanford: Stanford University Press, 1999).

SELECTED BIBLIOGRAPHY

Aguilar-San Juan, K., ed. *The State of Asian America: Activism and Resistance in the 1990s.* Boston: South End Press, 1994.

Alba, Richard D. *Ethnic Identity: The Transformation of White America.* New Haven: Yale University Press, 1990.

Almaguer, Tomas. *Racial Fault Lines: The Historical Origins of White Supremacy in California.* Berkeley: University of California Press, 1994.

Amritjit Singh, J. T. S., and Robert E. Hogan, eds. *Memory and Cultural Politics: New Approaches to American Ethnic Literatures.* Boston: Northeastern University Press, 1996.

Ancheta, Angelo N. *Race, Rights, and the Asian American Experience.* New Brunswick, N.J.: Rutgers University Press, 1998.

Anderson, Benedict O. "Exodus: Long Distance Nationalism." *Critical Inquiry* 20, no. 2 (1994): 314–27.

Appadurai, Arjun. *Modernity at Large: Cultural Dimensions of Globalization.* Minneapolis: University of Minnesota Press, 1996.

Aziz, Nurjehan, ed. *Her Mother's Ashes and Other Stories by South Asian Women in Canada and the United States.* Toronto: Tsar, 1994.

Bacon, Jean. *Life Lines: Community, Family, and Assimilation Among Asian Indian Immigrants.* New York: Oxford University Press, 1996.

Badr, Hoda. "Al-Noor Mosque: Strength Through Unity." In Helen R. Ebaugh and J. S. Chafetz, eds., *Religion and the New Immigrants,* 193–228. New York: Altamira Press, 2000.

Bahri, Deepika, and Mary Vasudeva, eds. *Between the Lines: South Asians and Postcoloniality.* Philadelphia: Temple University Press, 1996.

Balibar, Etienne, and Immanuel Wallerstein. *Race, Nation, Class: Ambiguous Identities.* London: Verso, 1991.

Barkan, Eliott R. "Race, Religion, and Nationality in American Society: A Model of Ethnicity—from Contact to Assimilation." *Journal of American Ethnic History* 14, no. 2 (1995): 38–76.

Bary, William T. D. *The Trouble with Confucianism.* Cambridge: Harvard University Press, 1991.

Batstone, David, and Eduardo Mendieta, eds. *The Good Citizen.* New York: Routledge, 1999.

Selected Bibliography

Bellah, Robert N. "Is There a Common American Culture?" *Journal of the American Academy of Religion* 66, no. 3 (Fall 1998): 613–25.

Bhardwaj, Surinder M. "The Temple as a Symbol of Hindu Identity in America." *Journal of Cultural Geography* 17, no. 2 (1998): 125–44.

Borjas, George J. *Heaven's Door: Immigration Policy and the American Economy.* Princeton: Princeton University Press, 1999.

Bozorgmehr, Mehdi. 1997. "Internal Ethnicity: Iranians in Los Angeles." *Sociological Perspectives* 40, no. 3 (1997): 387–409.

Carnoy, Martin. *Faded Dreams: The Politics and Economics of Race in America.* New York: Cambridge University Press, 1994.

Castells, Manuel. *The Information Age: Economy, Society, and Culture.* 3 vols. Oxford: Blackwell, 1996–1998.

Chan, Jeffery P., et al., eds. *The Big Aiiieeeee! An Anthology of Chinese American and Japanese American Literature.* New York: Meridian, 1991.

Chin, Frank, J. P. Chan, et al., eds. *Aiiieeeee! An Anthology of Asian-American Writers.* Washington, D.C.: Howard University Press, 1974.

Clifford, James. "Diasporas." *Cultural Anthropology* 9, no. 3 (1994): 302–38.

Colker, R. *Hybrid: Bisexuals, Multiracials, and Other Misfits Under American Law.* New York: New York University Press, 1996.

Dave, S., et al. "De-Privileging Positions: Indian Americans, South Asian Americans, and the Politics of Asian American Studies." *Journal of Asian American Studies* 3, no. 1 (2000): 67–100.

Davis, Michael. *Magical Urbanism: Latinos Reinvent the U.S. Big City.* New York: Verso, 2000.

Del Castillo, Richard, and Arnoldo De Leon. *North to Aztlan: A History of Mexican Americans in the United States.* New York: Twayne, 1996.

Ebaugh, Helen R., and J. S. Chafetz, eds. *Religion and the New Immigrants: Continuities and Adaptations in Immigrant Congregations.* New York: Altamira, 2000.

Eck, Diana. *A New Religious America.* San Francisco: HarperSanFrancisco, 2001.

——. *On Common Ground: World Religions in America.* New York: Columbia University Press, 1997.

Eisenstein, Zillah. *Global Obscenities: Patriarchy, Capitalism, and the Lure of Cyberfantasy.* New York: New York University Press, 1998.

Feldman, Alison, and Mehdi Bozorgmehr, eds. *Middle Eastern Diaspora Communities in America.* New York: Hagop Kevorkian Center for Near Eastern Studies at New York University, 1996.

Fiss, Owen. *A Community of Equals: The Constitutional Protection of New Americans.* Boston: Beacon, 1999.

Flores, William V., and Rita Benmayor, eds. *Latino Cultural Citizenship: Claiming Identity, Space, and Rights.* Boston: Beacon, 1997.

Selected Bibliography

Fong, Timothy P. *The Contemporary Asian American Experience: Beyond the Model Minority*. New Jersey: Prentice Hall, 1998.

Friedman, Lester D., ed. *Unspeakable Images: Ethnicity and the American Cinema*. Urbana: University of Illinois Press, 1991.

Fuchs, Lawrence H. *The American Kaleidoscope: Race, Ethnicity, and the Civic Culture*. Hanover, N.H.: University Press of New England, 1990.

Gaonkar, Dilip Parameshwar, ed. *Alternative Modernities*. Durham: Duke University Press, 2001.

Garber, Marjorie, and Rebecca L. Walkowitz, eds. *One Nation Under God? Religion and American Culture*. New York: Routledge, 1999.

Gillan, Maria M., and Jennifer Gillan, eds. *Unsettling America: An Anthology of Contemporary Multicultural Poetry*. New York: Penguin, 1994.

Glazer, Nathan. "Is Assimilation Dead?" *Annals of the American Academy of Political and Social Science* 530 (1993): 122–37.

Gooding-Williams, Robert, ed. *Reading Rodney King/Reading Urban Uprising*. New York: Routledge, 1993.

Gordon, Milton M. *Assimilation in American Life: The Role of Race, Religion, and National Origins*. New York: Oxford University Press, 1964.

Gracia, Jorge J. E., and Pablo De Greiff, eds. *Hispanics/Latinos in the United States: Ethnicity, Race, and Rights*. New York: Routledge, 2000.

Gregory, Stephen, and Roger Sanjek, eds. *Race*. New Brunswick, N.J.: Rutgers University Press, 1994.

Gupta, Akhil, and James Ferguson, eds. *Culture, Power, Place: Explorations in Critical Anthropology*. Durham: Duke University Press, 1997.

Hall, Stuart. "The Local and the Global." In Anne Mclintock, Aamir Mufti, and Ella Shohar, eds. *Dangerous Liasons: Gender, Nation, and Postcolonial Perspectives*. Minneapolis: University of Minnesota Press, 1997. 173–187.

Hall, Stuart, ed. *Representation: Cultural Representation and Signifying Practices*. London: Sage Publication, 1997.

Hefner, Robert W. *Civil Islam: Muslims and Democratization in Indonesia*. Princeton: Princeton University Press, 2000.

Hing, Bill O. *Making and Remaking America Through Immigration Policy, 1850–1950*. Stanford: Stanford University Press, 1993.

Hollinger, David A. "Multiculturalism and the Jews." *Tikkun* 13, no. 6 (1998): 68–69.

——. *Postethnic America: Beyond Multiculturalism*. New York: Basic Books, 1995.

hooks, bell. *Black Looks: Race and Representation*. Boston: South End Press, 1992.

Huntington, Samuel P. "The Clash of Civilizations?" *Foreign Affairs* 72, no. 3 (1993): 22–49.

——. *The Clash of Civilizations and the Remaking of World Order*. New York: Simon and Schuster, 1996.

Selected Bibliography

——. "The Erosion of American National Interests." *Foreign Affairs* 76, no. 5 (September–October 1997): 28–49.

Huyssen, Andreas. *Twilight Memories: Marking Time in a Culture of Amnesia.* New York: Routledge, 1995.

Johnson, J., and F. J. Costa. "Hindu Temple Development in the United States: Planning and Zoning Issues." *Journal of Cultural Geography* 17, no. 2 (1998): 115–22.

Karim, Persis M., and Mohammad M. Khorrami, eds. *A World Between: Poems, Short Stories, and Essays by Iranian Americans.* New York: George Braziller, 1999.

Kelley, Ron, and Jon Friedlander, eds. *Irangeles: Iranians in Los Angeles.* Los Angeles: University of California Press, 1993.

Khan, Shahnaz. *Muslim Women: Crafting a North American Identity.* Gainesville: University Press of Florida, 2000.

Kibra, Nazli. "Not Asian, Black, or White? Reflections on South Asian American Racial Identity." *Amerasia Journal* 22, no. 2 (1996): 77–86.

King, Rebecca Chiyoko. "Racialization, Recognition, and Rights: Lumping and Splitting Multiracial Asian Americans in the 2000 Census." *Journal of Asian American Studies* 3, no. 2 (2000): 191–217.

Kivisto, Peter A. "Religion and the New Immigrants." In J. William Swatos, ed., *A Future for Religion? New Paradigms for Social Analysis*, 92–108. Newbury Park, Calif.: Sage, 1992.

Koshy, Susan. "Category Crisis: South Asian Americans and the Questions of Race and Ethnicity." *Diaspora* 7, no. 4 (1998): 285–320.

Kurien, Prema. "Becoming American by Becoming Hindu: Indian Americans Take Their Place at the Multicultural Table." In R. Stephen Warner and J. G. Wittner, eds., *Gatherings in Diaspora: Religious Communities and the New Immigration*, 37–70. Philadelphia: Temple University Press, 1998.

Kwon, H-Y, K. C. Kim, and R. Stephen Warner. *Korean Americans and Their Religions.* University Park: Pennsylvania State University Press, 2001.

Leonard, Karen. *The South Asian Americans.* Westport, Conn.: Greenwood, 1997.

——. "State, Culture, and Religion: Political Action and Representation Among South Asians in North America." *Diaspora* 9, no. 1 (2000): 21–38.

Lind, Michael. *The Next American Nation: The New Nationalism and the Fourth American Revolution.* New York: Free Press, 1995.

Lippy, Charles. *Pluralism Comes of Age: American Religious Culture in the Twentieth Century.* Armonk, N.Y.: M. E. Sharpe, 2000.

Lipschutz, Ronnie D. *After Authority: War, Peace, and Global Politics in the Twenty-first Century.* Albany: State University of New York Press, 2000.

Long, Charles H. *Significations: Signs, Symbols, and Images in the Interpretation of Religion.* 2d ed. Aurora: Davies Group, 1995.

Selected Bibliography

Lowe, Lisa. *Immigrant Acts: On Asian American Cultural Politics*. Durham: Duke University Press, 1996.

Lubiano, Wahneema, ed. *The House That Race Built*. New York: Random House, 1998.

Lyman, Stanford M. "Marginalizing the Self." *Symbolic Interaction* 14, no. 4 (1993): 379–93.

Maira, Sunaina. "Henna and Hip Hop: The Politics of Cultural Production and the Work of Cultural Studies." *Journal of Asian American Studies* 3, no. 3 (October 2000): 329–69.

Massey, Douglas S., and N. A. Denton. *American Apartheid: Segregation and the Making of the Underclass*. Cambridge: Harvard University Press, 1993.

McCloud, Aminah Beverly. *African American Islam*. New York: Routledge, 1995.

McLaren, Peter. *Revolutionary Multiculturalism: Pedagogies of Dissent for the New Millennium*. Boulder: Westview, 1997.

Mignolo, Walter. *Local Histories/Global Designs*. Princeton, N.J.: Princeton University Press, 2000.

Mishra, V. "The Diasporic Imaginary: Theorizing the Indian Diaspora." *Textual Practice* 10, no. 3 (1996): 421–47.

Mizruchi, Susan L., ed. *Religion and Cultural Studies*. Princeton: Princeton University Press, 2001.

Naficy, Hamid. *An Accented Cinema: Exilic and Diasporic Filmmaking*. Princeton, N.J.: Princeton University Press, 2001.

——. *The Making of Exile Cultures: Iranian Television in Los Angeles*. Minneapolis: University of Minnesota Press, 1993.

Nakayama, Thomas K. " 'Model Minority' and the Media: Discourse of Asian America." *Journal of Communication Inquiry* 12, no. 1 (1988): 65–73.

Nattier, Jan. "Visible and Invisible: Jan Nattier on the Politics of Representation in Buddhist America." *Tricycle: The Buddhist Review* (Fall 1995): 42–49.

Oboler, Suzanne. " 'It Must Be a Fake!': Racial Ideologies, Identities, and the Question of Rights." In Jorge J. E. Gracia and P. D. Grieff, eds., *Hispanics/Latinos in the United States*, 125–44. New York: Routledge, 2000.

Okamura, Jonathan Y. *Imagining the Filipino American Diaspora: Transnational Relations, Identities, and Communities*. New York: Garland, 1998.

Okihiro, Gary Y. *Margins and Mainstreams: Asians in American History and Culture*. Seattle: University of Washington Press, 1994.

Omi, Michael, and Howard Winant. *Racial Formation in the United States: From the 1960s to the 1980s*. New York: Routledge, 1986.

——. *Racial Formation in the United States: From the 1960s to the 1990s*. New York: Routledge, 1994.

Ong, Aiwah. "Cultural Citizenship as Subject-Making: Immigrants Negotiate Racial and Cultural Boundaries in the United States." *Current Anthropology* 37, no. 5 (1996): 737–62.

Selected Bibliography

Palumbo-Liu, David. *Asian/American: Historical Crossings of a Racial Frontier.* Stanford: Stanford University Press, 1999.

Papastergiadis, Nikos. "The Limits of the Diaspora: A Conversation with Ashis Nandy." In *Dialogues in the Diasporas: Essays and Conversations on Cultural Identity,* 101–16. London: Rivers Oram Press, 1994.

Parekh, Bhikhu. 1994. "Some Reflections on the Hindu Diaspora." *new community* 20, no. 4 (July 1994): 603–20.

Park, Robert E. *Race and Culture.* Glencoe: Free Press, 1950.

Portes, Alejandro, and Ruben G. Rumbaut. *Immigrant America: A Portrait.* 2d ed. Berkeley: University of California Press, 1996.

Prashad, V. *The Karma of Brown Folk.* Minneapolis: University of Minnesota Press, 2000.

Radhakrishnan, Rajagopalan. *Diasporic Meditations: Between Home and Location.* Minneapolis: University of Minnesota Press, 1996.

Rajagopal, Arvind. "Hindu Nationalism in the U.S.: Changing Configurations of Political Practice." *Ethnic and Racial Studies* 23, no. 3 (May 2000): 467–96.

Robins, Kevin. "Interrupting Identities: Turkey/Europe." In Stuart Hall and Paul du Gay, eds., *Questions of Cultural Identity,* 61–88. London: Sage, 1996.

Rodowick, D. N. *Reading the Figural, or, Philosophy After the New Media.* Durham: Duke University Press, 2001.

Roof, Wade C. *Spiritual Marketplace: Baby Boomers and the Remaking of American Religion.* Princeton: Princeton University Press, 1999.

Root, Maria. "Multiracial Asians: Models of Ethnic Identity." *Amerasia Journal* 23, no. 1 (1997): 29–41.

——. *The Multiracial Experience: Racial Border as the New Frontier.* Thousand Oaks, Calif.: Sage, 1996.

Rosenblum, Nancy L., ed. *Obligations of Citizenship and Demands of Faith: Religious Accommodation in Pluralist Democracies.* Princeton: Princeton University Press, 2000.

Rudolph, Susanne, and James Piscatori, eds. *Transnational Religion and Fading Nation-States.* Boulder: Westview, 1997.

Rumbaut, Ruben G., and Silvia Predraza. *Origins and Destinies: Immigration, Race, and Ethnicity in America.* Belmont, Calif.: Wadsworth, 1996.

Salins, Peter D. *Assimilation, American Style.* New York: Basic Books, 1996.

Salyer, Lucy E. *Laws Harsh as Tigers: Chinese Immigration and the Shaping of Modern Immigration Law.* Chapel Hill: University of North Carolina Press, 1995.

Sassen, Saskia. *Globalization and Its Discontents: Essays on the New Mobility of People and Money.* New York: New Press, 1998.

Schlesinger, Arthur, Jr. *The Disuniting of America: Reflections on a Multicultural Society.* New York: Norton, 1992.

Selected Bibliography

Seager, Richard H. *Buddhism in America*. New York: Columbia University Press, 1999.

Shankar, Lavina D., and Rajini Srikanth, eds. *A Part, Yet Apart: South Asians in Asian America*. Philadelphia: Temple University Press, 1998.

Shankman, Arnold M. *Ambivalent Friends: Afro-Americans View the Immigrant*. Westport, Conn.: Greenwood, 1982.

Shepherd, George W., Jr., et al. *Racism and the Underclass: State Policy and Discrimination Against Minorities*. Westport, Conn.: Greenwood, 1991.

Shohat, Ella, and Robert Stam, eds. *Unthinking Eurocentrism: Multiculturalism and the Media*. London: Routledge, 1994.

Stevens-Arroyo, Anthony M., and G. R. Cadena, eds. *Old Masks, New Faces: Religion and Latino Identities*. New York: Bildner Center for Western Hemisphere Studies, 1995.

Swatos, J. William, ed. *A Future for Religion? New Paradigms for Social Analysis*. Newbury Park, Calif.: Sage, 1992.

Takaki, Ronald. *A Different Mirror: A History of Multicultural America*. Boston: Little, Brown, 1993.

——. *Strangers from a Different Shore*. New York: Penguin, 1989.

Tweed, Thomas A. *Our Lady of the Exile: Diasporic Religion at a Cuban Catholic Shrine in Miami*. New York: Oxford University Press, 1997.

——, ed. *Retelling U.S. Religious History*. Berkeley: University of California Press, 1997.

Tweed, Thomas A., and Stephen Prothero. *Asian Religions in America: A Documentary History*. New York: Oxford University Press, 1999.

Uberoi, J. P. S. *Religion, Civil Society, and the State*. New Delhi: Oxford University Press, 1999.

Visweswaran, Kamala. "Diaspora by Design: Flexible Citizenship and South Asians in U.S. Racial Formations." *Diaspora* 6, no. 1 (1997): 5–29.

Waldinger, Roger D., and Mehdi Bozorgmehr, eds. *Ethnic Los Angeles*. New York: Russell Sage Foundation, 1996.

Wallerstein, Immanuel. "Culture as the Ideological Battleground of the Modern World-System." *Theory, Culture, and Society* 7 (1990): 31–55.

Walzer, Michael. "The Idea of Civil Society." *Dissent* 39, no. 3 (Spring 1991): 293–304.

Warner, R. Stephen, and J. G. Wittner, eds. *Gatherings in Diaspora: Religious Communities and the New Immigration*. Philadelphia: Temple University Press, 1998.

Wei-Ming, Tu. *The Living Tree: The Changing Meaning of Being Chinese Today*. Stanford: Stanford University Press, 1994.

——, ed. *The Confucian World Observed: A Contemporary Discussion of Confucian Humanism in East Asia*. Honolulu: East-West Center, 1992.

Selected Bibliography

Werber, Pnina. "Introduction: The Materiality of Diaspora— Between Aesthetic and 'Real' Politics." *Diaspora* 9, no. 1 (2000): 5–20.

West, Cornel. *Race Matters.* New York: Random House, 1994.

Wildman, Stephanie M., ed. *Privilege Revealed: How Law, Language, and the American Mind-set Uphold the Status Quo.* New York: New York University Press, 1996.

Williams, Raymond B., ed. *A Sacred Thread: Modern Transmission of Hindu Traditions in India and Abroad.* Chambersburg, Pa.: Anima, 1992.

Winant, Howard. *Racial Conditions: Politics, Theory, Comparisons.* Minneapolis: University of Minnesota Press, 1994.

Wright, R. George. *Does the Law Morally Bind the Poor? Or What Good's the Constitution When You Can't Afford a Loaf of Bread?* New York: New York University Press, 1996.

Yang, F. *Chinese Christians in America: Conversion, Assimilation, and Adhesive Identities.* University Park, Pa.: Penn State University Press, 1999.

Yoo, David K., ed. *New Spiritual Homes: Religion and Asian Americans.* Honolulu: University of Hawaii Press, 1999.

Zukin, Sharon. *The Cultures of Cities.* Oxford: Blackwell, 1995.

INDEX

Afghanistan, 26, 45, 74, 78
Africa, 30, 66, 72, 76. *See also* Senegal
African American Muslims, 33, 49, 51, 82,
  137; and Muslim immigrants, 18–21,
  83, 84
African Americans: and American identity, 119, 148n1; and Anglo Americans,
  32–33, 141; and Asians, 40, 99, 119–20,
  135; and black/white bipolarism, 2, 10,
  42–43, 73, 150n18, 153nn35,36; Buddhist, 85, 128; citizenship of, 157n13;
  and common American culture, 81;
  diversity among, 14; in ethno-racial
  pentagon, 39, 73, 80, 121; in film, 12,
  119–20; and intermarriage, 120, 141;
  and internalization of prejudice, 137;
  in kaleidoculture, 23, 144; legacy
  claims of, 156n6; and model minorities, 168n21; and Native Americans,
  147nn8,10; and racialized class prejudice, 10, 11, 83; and social construction of race, 152n32; and South
  Asians, 20–21, 66, 83, 84, 151n24, 177n8
African Orthodox Church, 113, 128
Afrocentrism, 158n13
agnosticism, 33–34, 50, 171n8, 174n16
Alaskan natives, 73. *See also* Native
  Americans
Alba, Richard D., 152n27
Ali, Amir, 50–51
Ambedkar, B. R., 154n39
Amerasia Journal, 99
America: citizenship in, 142; culture of, 7,
  18, 21, 28–30, 43, 81–82, 103, 128, 139,
  141; and East Asia, 146n5; and Europe,
  23, 27, 28, 30, 37; exceptionalism of,
  30; identity in, 6, 28–30, 41, 119, 136,

148n1; imperialism of, 166n7; and
  India, 154n39; irreligion in, 174n16;
  kaleidoculture in, 22, 83, 140, 142;
  minorities in, 135–36; modernity of,
  162n8; as North America, 148n12;
  polity of, 36–37; Protestantism in, 36,
  37, 81, 89; religion of, 17–18, 21, 22,
  23–45, 61–62, 83, 110, 117–18, 127–28
American dream, 18, 47, 154n42
Americanization, 37, 82–83, 121, 139,
  159n21
American Kaleidoscope (Fuchs), 151n21
American Medina (Schmidt), 20–21
Amirahmadi, Hooshang, 171n6
Amritsar, attack on Sikhs at, 96–97
Anderson, Benedict, 82, 89, 170n5
Angela's Ashes (McCourt), 112
Anglo Americans: and African Americans, 32–33, 141; and American culture, 21, 29, 30, 43, 103, 141; and Asian
  Americans, 82, 85, 99; and
  black/white bipolarism, 42; and Buddhism, 85, 86, 127–28; and class, 83;
  diversity among, 14; dominance of, 11,
  43, 158n13; and ethno-racial pentagon,
  39; and Euro-Americans, 80–81; in
  film, 12, 119–20; and Hinduism, 52,
  127–28; and images, 117; and immigration debate, 75, 78; and judicial system, 16; in L.A., 102; and other
  groups, 13, 32–33, 99, 136, 144; and
  religion, 117–18, 127–28; and social
  construction of race, 152n32; and
  Utne Reader, 173n5
Anglo-conformity, 32–33, 43, 64, 138–39,
  153n36, 155n51, 159n23
Anglo-Iranians, 100

Index

Anglo-Protestants, 37, 136–38, 140, 154nn-43,44. *See also* Protestantism
Appadurai, Arjun, 3, 63–64, 130, 142
Appiah, K. Anthony, 81
Arab Americans, 49, 86, 144; and September 11 attacks, 4, 39, 45, 161n38
al-Arian, Abdullah, 4
Asad, Talal, 126
Ashcroft, John, 45
Asian Americans: and African Americans, 40, 99, 119–20, 135; and Anglo Americans, 82, 85, 99; and cyber society, 63–65; diversity among, 13–14, 21; in ethno-racial pentagon, 39, 80, 120–21; identity of, 84, 134–35; intermarriage with, 120; and law, 16, 138, 176n6; marginalization of, 74; and media, 120, 138; and multiculturalism, 81; and Progressive Patriotic Protestantism, 17, 144; and racialized class prejudice, 11, 84–86; religions of, 41, 120, 158n15; as scholars, 3, 156n6; and September 11 attacks, 45, 176n3; stereotypes of, 16, 20; as threat, 170n42; *vs.* Arab Americans, 4–5. *See also* South Asian Americans
Asian American studies, 23, 138, 177n8
Asian immigrants: agnostic, 33–34; and American religion, 61–62, 110; assimilation of, 150n18; and black/white bipolarism, 42; and citizenship, 72, 129, 139; and civil society, 61; in ethno-racial pentagon, 18, 73; and 1965 Immigration Act, 8, 99, 138; and other minorities, 8, 19, 99; and racialized class prejudice, 118–21; religions of, 7, 8, 123, 125, 126–27, 129, 131; and spirituality, 108, 110, 120; statistics on, 5, 74. *See also* South Asian immigrants
assimilation: and Anglo-conformity, 41, 44; in cities, 163n13; and civil society, 57; and consumerism, 170n42; and intermarriage, 141–42; of Iranians, 88, 89, 100; and modernity, 138; of Muslims, 82–83; and race, 41–42; and reli-

gion, 37, 92; *vs.* cultural citizenship, 136; to whiteness, 42, 150n18
authoritarianism, 25, 60, 134, 169n36
Ayodhya Mandir/Babri Masjid conflict, 51–52

baby boomers, 116–18
Bahaism, 145n3
Bangladesh, 74, 78, 80
Barbarians Are Coming, The (Louie), 12
Bauer, Gary, 43
Beck, Lillian, 166n4
Belal, Ould, 134
Bellah, Robert N., 36, 81–82, 108
Bennett, William, 156n8
Berkeley, University of California at, 38–39
Bhaba, Homi, 149n9
Bhagwati, Jagdish, 75–76, 77
Bharatiya Janata Party (BJP; India), 142
Bhindranwale, Sant, 96–97
Bhutan, 74
biculturalism, 97
bipolarism, black/white, 2, 10, 42–43, 73, 150n18, 153nn35,36
Bloch, Marc, 84
Bloom, Harold, 17
Borjas, George, 5–6, 7, 155n51
Bosnia, 44, 56
Boston Review (journal), 76–77, 81
Braudel, Fernand, 72
Brimelow, Peter, 75
Britain, 66, 76, 79–80, 92
Brother from Another Planet (film), 118
Bruce, Dickson D., Jr., 160n35
Bruce, Steve, 126
Buchanan, Pat, 157n8
Buddhists, 7, 113, 116, 145n4, 164n22; African-American, 85, 128
Bush, George W., 4, 143

California, 3, 108, 129, 171n8; University of, 38–39. *See also* Los Angeles
Canada, 5, 30, 80, 98, 148n12; Muslims in, 4, 150n11
capital, 28; cultural, 102; symbolic, 136, 137

Index

capitalism: and civil society, 48, 55, 57, 66; and class, 101; and cyber society, 64; frontier, 37; global, 56, 84, 104, 127, 143, 157n8; informational, 62–63; liberal, 57; and migration, 167n16; and religion, 117, 127, 143

Caribbean immigrants, 19

Carnoy, Martin, 168n21

Carter, Stephen, 18, 156n8

Castells, Manuel, 62–63, 112, 122, 123, 124, 164n26

Catholics: and American religion, 36–37, 113, 127–28, 136; Asian, 7, 145n3; and civil society, 54; Filipino, 31–32; in film, 119–20

Chafetz, Janet S., 35, 158n20

Chakrabarty, Dipesh, 126

Chang, Lan, 12

Chicago, 20, 48–50, 129

Chicano Americans, 13. *See also* Mexican Americans

China, 26, 74, 134

Chinese Americans, 11–12, 86, 119–20, 152n25, 170n42, 172n21

Chishti, Muzaffar, 77

Christianity: activists in, 164n22; and American culture, 7, 81–82; and American religion, 17; among Asian immigrants, 7, 98, 131; Anglo-American perceptions of, 126, 127–28; Asian, 65, 145n3; changes within, 110; diversity of, 113, 116, 127, 158n15; growth of, 145n4. *See also* Catholics; Protestantism

church and state, separation of, 36, 61, 66–67, 89

cities: assimilation in, 163n13; Canadian, 148n12; and civil society, 55, 66; culture of, 172n23; and cyberspace, 62, 63–64; in film, 118; immigrants in, 3, 101, 102–3, 129; kaleidoculture in, 41, 103; neighborhoods of, 102–3; premodern, 56–57; religion in, 16, 88, 163n13; Sikhs in, 95, 96, 97, 98; world, 160n31, 175n29

citizenship, 11, 12, 88; of African Americans, 157n13; for Asian immigrants, 64–65, 72, 129, 139; and civil society, 15, 55, 66; cultural, 10, 16, 21, 39, 64–65, 66, 86, 101, 129, 136, 138–39, 148n11, 156n6, 165n31; cyber, 63–64, 123; and ethno-racial pentagon, 38; European, 171n5; Indian, 142; world, 77

civility, 55, 57, 143

civilizational purity, 14, 34

civil rights, 55, 176n6. *See also* human rights; individual rights

civil rights movement, 19, 154n43, 155n50

civil society, 22, 36, 47–67; and capitalism, 48, 55, 57, 66; and cities, 55, 66; and citizenship, 15, 55, 64, 66, 86; and colonialism, 163n14; and culture, 56, 58, 86, 141; and cyberspace, 48, 62, 64, 67; in Eastern Europe, 53–54, 60; and fundamentalism, 17; global, 66, 143, 162n12; and identity, 60, 84, 124, 125; and individual rights, 53–56; and Islam, 57–60; and kaleidoculture, 136–37; and the market, 17, 56, 59, 61, 137, 141; and politics, 48, 54, 66; polyvalent, 66, 137; premodern, 56–57; and private property, 55, 56; and private sphere, 48, 57, 141; and public sphere, 48, 54, 57, 141, 162n8; and religion, 47, 48, 53, 54, 58, 59, 61, 65, 66, 141; scope of, 53–56; and the state, 47, 48, 53–54, 57, 59, 137, 141, 164n23; and technicalism, 61–63; transnational, 48, 65, 89, 102

Clash of Civilizations and the Remaking of the World Order, The (Huntington), 34

class: in American Buddhism, 85–86; and culture, 27, 112; in film, 118; and hybridity, 28; and immigrants, 15, 77, 100–102, 143, 155n51; in Iran, 92–94, 171n6; and kaleidoculture, 38; knowledge, 117, 154n44, 155n50; middle, 18, 0

informational politics, 62–63; and labor, 66, 136; and localization, 130; and media, 130, 173n3

global network society, 62–63

189

Index

government, 15, 118, 134. *See also* Immigration and Naturalization Act of 1965; U.S. Census; welfare
Graham, Billy, 113
Graham, Franklin, 33
Gramsci, Antonio, 53, 124, 164n23
Greek Orthodox Church, 113
Greenberg, Irving, 105, 128, 153n36
Griffiths, Paul, 126
Gupta, Akhil, 69
gurudwaras (Sikh temples), 97, 98

Habermas, Jurgen, 54
Habits of the Heart (Bellah), 108
Haley, Alex, 152n32
Hall, Stuart, 123, 124–25, 130
Hansen, Marcus, 40
Hart-Celler Act. *See* Immigration and Naturalization Act of 1965
Havel, Vaclav, 55
Hegel, G. W. F., 164n23
Herberg, Will, 28, 36–37, 156n6, 159n21
Hernstein, Richard J., 75
heteronomic networks, 62, 165n27
hierarchy: among immigrants, 143; and civil society, 66; cultural, 112, 122; in cyberspace, 61, 62–63, 64, 67, 165n34; and ethno-racial pentagon, 38. *See also* class; elites
Hindu Americans, 52, 64–65
Hinduism, 7, 25, 51–52, 127–28, 145n4, 154n39, 162n5
Hindus: and Muslims, 51–52, 162n5; nationalism of, 95, 97, 142; and Sikhs, 60, 61, 65, 95–97, 162n5
Hispanic Americans, 8, 11, 13, 156n6, 168n21
Hispanic immigrants, 42, 61, 73
Hispanics, 155n45; *vs.* Latinos, 13, 152n31
Hodgson, Marshall, 62
Hoffman, Dustin, 119
Hollinger, David, 3, 14, 24, 140, 149nn8,9, 159n26
hooks, bell, 85, 128, 147n10, 152n29
humanities, 35, 122

human rights, 64, 138. *See also* civil rights; individual rights
Hunger (Chang), 12
Hunter, James, 156n8
Huntington, Samuel, 18, 24, 35, 37, 38, 159n29, 163n14; and black/white bipolarism, 43; on religion and culture, 25–26, 31, 34
hybridity: cultural, 101, 151n24, 160n35; and gender, 23, 28, 156n3; and henna, 151n24, 177n8; and identity, 84, 99; of Iranian Americans, 103; racialized, 23, 28, 73; religious, 108–10, 175n25
hypervisualization, 16, 117, 121–29

Idea of Civil Society, The (Seligman), 47
identity: and African Americans, 119, 148n1; American, 6, 28–30, 41, 119, 136, 148n1; of Asian Americans, 84, 134–35; and civil society, 60, 84, 124, 125; and culture, 123, 124; ethnic, 152n27; of European immigrants, 152n27; hybrid, 84, 99; and location, 82, 102–3; and religion, 99, 100, 102, 124, 125, 129, 151n21; symbolic, 152n27; and technology, 131; transnational, 104; white, 149n6
"Image" (Miles), 105
images: media, 116–17, 121; religious, 105–16; *vs.* text, 122
IMAN (Inner-City Muslim Action Network), 49–50
"Immigrant as Pariah, The" (Fiss), 77–78
immigrants: in Britain, 76, 80; in cities, 3, 101, 102–3, 129; and civil society, 47–67; and class, 15, 77, 100–102, 143, 155n51; culturalist view of, 5; in cyberspace, 64, 104, 125, 131; diversity among, 13–14, 21, 75; and ethno-racial pentagon, 39; generational shift among, 8; illegal, 1, 3, 5, 7, 74, 75, 77–78, 143, 148n3; and informational politics, 63; involuntary, 135; and law, 3, 16; legal, 1, 3, 7, 74, 143; long-distance nationalism of, 3, 33, 82, 89, 100, 103–4, 137, 170n5; marginaliza-

Index

tion of, 44; and media, 104; as model minorities, 155n51; official vs. unofficial biases against, 80–81; as participants in critical theory, 3–4, 8; and polyvalence, 48; prejudice against, 65, 69–86, 120; professional, 101, 148n3; and race, 42; and religion, 16, 61, 79, 98–99; restrictions on, 155n51; rivalry among, 40; statistics on, 74, 148n3; stereotypes of, 19–20; subjectivity of, 142; voluntary, 119, 136; and Western culture, 30; and whiteness, 73. *See also particular ethnicities and nationalities*

immigration: and culture, 76, 77, 78, 79, 80; and cyberspace, 142; dangers of, 6, 7; debate on, 75–76, 78–80; future impact of, 40–41; policy on, 6, 19–20; and religion, 76, 77

Immigration Act of 1990, 80

Immigration and Naturalization Act of 1965 (Hart-Celler Act), 1, 5; and American religion, 110, 113, 121; and Asian Americans, 138; and Asian immigrants, 8, 99; and Asian religions, 127, 129; and civil rights movement, 19; and corporate multiculturalism, 131; and ethno-racial pentagon, 73; impact of, 7, 41, 71, 123, 148n3, 155n48; and Iranian immigrants, 91; and minority discourse, 147n10; and occupational preference, 79–80; and polyvalence, 37; and South Asian immigrants, 79, 80, 101

Inada, Lawson Fusao, 133, 134, 139

India: fundamentalism in, 154n39; and Hindu immigrants, 51–52, 64–65; Hinduism in, 113, 142; immigrants from, 76, 78, 104; and Pakistan, 26; Sikhs in, 95–97. *See also* South Asia

individualism, 23, 28, 81, 108, 149n7, 162n8

individual rights, 48, 53–56. *See also* civil rights; human rights

Indonesia, 59, 65

Indo-Pakistanis, 49, 50

information age, 36, 106–7, 122, 123

Institute of Islamic Information and Education (III&E), 49–51, 64–65, 84

intermarriage, 41, 52, 79, 99; and racialized class prejudice, 20, 120, 141–42, 168n20

Internet. *See* cyberspace

Iran, 88–89, 91–94, 95, 171n6

Irangelinos, 86, 102, 103

Iranian Americans, 86, 88, 100–102, 103, 104

Iranian immigrants, 88, 89, 94–95, 98–99, 100, 102

Iraq, 93

Islam: African American, 18–19, 51; American, 82–84, 137; Anglo-American perceptions of, 127–28; and civil society, 57–60; and cyber society, 64; egalitarianism in, 25; fundamentalism in, 50, 154n39, 158n17; growth of, 145n4; ignorance of, 49–51; and internal reform, 110; Iranian, 88–89, 98, 99; and racism, 21; Relgious Right on, 33; in Saudi Arabia, 65; sects of, 65, 95, 150n11; in Senegal, 163n21; since September 11 attacks, 144; as threat to Western civilization, 25–26; universal, 50–51. *See also* African American Muslims; Muslims

Islamic Retribution Bill (Iran), 93

Italian Americans, 119

Jainism, 127, 145n3

Jains, 113, 116, 162n5

Japan, 163n13

Japanese Americans, 152n25, 170n42, 172n21; incarceration of, 161n38, 176n3

Jencks, Christopher, 19–20, 155n51

"Jewish Denominationalism" (Greenberg), 105

Jews, 14, 36–37, 136, 153n36; in media, 112, 113, 115, 116

Journal of Asian American Studies, 177n8

Judaism, 7, 107, 110, 127–28, 145n4

Index

kaleidoculture: African Americans in, 23, 144; in America, 22, 83, 140, 142; and Asian Americans, 135; in cities, 41, 103; and civil society, 136–37; and cultural citizenship, 139; in cyberspace, 132; immigrants in, 48; and media, 116, 121; and Progressive Patriotic Protestantism, 38, 139, 144; and racialized class prejudice, 13, 41–45; and transnationality, 104; *vs.* multiculturalism, 9, 12, 24, 37–38. *See also* polyvalence
Kallen, Horace, 37
Kant, Immanuel, 37, 138
Kashmir, 26, 96
Kasravi, Ahmad, 90, 92
Kemalist ideology, 57, 58, 59
Kenya, 66, 76
Khalistan, 142
Khatami, Ayatollah, 94
Khomeini, Ayatollah, 90, 93
King, Martin Luther Jr., 33
Kivisto, Peter, 31–32, 157n10
Korea, 166n7
Korean immigrants, 7, 31–32, 74, 145n3, 172n21
Kosmin, Barry, 88, 95, 98
Krishna Consciousness Movement (ISKCON), 52
Kristeva, Julia, 149n9

labor, 6, 79, 127, 143, 148n1, 159n28; in cities, 102, 129; and globalization, 66, 136
Lachman, Seymour, 88, 95, 98
Last of the Mohicans, The (film), 119
Latin America, 5, 74
Latino Americans, 23, 103, 135–36, 144, 158n15; class of, 100–101; cultural citizenship of, 129, 148n11; in ethno-racial pentagon, 39, 80; Muslim, 49
Latino immigrants, 5, 8, 40, 73, 91, 150n18; and 1965 Immigration Act, 1, 7
Latinos, 13, 152n31, 168n26
law: and Asian Americans, 16, 138, 176n6; and economistic view, 5; and immi-

grants, 3, 16; in Iran, 93; and racialized class prejudice, 22. *See also* Immigration and Naturalization Act of 1965
Lawrence, Bruce, 38, 71
Lee, Bruce, 11
Lee, Spike, 118–19
Leonard, Karen, 82–83, 129
Levine, Lawrence, 40, 41, 43
Life (magazine), 28, 110–16, 117, 127, 132
Limbaugh, Rush, 43
Lincoln, Bruce, 130
Lind, Michael, 131, 139
Lindsay, Hal, 153n37
Little Big Man (film), 119
location, 131, 139, 146n5; double, 137; and identity, 82, 102–3; and religion, 10, 124, 125, 127
Long, Charles H., 32–33, 157n13
Longowal, Sant Harchand Singh, 97
la longue durée, 72
Los Angeles (L.A.), 86, 91, 98, 100–103, 129
Louie, David, 12
Lowe, Lisa, 72–73, 166n7
Lum, Wing Tek, 133, 134

Malaysia, 36, 76
Malcolm X, 33, 160n35
Malia, Martin, 162nn11, 12
Maneta, Norman, 144, 176n3
marabouts (Sufi leaders), 59–60, 163n21
marginalization, 12–13, 15, 44, 63, 64, 74, 101
market, the, 28, 138; and civil society, 17, 56, 59, 61, 137, 141; in cyberspace, 63, 165n34; and religion, 23–45, 117. *See also* economy
Marty, Martin, 145n4, 156n8
Marxism, 117
Marx, Karl, 53, 164n23
Mauritanians, 134
May, Henry, 17, 37
Mazrui, Ali, 83
McCarthy, Thomas, 138–39
McCloud, Aminah, 18

Index

Index

Native Americans, 2, 14, 144; and African Americans, 147nn8,10; and Asians, 99, 135; in ethno-racial pentagon, 39, 73, 80, 121; in film, 119; intermarriage with, 120; as Other, 42, 119; and race, 10–11; in U.S. Census, 135, 146n6

Nattier, Jan, 85, 169n40

neoconservatism, 18, 139, 142, 147n10, 154nn43,44

neoliberalism, 56, 118, 139, 147n10, 153n36

Nepal, 74

netizens, 123

New Religious America, The (Eck), 31

no-religioners, 33–34. *See also* agnosticism; secularism

North Africa, 26, 73

North America, 79, 162n5; civil society in, 56–57; immigrants in, 63, 98, 113, 138; and Mexico, 154n45; U.S. as, 148n12. *See also* America; Canada

Nussbaum, Martha, 77, 149nn7,9, 154n39

occupational preferences, 6, 79–80

Office of Management and Budget (OMB), 73

Okihiro, Gary Y., 170n42

On Common Ground: World Religions in America (Eck; CD-ROM), 31–32, 35, 99, 121, 128, 157n9, 169n35

One Nation Under God? (Garber and Wilkowicz), 23

One Nation Under God (Kosmin and Lachman), 88

Operation Bluestar, 96–97

Otherness: and Anglo-Protestant norm, 136–38; of Asian Muslims, 45; and civic religion, 61–62; in the media, 105, 121, 128; of Native Americans, 42, 119; in popular culture, 121; since September 11 attacks, 144; and whiteness, 42

Ottoman Empire, 58

Pacific Islanders, 73

Pakistan, 26, 73, 80, 96

Pakistani immigrants, 78

Palestinians, 4, 25

palimpsest metaphor, 151n22

Palumbo-Liu, David, 3, 146n5, 166n7, 170n42

Park, Robert, 69, 84–85, 141, 142, 153n36

patriarchy, 52, 63

"Patriotism and Cosmopolitanism" (Nussbaum), 77

Pawnbroker, The (film), 118

Pentecostals, 113

Philippines, 145n3, 166n7. *See also* Filipino immigrants

Piscatori, James, 89, 170n5

Playing in the Dark (Morrison), 42

pluralism: and American identity, 41; as balkanization, 44; within Christianity, 158n15; and civil society, 55, 56, 60; and commercialism, 117–18; institutionalized, 57; and nationalism, 33; premodern, 56–57; and relativism, 171n8; religious, 14, 24–25, 37, 56–57, 59, 108–10, 117–18, 129, 132, 141; religious *vs.* cultural, 28, 37, 156n6; as threat, 44; *vs.* cosmopolitanism, 3; *vs.* diversity, 24–25. *See also* multiculturalism

politics, 2, 10, 18, 41, 78, 135; and civil society, 48, 54, 66; of difference, 150n11; informational, 62–63; and religion, 17, 65; transnational, 104

polyvalence, 10, 22, 140, 144; and Asian Americans, 135, 138; and civic religion, 61; and civil society, 66, 136–37; cultural, 9, 41, 156n6; and cultural citizenship, 139; in cyberspace, 132, 142–43; and double consciousness, 160n35; and immigrants, 48; in media, 116, 118, 121; and multiculturalism, 24, 131; and 1965 Immigration Act, 37; and Otherness, 137–38; and racialized class prejudice, 13; religious, 41, 141, 156n6; and September 11 attacks, 45; and transnationality, 104; *vs.* diversity, 9, 12. *See also* kaleidoculture

population statistics, 5, 74, 103, 113, 148n3

power structures, 11, 21, 118, 124, 131, 147n10

Index

Index

religion: American (*continued*)
civil society, 47, 48, 53, 54, 58, 59, 61, 65, 66, 141; and class, 10, 18, 31, 52, 151n21, 172n28; and conflict, 24, 25–26, 32, 159n29; and consumerism, 117–18, 124, 125; and cultural studies, 140; and culture, 10, 23, 26–30, 51, 98–99, 121, 131, 132, 135, 140, 156n5, 157nn8,9; in cyberspace, 40–41, 64, 105–8, 117, 122–23, 125, 130; and doubling, 137; Eck on, 31–33; freedom of, 45, 118; and hypervisualization, 122; and identity, 99, 100, 102, 124, 125, 129, 151n21; ideologies of, 130, 157n9; New Age, 108–10, 172n28; and protest, 134; and racialized class prejudice, 10, 21, 141, 143, 145n3, 171n8; smorgasbord, 116, 131; social significance of, 130; and the state, 17, 36, 61, 65, 66–67, 89, 91–92; and transnationality, 45, 64, 89, 91, 102; types of, 27; in U.S. Census, 88, 89; and women, 18, 108, 172n15. *See also* agnosticism; secularism; *particular faiths*
Religion, Civil Society, and the State (Uberoi), 47
Religion One, 27, 35, 36, 126, 129, 131, 140, 143
Religion Two, 28, 36, 126, 129, 141, 143
Religious Right, 18, 33, 158n15
religious studies, 5, 28–29, 35–36, 140, 175n35
representation, 123, 124, 125, 129, 131, 152n29, 165n34
reproduction, 124, 125, 129
Robbins, Bruce, 149n9
Robertson, Pat, 18
Rodowick, D. N., 165n34
Rosaldo, Renato, 39
Rudolph, Suzanne, 89, 170n5
Russia, 56, 60. *See also* Soviet Union
Russian Orthodox Church, 113

Said, Edward, 34
Sanjek, Roger, 168n20
Sasken, Sassia, 64
Saudi Arabia, 50, 65

Schlesinger, Arthur, 6, 141, 142, 157n13
secularism, 33–34, 50, 65, 89, 126, 174n16; and frontier mentality, 98, 171n8; of Iranian immigrants, 94–95, 98–99; limits of, 36; in Turkey, 58
Seligman, Adam, 47, 55, 162nn8,12
Senegal, 59–60, 65, 163n21
September 11 attacks, 18, 29, 33, 84; and Arab Americans, 4, 39, 45, 161n38; arrests following, 134, 161n38; profiling since, 143–44, 176n3; and separation of church and state, 66–67
Shintoism, 146n4
Sikhism, 127, 145n4, 154n39
Sikhs, 7, 95–98, 113, 116, 142; and Hindus, 60, 61, 65, 95–97, 162n5
Singapore, 76
Singh, Guru Gobind, 95
Singh, Sant Fateh, 96
Singh, Tara, 96
Singhal, Ashok, 52
Smith, Jonathan Z., 10, 126
social sciences, 35
social structure, 58, 59–60. *See also* hierarchy
Social Text (journal), 76
Souls of Black Folk, The (Du Bois), 1
South Africa, 76
South Asia, 74, 162n5. *See also* India
South Asian Americans, 32, 50, 101, 104, 138; and African Americans, 20–21, 66, 83, 84, 151n24, 177n8
South Asian immigrants, 69–70, 74–76, 104, 146n5; in Africa, 66, 76; in cities, 129; in film, 1, 12, 66, 76, 148n2; in immigration debate, 78–80; Muslim, 83, 84; and 1965 Immigration Act, 79, 80, 101
South Asians, 95, 165n31; and class, 32, 76, 101, 167n16; Muslim, 51–52, 65, 162n5
Southeast Asia, 36, 74, 146n5
Southeast Asian immigrants, 79
Soviet Union, 25, 34, 56
Spanish explorers, 10–11
spirituality: Asian, 108, 110, 120; as consumer product, 117–18; and corporate

Index

multiculturalism, 131; New Age, 108–10; smorgasbord of, 116, 131. *See also* religion
Sri Lanka, 74, 80
state, the, 62, 81; and civil society, 47, 48, 53–54, 57, 59, 137, 141, 164n23; and religion, 17, 61, 65, 91–92; separation of church and, 36, 61, 66–67, 89
stereotypes, 11–12, 15, 16, 19–20, 62, 160n35
Sufism, 59–60, 164n22
Sukarno, 59

Takaki, Ronald, 146n5, 151n25
"Taking It to the Streets" (1997 IMAN festival), 49–50
Taoism, 145n3
Taylor, Charles, 138–39
techgnosis, 104, 172n28
technicalism, 61–63
technology, 36, 104, 110, 131; and hypervisualization, 121–22, 128
Teitelbaum, Michael, 75, 159n28
television, 101, 102, 172n21
Third World Newsreel, 119
Time (magazine), 105–7, 110, 116, 117
Tocqueville, Alexis de, 53
Todorov, Tzvetan, 149n9
transnationality, 3, 104, 131, 162n5; and civil society, 48, 65, 89, 102; corporate, 136; in cyberspace, 63, 142; of empires, 57, 80; and religion, 45, 64, 89, 91, 102
Transnational Religion and Fading Nation-States (Rudolph and Piscatori), 89
Tricycle: The Buddhist Review (journal), 85
Turkey, 57–59, 65
Tweed, Thomas A., 7, 102, 103, 156n8

Uberoi, J. P. S., 47, 60–61, 64–65, 164n23
universalism, 3, 50–51, 149nn8,9
U.S. Census, 75, 80, 103; and Americanization, 82; Anglo-conformity of, 137, 139; and black/white bipolarism, 42; classifications of, 153n35, 166n9; and ethno-racial pentagon, 14, 38, 73; Native Americans in, 135, 146n6; religion in, 88, 89

Utne Reader (magazine), 108–10, 116, 117, 120, 131, 173n5

Vietnamese Americans, 79
Vietnamese immigrants, 40
Vietnam War, 74, 79, 133, 166n7
violence, 32, 40, 45, 96–97
Vishwa Hindu Parishad (VHP), 51–52, 64–65

Wallerstein, Immanuel, 27, 39
Walzer, Michael, 58–59, 149n9
Ward, Keith, 126
Washington, Booker T., 141
Weber, Max, 55
welfare, 14, 22, 73, 75, 153n36
Wellesley College, symposium at (1998), 24–25
Wentz, Richard E., 159n21
West, the: civilization of, 34, 43; civil society in, 54–55, 65; culture of, 30, 97; and Islamic fundamentalism, 25–26, 158n17; and modernity, 138
West Asia, 26
West, Cornel, 23, 27, 28, 29, 66, 160n35
whiteness, 10, 73, 149n6, 153n34; of Jews, 153n36; as norm, 42, 150n18. *See also* bipolarism, black/white
White Revolution (Iran; 1963), 92
White Skins, Black Masks (Fanon), 99
Wiener, Myron, 77
Williams, Raymond, 8, 58
Winant, Howard, 2, 10
Wolfe, Alan, 156n8
women, 4, 18, 108, 112, 114, 150n11, 172n15
Woods, Tiger, 11, 147n8
World Wide Web. *See* cyberspace

"yellow peril," 72, 170n42
Yoo, David, 23
Yugoslavia, 44, 56

Zarrin, Ali, 88, 94, 170n1
Zionism, 25, 50
Zoroastrianism, 145n3